Microsoft® Word 7 Projects for Windows 95

James A. Folts
Oregon State University

The Benjamin/Cummings Publishing Company, Inc.
Menlo Park, California • Reading, Massachusetts
New York • Don Mills, Ontario • Harlow, U.K. • Amsterdam
Bonn • Paris • Milan • Madrid • Sydney • Singapore • Tokyo
Seoul • Taipei • Mexico City • San Juan, Puerto Rico

Senior Editor: *Maureen A. Allaire*
Project Editor: *Nancy E. Davis, Kathy G. Yankton*
Assistant Editor: *Heide Chavez*
Executive Editor: *Michael Payne*
Project Manager: *Adam Ray*
Associate Production Editor: *Jennifer Englander*
Marketing Manager: *Melissa Baumwald*
Custom Publishing Operations Specialist: *Michael Smith*
Senior Manufacturing Coordinator: *Janet Weaver*
Composition and Film Manager: *Vivian McDougal*
Copy Editor: *Robert Fiske*
Technical Editor: *Lynda Fox Fields*
Proofreader: *Holly McLean Aldis, Roseann Viano*
Indexer: *Mark Kmetzko*

ISBN 0-8053-1234-X bundled version
ISBN 0-8053-1701-5 stand alone version

1 2 3 4 5 6 7 8 9 10—DOW—00 99 98 97 96

Ordering from the SELECT System

For more information on ordering and pricing policies for the SELECT System of microcomputer applications texts and their supplements, please contact your Addison-Wesley • Benjamin/Cummings sales representative or call our SELECT Hotline at 800/854-2595.

The Benjamin/Cummings Publishing Company, Inc.
2725 Sand Hill Road
Menlo Park, CA 94025
http://www.aw.com/bc/is
bc.is@aw.com

Getting Started

Welcome to the *SELECT Lab Series.* We invite you to explore how you can take advantage of the newest Windows 95 features of the most popular software applications using this up-to-date learning package.

Greater access to ideas and information is changing the way people work. With Windows 95 applications you have greater integration capabilities and access to Internet resources than ever before. The *SELECT Lab Series* helps you take advantage of these valuable resources with special assignments devoted to the Internet and additional connectivity resources which can be accessed through our web site, **http://www.aw.com/bc/is.**

The key to using software is making the software work for you. The *SELECT Lab Series* will help you learn to use software as a productivity tool by guiding you step-by-step through case-based projects similar to those you will encounter at school, work, or home. When you are finished with this learning package, you will be fully prepared to use the resources this software offers. Your success is our success.

A Guided Tour

To facilitate the learning process, we have developed a consistent organizational structure for each module in the *SELECT Lab Series.*

You begin using the software almost immediately. A brief **Overview** introduces the software package and the basic application functions. **Getting Help** covers the on-line Help feature in each package. **A Note to the Student** explains any special conventions or system configurations observed in a particular module.

Each module contains six to eight **Projects,** an **Operations Reference** of all the operations covered in each module, an extensive **Glossary** of **key terms,** and an **Index.**

The following figures introduce the elements you will encounter as you use each SELECT module.

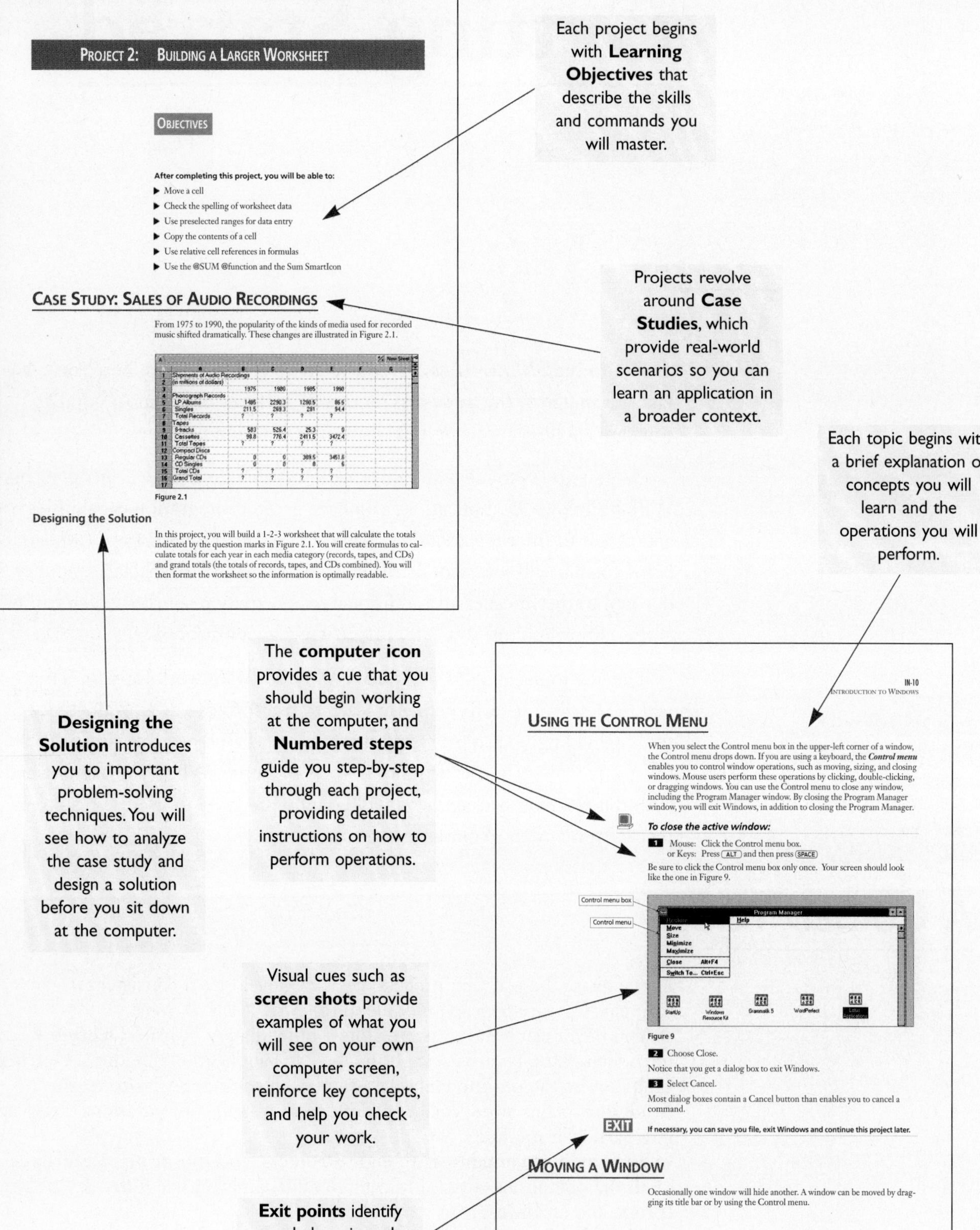
Project 2: Building a Larger Worksheet
Objectives
After completing this project, you will be able to:
▶ Move a cell
▶ Check the spelling of worksheet data
▶ Use preselected ranges for data entry
▶ Copy the contents of a cell
▶ Use relative cell references in formulas
▶ Use the @SUM @function and the Sum SmartIcon
Case Study: Sales of Audio Recordings
From 1975 to 1990, the popularity of the kinds of media used for recorded music shifted dramatically. These changes are illustrated in Figure 2.1.
Figure 2.1
Designing the Solution
In this project, you will build a 1-2-3 worksheet that will calculate the totals indicated by the question marks in Figure 2.1. You will create formulas to calculate totals for each year in each media category (records, tapes, and CDs) and grand totals (the totals of records, tapes, and CDs combined). You will then format the worksheet so the information is optimally readable.
Each project begins with **Learning Objectives** that describe the skills and commands you will master.
Projects revolve around **Case Studies**, which provide real-world scenarios so you can learn an application in a broader context.
Each topic begins with a brief explanation of concepts you will learn and the operations you will perform.
Designing the Solution introduces you to important problem-solving techniques. You will see how to analyze the case study and design a solution before you sit down at the computer.
The **computer icon** provides a cue that you should begin working at the computer, and **Numbered steps** guide you step-by-step through each project, providing detailed instructions on how to perform operations.
Visual cues such as **screen shots** provide examples of what you will see on your own computer screen, reinforce key concepts, and help you check your work.
Exit points identify good places in each project to take a break.
IN-10
Introduction to Windows
Using the Control Menu
When you select the Control menu box in the upper-left corner of a window, the Control menu drops down. If you are using a keyboard, the *Control menu* enables you to control window operations, such as moving, sizing, and closing windows. Mouse users perform these operations by clicking, double-clicking, or dragging windows. You can use the Control menu to close any window, including the Program Manager window. By closing the Program Manager window, you will exit Windows, in addition to closing the Program Manager.
To close the active window:
1 Mouse: Click the Control menu box.
or Keys: Press ALT and then press SPACE
Be sure to click the Control menu box only once. Your screen should look like the one in Figure 9.
Control menu box
Control menu
Program Manager
Figure 9
2 Choose Close.
Notice that you get a dialog box to exit Windows.
3 Select Cancel.
Most dialog boxes contain a Cancel button than enables you to cancel a command.
EXIT
If necessary, you can save you file, exit Windows and continue this project later.
Moving a Window
Occasionally one window will hide another. A window can be moved by dragging its title bar or by using the Control menu.

Key Terms are boldfaced and italicized and appear throughout each project.

WRD-12
Word for Windows

Opening a New Document

Word for Windows normally opens with a blank window and is ready to create a new document. If someone was using the computer before you, however, the window may already contain text. In that case, you will need to open a blank window for your new document. (If Word for Windows is not running already, start it by double-clicking the Word for Windows icon on the Windows desktop.)

To open a blank window for a new document:

1 Select New on the File menu or press (ALT) + (F7) and then type n

The New dialog box appears, as shown in Figure 1.1. This dialog box allows you to select from a variety of *templates* and *wizards*. ***Templates*** are preformatted skeleton documents ranging from memos to newsletters. ***Wizards*** ask a series of questions about a document format and then use that information to build a document for you to use. Right now, you need the default general-purpose template named Normal.

Figure 1.1

2 If Normal does not appear in the Template box, type `Normal`

3 Select OK.

Tip You can open a new document with a click of the mouse. Use the New document button on the standard toolbar to open a Normal document with a single click.

The document area of the screen will be blank except for the blinking vertical *insertion point* (|), *the end-of-document mark* (__), and possibly a *paragraph mark* (¶). The ***insertion point*** marks the position where text will be inserted or deleted when you type at the keyboard. The ***end-of-document mark*** shows where the document ends; you cannot insert characters after the end-of-document mark. A ***paragraph mark*** indicates the end of a paragraph and forces the beginning of a new line. The paragraph mark may not show on your screen. If not, you will learn shortly how to make it visible.

Margin figures show on-screen tools that are often convenient alternatives to menu commands presented in the numbered steps.

Tips, Reminders, Cautions, and **Quick Fixes** appear throughout each project to highlight important, helpful, or pertinent information about each application.

Study Questions (Multiple Choice, Short Answer, and For Discussion) may be used as self-tests or homework assignments.

Short Answer

1. What are the two main services offered by My Computer?
2. What objects are considered physical locations in My Computer?
3. Why is a directory structure sometimes called a tree?
4. How do you run a program from My Computer?
5. How do you create a new folder?
6. Will copying a file result in the original being changed in any way?
7. Why should you drag and drop objects using mouse button 2?
8. Will renaming a file cause a second copy of that file to be generated?

For Discussion

1. Why was the ability to create folders for file management on the PC. so important?
2. My Computer will open a new window every time the user double-clicks on a drive or folder ol How could this create a problem?
3. Why should you expect there to be some sort of access restrictions on network drives?

Review Exercises

Examining the File System

Use My Computer to examine the root folders of your computer's local hard drive(s). If the computer part of a network, take a look at the network drives as well. Get some practice resizing, moving, and cl the many windows that will be created during this exercise. Draw a tree that shows how information i organized on your system and network—make note of the major folders in the root directories, and lo for other folders within these. You don't have to list the thousands of individual files!

Launching Programs from My Computer

Use My Computer to explore your student data diskette. Without using the Find command, look for t program file AirMail and use My Computer to run the program. After closing AirMail, look on your l hard drive(s) for a folder called Program Files. This is a standard directory on Windows 95 systems, though it may not be present, or may have a different name, on your system. Use My Computer to op the Program Files folder, and examine what's inside. There are probably more folders within Program Files; if an Accessories folder is present, open it and then use My Computer to launch MS Paint or W Pad.

Assignments

Drag-and-Drop Manipulation of Files and Folders

In this assignment, you will use My Computer to "juggle" files and folders. This will provide extensive practice with window management and using the mouse for drag-and-drop operations.

Open the Temp folder on your student data diskette. Create a folder within it called Reports. Open the Reports folder and create three new text documents called Rain Forest, Desert, and Coral Reef. Using drag-and-drop, *move* the Reports folder (which will include the files you just created) to the Text folder of the student data diskette. Select the two files Rain Forest and Coral Reef and, again using drag-and-drop, *copy* them to the Work subdirectory. Rename the file Desert to Tundra. Finally, delete the Reports folder (which will also delete the files it contains).

Review Exercises present hands-on tasks to help you build on skills acquired in the projects.

Assignments require critical thinking and encourage synthesis and integration of project skills.

Each project ends with **The Next Step** which discusses the concepts from the project and proposes other uses and applications for the skills you have learned, a **Summary,** and a list of **Key Terms and Operations**.

The Next Step

Access has many functions that are part of the
You've already seen the Now() function in sev
If you're interested in extending your knowle
good place to start is the manual.
There are several other Report Wizards we
reports have no Detail band. Tabular reports l
forms. The AutoReport Wizard will attempt
that makes the most sense—at least, to the W
Word Mail Merge, exports data in a format th
Merge feature can read. This is handy for pro
Experiment with fonts and print styles, an

Summary and Exercises

Summary

- Access includes ReportWizards for single-column, grouped, and tabular formats, as well as mailing labels. Wizards are also included that generate automatic reports and export data to Microsoft Word's Mail Merge format
- To build a report with fields from two or more tables, you can query by example to create a view first, and then create the report based on that view.
- Grouping lets you create reports with records collated according to the values in one or more fields.
- Grouping also lets you create subtotals for groups as well as a grand total for the report.
- You can display today's date with the Now() function.
- You can change the format in which the date is printed.
- The mailing label ReportWizard handles standard Avery label layouts.
- To insert text characters in a mailing label, you must use the text buttons provided by the ReportWizards.
- The UCase() function is helpful when you want to make sure report output is entirely upper case.

Key Terms and Operations

Key Terms
group
group footer
group header
inner join
Now()
outer join
page footer
page header
report footer
report header
UCase()

Operations
Create a new report
Page Preview
Report Design
Sample Preview

Following the Numbered Steps

To make the application modules easy to use in a lab setting, we have standardized the presentation of hands-on computer instructions as much as possible. The numbered step sections provide detailed, step-by-step instructions to guide you through the practical application of the conceptual material presented. Both keystroke and mouse instructions are used according to which one is more appropriate to complete a task. The instructions in the module assume that you know how to operate the keyboard, monitor, and printer.

Tip When you are using a mouse, unless indicated otherwise, you should assume that you are clicking the left button on the mouse. Several modules provide instructions for both mouse and keyboard users. When separate mouse and keyboard steps are given, be sure to follow one method or the other, but not both.

Each topic begins with a brief explanation of concepts. A computer icon or the ▶ symbol and a description of the task you will perform appear each time you are to begin working on the computer.

For Example:

To enter the address:

1 Type `123 Elm Street` and press (ENTER)

Notice that the keys you are to press and the text you are to type stand out. The text you will type appears in a special typeface to distinguish it from regular text. The key that you are to press mimics the labels of the keys on your keyboard.

When you are to press two keys or a key and a character simultaneously, the steps show the keys connected either with a plus sign or a bar.

For Example: (SHFT) + (TAB)
(CTRL) + C

When you are to press keys sequentially, the keys are not connected and a space separates them.

For Example: (CTRL) (PGDN)
(HOME) (HOME) (↑)

Be sure to press each key firmly, but quickly, one after the other. Keys begin repeating if you hold them down too long.

In some instances margin figures of single icons or buttons will appear next to the numbered steps. Margin figures provide visual cues to important tools that you can select as an alternative to the menu command in the numbered step.

For typographical conventions and other information unique to the application, please see *A Note to the Student* in the Overview of each module.

The *SELECT* Lab Series—A Connected Learning Resource

The *SELECT Lab Series* is a complete learning resource for success in the Information Age. Our application modules are designed to help you learn fast and effectively. Based around projects that reflect your world, each module helps you master key concepts and problem-solving techniques for using the software application you are learning. Through our web site you can access dynamic and current information resources that will help you get up to speed on the Information Highway and keep up with the ever changing world of technology.

Explore our web site **http://www.aw.com/bc/is** to discover:

- **B/C Link Online:** Our on-line newsletter which features the latest news and information on current computer technology and applications.
- **Student Opportunities and Activities:** Benjamin/Cummings' web site connects you to important job opportunities and internships.
- **What's New:** Access the latest news and information topics.
- **Links:** We provide relevant links to other interesting resources and educational sites.

The TechSuite

This module may be part of our new custom bundled system—the **Benjamin/Cummings TechSuite.** Your instructor can choose any combination of concepts texts, applications modules, and software to meet the exact needs of your course. The TechSuite meets your needs by offering you one convenient package at a discount price.

Supplements

Each module has a corresponding Instructor's Manual with a Test Bank and Transparency Masters. For each project in the student text, the Instructor's Manual includes Expanded Student Objectives, Answers to Study Questions, and Additional Assessment Techniques. The Test Bank contains two separate tests (with answers) consisting of multiple choice, true/false, and fill-in questions that are referenced to pages in the student's text. Transparency Masters illustrate 25 to 30 key concepts and screen captures from the text.

The Instructor's Data Disk contains student data files, answers to selected Review Exercises, answers to selected Assignments, and the test files from the Instructor's Manual in ASCII format.

Acknowledgments

The Benjamin/Cummings Publishing Company would like to thank the following reviewers for their valuable contributions to the *SELECT Lab Series*.

Joseph Aieta
Babson College

Tom Ashby
Oklahoma CC

Bob Barber
Lane CC

Robert Caruso
Santa Rosa Junior College

Robert Chi
California State Long Beach

Jill Davis
State University of New York at Stony Brook

Fredia Dillard
Samford University

Peter Drexel
Plymouth State College

Ralph Duffy
North Seattle CC

David Egle
University of Texas, Pan American

Jonathan Frank
Suffolk University

Patrick Gilbert
University of Hawaii

Maureen Greenbaum
Union County College

Sally Ann Hanson
Mercer County CC

Sunil Hazari
East Carolina University

Bruce Herniter
University of Hartford

Lisa Jackson
Henderson CC

Cynthia Kachik
Santa Fe CC

Bennett Kramer
Massasoit CC

Charles Lake
Faulkner State Junior College

Ron Leake
Johnson County CC

Randy Marak
Hill College

Charles Mattox, Jr.
St. Mary's University

Jim McCullough
Porter and Chester Institute

Gail Miles
Lenoir-Rhyne College

Steve Moore
University of South Florida

Anthony Nowakowski
Buffalo State College

Gloria Oman
Portland State University

John Passafiume
Clemson University

Leonard Presby
William Paterson College

Louis Pryor
Garland County CC

Michael Reilly
University of Denver

Dick Ricketts
Lane CC

Dennis Santomauro
Kean College of New Jersey

Pamela Schmidt
Oakton CC

Gary Schubert
Alderson-Broaddus College

T. Michael Smith
Austin CC

Cynthia Thompson
Carl Sandburg College

Marion Tucker
Northern Oklahoma College

JoAnn Weatherwax
Saddleback College

David Whitney
San Francisco State University

James Wood
Tri-County Technical College

Minnie Yen
University of Alaska, Anchorage

Allen Zilbert
Long Island University

Contents

PROJECT 4: PARAGRAPH FORMATTING 76

PROJECT 5: SECTION FORMATTING 97

PROJECT 6: WRITING AND EDITING TOOLS 121

PROJECT 7: BUILDING TABLES 137

PROJECT 8: USING DESKTOP PUBLISHING 156

OPERATIONS REFERENCE 183

FORMATTING REFERENCE 187

GLOSSARY 189

INDEX 192

Overview

Objectives

After completing this overview, you should be able to:

- Start the Word for Windows program
- Customize the Word for Windows screen
- Get help
- Exit Word for Windows

People have been processing words for centuries using chisels, quills, pens, and pencils. In the mid-1800s, the first typewriters added mechanical precision and speeded matters up somewhat, but they were still clumsy and relatively inefficient. Revision and editing required cutting and pasting, and ultimately retyping. It was not uncommon for a letter or manuscript to be retyped several times before it was complete. If the manuscript was for publication, it would then need to be completely retyped by a typographer to put it into publishable form.

The first real word processor was the IBM Magnetic Tape/Selectric typewriter, introduced in 1964. It recorded the typist's keystrokes on a magnetic tape and allowed the tape to be revised and then played back on an electric typewriter directly from the tape. It was awkward and slow by today's standards, but it reduced the amount of retyping needed to produce finished documents. Today, ***word processing*** involves the use of a computer to write, edit, format, store, and print documents.

Using a Word Processor

Not only have modern word processors eliminated cutting, pasting, and retyping, but they also have combined writing, revising, editing, and often the publication process itself into one integrated system. With your word processor, you can pull together elements from many sources, such as charts, graphs, photographs, or drawings, as well as words. You can format your documents as only commercial typesetters could a decade ago—using different typefaces and sizes, using columns and borders, or including graphics with your words. Word processing will make your written communication easier and probably more effective and more attractive.

Most people who use personal computers use them for word processing. Many use them for nothing else. Word processors vastly simplify the creation and development of documents. Text that is typed on the computer keyboard is stored on a magnetic disk. The text can be called back up on the computer screen and revised and saved repeatedly. At any time in the preparation process, the text can be printed out.

Modern word processors offer a variety of tools to assist in the document preparation process. Today's full-fledged word processors do much more than manipulate words. They are an integral part of the desktop publishing process, allowing you to combine words, pictures, charts, equations—even sound and movies—in your documents. They allow extensive formatting choices and can print on anything from a simple dot-matrix printer to a complex typesetting machine. Or they can prepare documents that will never be printed on paper, but instead appear solely in electronic form as e-mail or as a page on the World Wide Web.

Using Word for Windows

Word processing programs vary widely in their capabilities and ease of use. Microsoft Word for Windows 95 is an industrial-strength word processor, as capable of producing the Great American Novel or a complex technical manual as it is preparing a one-page memo or the envelope to put that memo in. Word for Windows 95 probably contains more features and capabilities than you'll ever need. Despite its power, however, you should find it relatively easy to learn and use for basic writing needs. As your needs as a writer grow, those advanced features will be there for you to use, but they won't be in the way in the meantime.

Word for Windows 95 can make your writing easier and more polished. Correcting and editing your writing with a word processor allows your ideas to flow onto paper more easily. Then you can use a variety of features to revise and develop your document. You can easily insert, delete, and correct words. You can move, copy, and delete blocks of text. Word for Windows can consult its electronic dictionary on the fly to check the spelling of each word as you type. You can use the electronic thesaurus to find alternative word choices while you're writing or revising. You can use a grammar checker that looks for common style and usage problems. Word for Windows 95 will even correct keyboarding errors as you type. For example, if you accidentally type *adn,* it will automatically substitute *and.*

Sophisticated formatting capabilities allow you to create professional-quality documents that look as though they came from a printshop rather than out of a printer. Word for Windows 95 is a ***WYSIWYG*** word processor, which means what you see is what you get. Because what you see on the screen is what you will get from your printer, you can see how formatting changes will affect your final document. With a click of the mouse, you can create numbered lists, bulleted lists, or indentations. With another click, you can create a table and then format it to present data you either type in or import from spreadsheets or databases. Click again for the Word for Windows integrated drawing program. For a term paper or lab report, you can add headers and footers, footnotes, or a table of contents. You can add columns and pictures to the format for your organization's newsletter. Word for Windows also contains a variety of templates and automatic formatting features to help you give your documents a polished, professional look.

Word for Windows 95 is a powerful writing, editing, and publishing tool. You'll find your investment in learning how to use it rewarded in added ease and flexibility in writing, in the creative options it lends to your written communication, and in the polish it allows you to give your written presentation.

STARTING WORD FOR WINDOWS 95

In this module, you will create, edit, save, and print several documents. Work all numbered steps in order so that your document content and screen displays will coincide with those described. Your screen display may differ slightly, depending on your system configuration. You can interrupt your work at the end of any series of numbered steps and exit Word for Windows. If you wish to retrieve the document later and continue where you stopped, be sure to save your document ***(file)*** before exiting. You can print your document at any point.

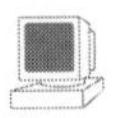

To start Word for Windows 95:

1 Make sure that Windows 95 is running on your computer.

2 Click the Start button in the bottom-left corner of your monitor screen.

3 Launch Word from the Start menu.

Start

Microsoft Excel
Microsoft Word
MS-DOS Prompt
Netscape
Windows Explorer

You may need to navigate through the Programs and Microsoft Office options to access Microsoft Word, depending on the way your system and desktop are organized. Check with your instructor or lab assistant if you need help with this step.

The Word for Windows 95 screen will appear on the monitor, as shown in Figure 0.1.

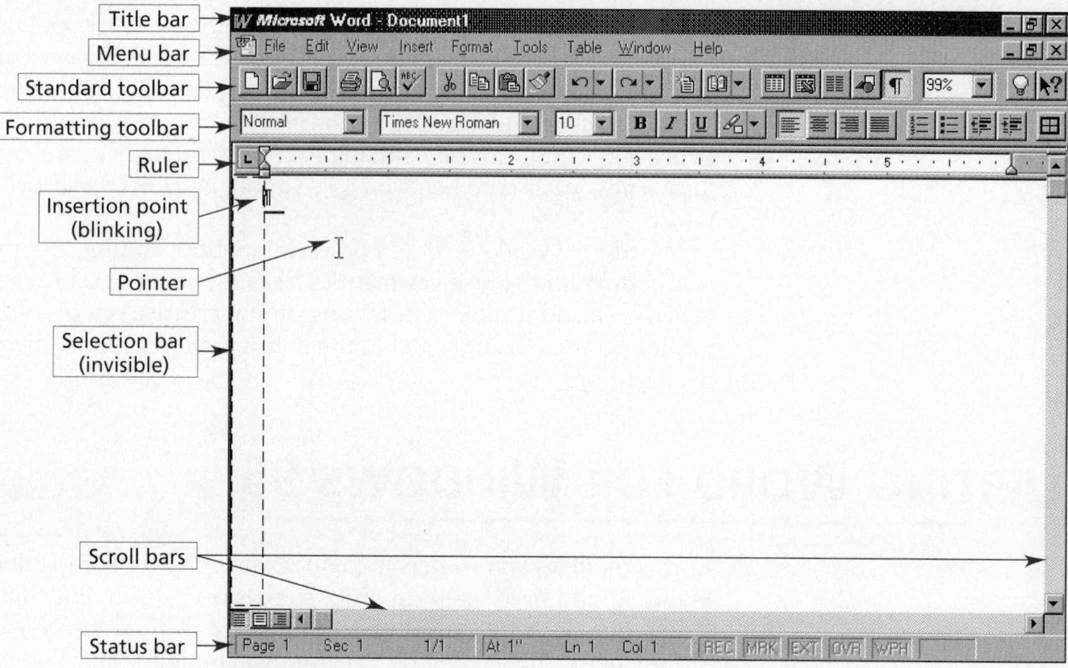

Figure 0.1

The Word for Windows Screen

The Word for Windows screen is organized into several areas that allow you not only to view your document, but also to manipulate it in a variety of ways.

Title bar: contains the title of the application (Microsoft Word) and the name of the document file you're working on (probably Document1 if you haven't named the file yet).

Menu bar: gives you access to word processing commands.

Standard toolbar: contains buttons that allow you to perform many word processing tasks with one click of the mouse.

Formatting toolbar: contains information, lists, and buttons related to formatting your document.

Ruler: displays and allows you to control margins, indents, tab settings, and so on.

Scroll bars: are used to move around in your document; the horizontal scroll bar also includes buttons to display your document in different ways.

Status bar: gives basic information about your document or about word processing modes.

Selection bar: is an invisible area at the left edge of the screen used to select part of your document with a mouse.

You can customize the Word for Windows screen to suit your preferences and working habits. The Standard toolbar, Formatting toolbar, and ruler can all be individually turned on or off. You can also add other specialized toolbars. You can even display your document full screen, with no menus, rulers, or toolbars showing.

To turn the Standard toolbar off and on:

1 Choose Toolbars from the View menu.
The dialog box shown in Figure 0.2 will appear on the screen.

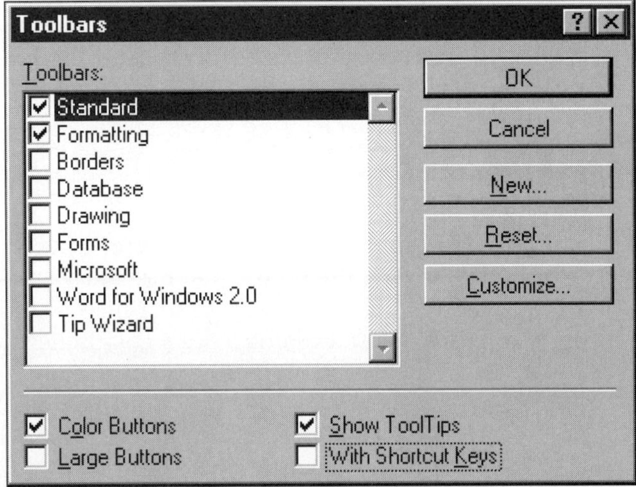

Figure 0.2

2 Click Standard to clear the check box.

3 Select OK.
Note that the Standard toolbar disappears. You can turn it back on by reversing the procedure. This time you will use the right mouse button, used in a number of different contexts, to pop up a shortcut menu.

4 Position the mouse pointer anywhere on the Formatting toolbar, and click the *right* mouse button to produce the pop-up menu shown in Figure 0.3.

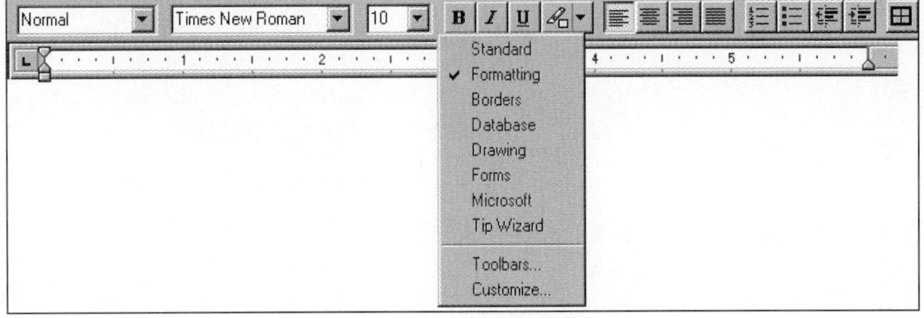

Figure 0.3

5 Select Standard from the pop-up menu to turn the toolbar back on.
You use the View menu to turn the ruler on and off. When the ruler is visible, a check mark appears beside it on the menu list.

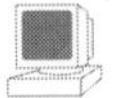

To turn the ruler off and on:

1 Select Ruler from the View menu to turn it off.

2 Select Ruler from the View menu a second time to turn it back on.
If you want to see your text alone, with no menus or toolbars showing, you can switch to full-screen view.

To change to full-screen view:

1 Choose Full Screen from the View menu.
When you want the menus and toolbars back, you can drop out of full-screen view easily.

2 Press ESC or click the center of the Full Screen button, located near the bottom of the screen, to exit full-screen view.

Getting Online Help

Word for Windows offers several types of online Help. You can point at icons using the mouse pointer, and Word will tell you what the icons are used for. You can use a similar help feature to find out how to fill in dialog boxes. Word even includes a comprehensive online manual, with a table of contents and an index, and also allows you to type in questions in your own words to find out how to use various Word features.

The simplest of Word's help tools are ToolTips, which will help you identify the icons on toolbars until you learn the ones you use the most.

To use ToolTips:

1 Turn on the Standard toolbar if it is not already visible.

2 Position the mouse pointer over the third icon from the left edge of the toolbar, and let it rest there for a few seconds.
Notice that a small box appears, identifying the icon as the Save button. Notice also that the status bar, at the bottom of the screen, explains what the button is used for in more detail.

3 Point at other icons on any of the toolbars to see what they do.
ToolTips give you only limited information about icons. To find out about other Word features, you can use the Help button, at the right edge of the Standard toolbar. For instance, you can use the Help button to find out a little more about the Save icon or to find out about the Save As option on the File menu.

To use the Help button:

1 Click the Help button at the right edge of the Standard toolbar.

Notice that the mouse pointer changes shape to include a question mark. When you click icons or menu options while the mouse pointer has this help shape, Word will give you information rather than activating the icon or option.

2 Click the Save icon to open a Help box that explains what the icon does.

3 Click anywhere on the screen to close the Help box.

4 Click the Help button again to get the question-mark mouse cursor shape.

5 Select Save As from the File menu to find out what the Save As command does.

6 Click anywhere on the screen to close the Help box.

To find out even more information about Word features, you can consult the online manual contained in the Help Topics dialog box. You can access this information using its table of contents, its index, its database (find), or the Answer Wizard, where you type in questions in your own words.

To get help about naming documents when you save them:

1 Select Microsoft Word Help Topics from the Help menu.
The Help Topics dialog box will appear on your screen, as shown in Figure 0.4.

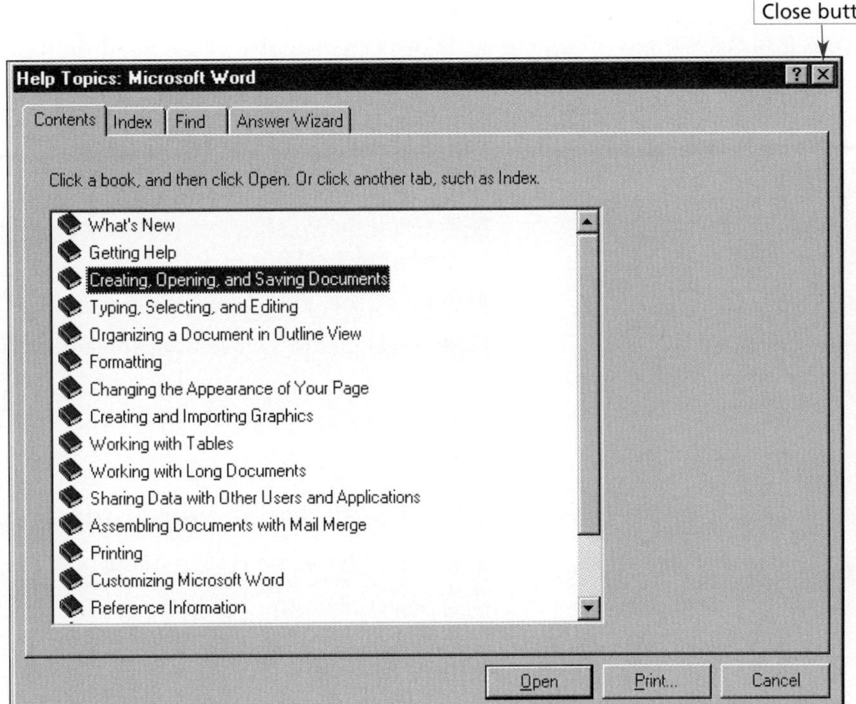

Figure 0.4

2 Click the Contents tab if it isn't already on top.

3 Click the Creating, Opening, and Saving Documents book, then click the Open button.

4 Double-click the Saving and Closing Documents book.

5 Double-click the Naming documents topic.

6 Close the Help box by pressing ESC or clicking the close button in the upper-right-hand corner of the Help box.

To get help about saving documents using the help index:

1 Select Microsoft Word Help Topics from the Help menu.

2 Click the Index tab.

3 Type **save** to locate topics about saving.

4 Double-click the "open document(s)" subtopic (located under the saving documents topic).

5 Scroll down the Help box until you see a list of topics under the heading "What do you want to do?"

Notice that the mouse pointer changes shape from an I-beam to a hand when you position it over the list of topics. The pointed hand indicates a link to further information about a related topic. If you click a link, you'll get more information about the topic it points to.

6 Click the topic "Save a new, unnamed document" to get step-by-step information about saving a new document.

7 Close the Help box.

Word can also give you a hand in filling out dialog boxes by displaying ScreenTips.

To use Screen Tips to get help in using the Answer Wizard:

1 Select Answer Wizard from the Help menu.

2 Click the small question-mark icon in the upper-right corner of the help window.

3 Click the Type your request text box near the top of the help window.

4 Click again to close the explanation box.

If you're not sure where to look for help in the index or contents, the most flexible help tactic is to use the Answer Wizard, already open on your screen.

To get help about Help using the Answer Wizard:

1 Clear the Type your request text box and type `help me` into the box.

2 Select Search.
A listing of possibly relevant topics will appear in the Select a Topic box.

3 Double-click *Getting assistance while you work* to display a help window that identifies various parts of the Help Topics dialog box.

4 Click the various links in the help window to review ways of getting help while you're using Word.

5 Close the help window.

Exiting Word for Windows

Word for Windows 95 has a safety feature to prevent the loss of text. If you attempt to quit the program without first saving your file, Word will automatically ask if you want to save changes to your file. To see how this safety feature works, you must first type something on the screen.

To exit Word for Windows:

1 Type some text on the screen. It can be anything: your name, the name of your dog or cat, the name of your favorite rock star.

2 Choose Exit from the File menu (or click the Close box at the upper-right corner of the Word window).
Because you made changes to your document before quitting, you'll get the warning shown in Figure 0.5.

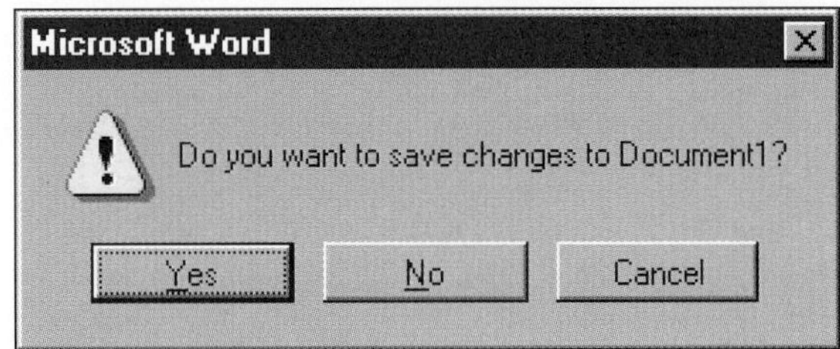

Figure 0.5

If you select Yes, the Save As dialog box will appear so that you can save your file (you'll see how to do that in the next project). If you select No, Word will quit without saving changes to the file. If you select Cancel, Word will return you to the document without quitting.

3 Select No.
This should return you to the Windows desktop.

This concludes the Overview. You can either exit Word or go on to work the Study Questions.

Summary and Exercises

Summary

- Word processing is using a computer to write, edit, format, store, and print documents.
- Word for Windows is a powerful word processing program with extensive features for creating, saving, retrieving, editing, and printing documents.
- You can modify the Word for Windows screen to suit your working habits.
- Whenever you need help with menus, commands, or concepts, you can use the Word for Windows online Help facility instead of having to page through a manual.

Key Terms and Operations

Key Terms
file
Formatting toolbar
menu bar
ruler
scroll bar
selection bar
Standard toolbar
status bar
title bar
word processing
WYSIWYG

Operations
Start Word
Get online Help
Exit Word

Study Questions

Multiple Choice

1. If you try to quit Word for Windows 95 without first saving changes to your document:
   a. The changes will be lost.
   b. Word for Windows will save the changes automatically.
   c. You will be asked if you want to save changes before quitting.
   d. You will destroy your document file.
2. To change the pointer to its Help shape (a question mark) so as to access ScreenTips:
   a. Press CTRL+H
   b. Click the Help button.
   c. Double-click the Help menu.
   d. Press and hold down the ALT and SHIFT keys.
3. What is the major reason a word processor like Word for Windows 95 saves time and effort?
   a. You don't have to retype the entire document each time you make changes or additions.
   b. You can type faster on a computer.
   c. You can format text using different typefaces and sizes.
   d. You can integrate pictures and text.
4. You can turn toolbars on and off by:
   a. pressing CTRL+T
   b. using the Tools menu.
   c. double-clicking the toolbar.
   d. clicking the toolbar using the right mouse button.
5. You normally start Word for Windows:
   a. at the DOS prompt.
   b. from the Windows Start button.
   c. from within the document you are editing.
   d. from the Windows 95 Explorer.

Short Answer

1. The __________ at the bottom of the screen gives basic information about your document or about word processing modes.
2. __________ is an acronym indicating that the screen shows your document exactly as the document will be printed.
3. Word's __________ allows you to ask for help in your own words.
4. A __________ contains a row of buttons that allow you to perform common word processing tasks with a click of the mouse.
5. To retrieve a document to edit it later, you must first save it as a __________.

For Discussion

1. How do you start Word on your system?
2. Describe three ways to access the Help system in Word for Windows 95.
3. What writing and editing functions are included in a modern word processor such as Word for Windows 95?

PROJECT 1: CREATING A DOCUMENT

Objectives

After completing this project, you should be able to:

- Open a new document
- Enter text
- Display nonprinting characters
- Move around in a document
- Check spelling as you type
- Save a document
- Insert graphics
- Make backup copies of your document

In this project, you will create a new document, type text, move around in the document, make simple corrections, and save the document. You'll begin preparing a flyer for a film festival. When you finish this project, you'll know the rudiments of word processing with Word for Windows 95.

CASE STUDY: CREATING A FILM FLYER

Assume that you are in charge of publicity for a film festival being organized by a campus organization. As part of the publicity effort, you and your committee have decided to produce a flyer that can be handed out to individuals and also be posted on bulletin boards.

The flyer must be bold and informative. It must attract attention at a distance, then give readers enough information to entice them to see the movies.

Designing the Solution

The festival will feature science fiction films from the 1950s that star monsters, usually either from outer space or awakened by untimely atomic explosions. Some of the movies are well made; others are decidedly "B" movie material. All are escapist, very retro, and, you hope, fun for the audience.

You want to create a flyer that captures the spirit of the festival and attracts attention. You decide to put the title of the festival at the top in bold type, then list the films below in chronological order. You'll also include information about each of the films because prospective audience members are not likely to have heard of many of them. In addition, the flyer will give dates, times, location, and admission charge for the showings.

Most writing projects are not strictly linear—that is, you rarely begin writing with the first word and write straight through to the last, ending with a final product. Instead, most of us get a few ideas down on paper, add more words, move things around, delete some words and add others, revise and reshape, change words, smooth transitions, and so on. A word processor can be a powerful tool in this evolutionary process because you can make changes without throwing any of your work away.

The festival flyer is a fairly simple document, but even it will evolve over the next four projects. You'll begin by typing the beginnings of the text. You'll add more text. You'll revise and rearrange text, as is typical in the preparation of any document produced by a committee. Then you'll polish the final product by choosing the type style and formatting the paragraph arrangement. In the end, you'll have an eye-catching flyer that will attract attention to the film festival.

Opening a New Document

Word for Windows 95 normally opens with a blank window and is ready to create a new document. If someone was using the computer before you, however, the window may already contain text. In that case, you'll need to open a blank window for your new document. (If Word for Windows isn't running already, launch it now.)

To open a blank window for a new document:

1 Choose New from the File menu.

The New dialog box will appear, as shown in Figure 1.1. This dialog box allows you to select from a variety of templates and wizards. ***Templates*** are preformatted skeleton documents ranging from memos to newsletters. A template is like a blank, formatted document that you can fill in with your own text. ***Wizards*** ask a series of questions about a document format and then use your answers to build a document for you to use. To create the flyer, you will use the default general-purpose template, named Blank Document.

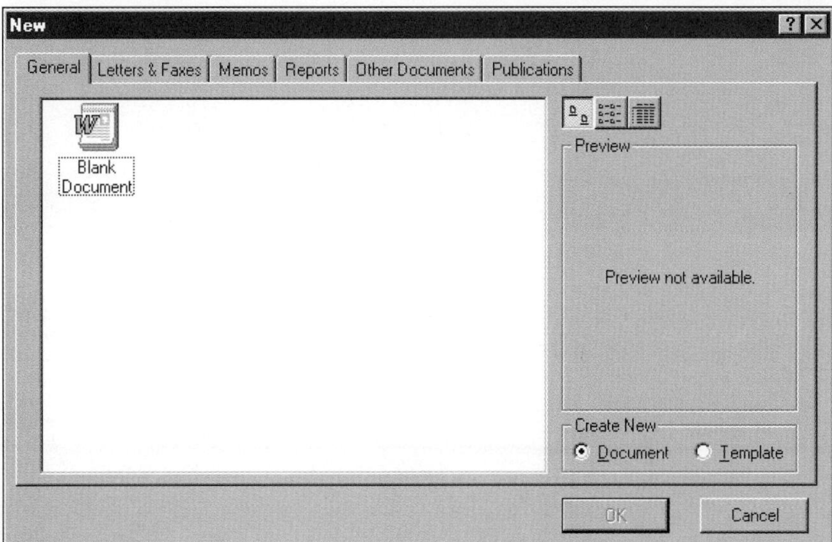

Figure 1.1

2 Select the General tab if it is not already on top.

3 Select Blank Document by double-clicking the icon, or by clicking the icon then selecting OK.

> ***Tip*** You can click the New button on the Standard toolbar to open a document based on the Blank Document template.

The document area of the screen will be blank except for the blinking insertion point (|), the end mark (__), and possibly a paragraph mark (¶). The ***insertion point*** marks the position where text will be inserted or deleted when you type on the keyboard. The ***end-of-document mark*** (end mark) shows where the document ends; you cannot insert characters after the end mark. A ***paragraph mark*** indicates the end of a paragraph and forces the beginning of a new line. The paragraph mark may not show on the screen. If not, you'll see shortly how to make the paragraph mark visible.

ENTERING TEXT

In this project, you will create and edit the film flyer, the beginnings of which are shown in Figure 1.2.

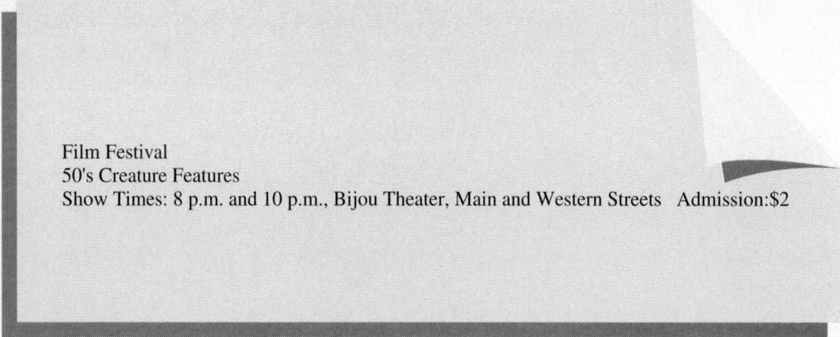

Figure 1.2

Don't worry if you make errors as you type. These errors will just give you more to practice with when you learn how to make corrections later.

To enter the first lines of the film flyer:

1 Type **`Film Festival`** and press ENTER
Notice as you type that the insertion point moves just ahead of the last character you typed. Note also that pressing ENTER forces the beginning of a new line.

2 Type **`50's Creature Features`** and press ENTER

3 Type **`Show Times: 8 p.m. and 10 p.m., Bijou Theater, Main and Western Streets`** and press TAB

4 Type **`Admission: $2`** and press ENTER

You have begun the flyer. Before continuing with it, you will learn how to display nonprinting characters and how to move the insertion point around in the document.

DISPLAYING ALL CHARACTERS

Most of the characters you've just typed are printable: they will appear on the sheet of paper that eventually comes out of your printer. But some, like the spaces between words, will not be printed. ***Nonprinting characters*** include not only spaces, but also paragraph marks (inserted with ENTER) and tab characters (inserted with TAB). Often it's helpful to be able to see some or all of these characters on the screen. Word for Windows allows you to turn nonprinting characters on or off to suit yourself.

You can change the display of nonprinting characters by using the Tools menu.

To display nonprinting characters using the Tools menu:

1 Choose Options from the Tools menu.
The Options dialog box, shown in Figure 1.3, appears. You can customize Word for Windows in many ways by changing the settings in this dialog box. Right now, we're interested only in the options on the View tab.

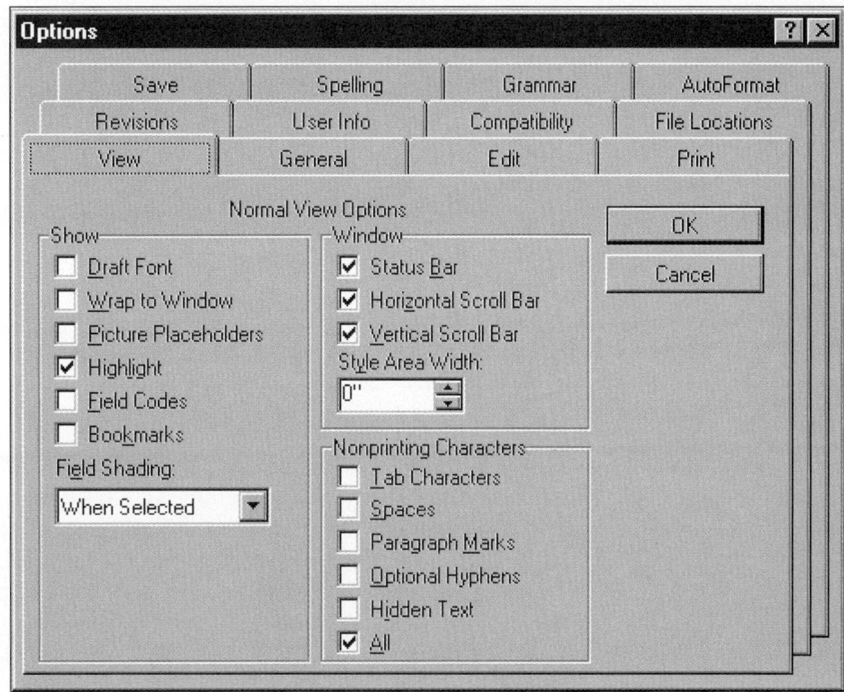

Figure 1.3

2 If it is not already visible, select the View tab, shown in Figure 1.3.

3 Select All within the Nonprinting Characters box, so a check mark appears inside the box to its left.

4 Clear all other check boxes (except All) under Nonprinting Characters.

5 Select OK.

The View tab in the Options dialog box allows you to specify precisely which nonprinting characters you want to display and which you want to stay hidden. If you just want to quickly flip back and forth between displaying and hiding nonprinting characters, however, it is much faster to use the Show/Hide ¶ button on the Standard toolbar.

To use the Show/Hide ¶ button to turn nonprinting characters on and off:

1 Make sure the Standard toolbar appears at the top of the screen. If the toolbar does not appear, choose Toolbars from the View menu and use the Toolbars dialog box to turn the toolbar on.

2 Click the Show/Hide ¶ button near the right side of the Standard toolbar.

Note that each time you click the Show/Hide ¶ button, the paragraph marks (¶) at the end of each line toggle on or off. Notice also that spaces between words, represented by a small raised dot (·), toggle on or off. And notice that the tab character, represented by an arrow (→), toggles on or off as well.

Figure 1.4 shows the screen with all nonprinting characters displayed.

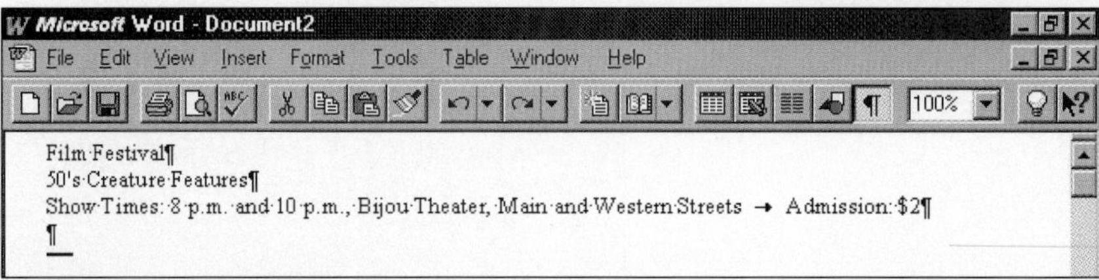

Figure 1.4

Moving Around in a Document

The blinking insertion point indicates a specific location in a document: a position where some action might take place, such as changing a character or inserting and deleting text. Note that the insertion point and the mouse pointer are similar but different. The insertion point blinks and is a plain vertical line; the pointer does not blink and is shaped like an I-beam.

You can reposition the insertion point using either the mouse or the keyboard. To use the mouse, move the pointer to the new location and click once.

To position the insertion point with the mouse:

1 Position the pointer between the *e* and *a* in *Creature.*

2 Click the left mouse button.

The blinking insertion point is now positioned between the *e* and *a.*

The insertion point can only be positioned within the text of your document. The insertion point will not move into the white space at the right of the text. If you try to position it there, the insertion point will move to the end of the nearest line.

You can also use the keyboard to move the insertion point. Table 1.1 describes the actions associated with various keystrokes.

Table 1.1

Keys	Action
↑, ↓, ←, →	Moves the insertion point up or down one line, or left or right one character
HOME	Moves the insertion point to the beginning of the line
END	Moves the insertion point to the end of the line
PGUP	Moves the insertion point up one screen
PGDN	Moves the insertion point down one screen
CTRL + → (or ←)	Moves the insertion point to the beginning of the next (or previous) word
CTRL + ↓ (or ↑)	Moves the insertion point to the beginning of the next (or previous) paragraph
CTRL + PGUP (or PGDN)	Moves the insertion point to the top (or bottom) of the screen
CTRL + HOME (or END)	Moves the insertion point to the beginning (or end) of the document

In the steps that follow, be sure that NUM LOCK is turned *off* if you are using the numeric keypad. Note as you move the insertion point how the center portion of the status bar at the bottom of the screen indicates changes in the position of the insertion point.

To move the cursor one line or one character at a time:

1 Press ↑ until the insertion point reaches the top of the screen.

2 Press ↓ until the insertion point reaches the bottom of the current document.

3 Position the insertion point somewhere in the middle of the line that begins with *Show Times.*

4 Press → until the insertion point reaches the end of the line.

5 Press ← until the insertion point reaches the beginning of the line. Practice moving with the arrow keys until you are comfortable with them.

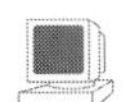

To move the insertion point to the beginning or end of a line:

1 Position the insertion point somewhere within a line of text.

2 Press HOME to move the insertion point to the beginning of the line.

3 Press END to move the insertion point to the end of the line.

To move the insertion point from word to word:

1 Position the insertion point somewhere within a line of text.

2 Press CTRL+→ several times to move from one word to the next word in your document.

3 Press CTRL+← several times to move backward from word to word.

MAKING MINOR CORRECTIONS

One of the advantages of a word processor is that you can make corrections at any time during the document preparation process. If the ideas are flowing, you probably won't want to take the time to check the spelling of a word until later. But sometimes you'll notice a typo that you can't put out of your mind until you correct it. You can make minor corrections using the BACKSPACE or DEL key. You can also reverse previous typing or editing by using Word's Undo feature. (In Project 2, you'll learn to use even more extensive editing and correcting tools.)

Assume you want to insert *price* after *Admission* on the third line of the flyer.

To make corrections using BACKSPACE:

1 Position the insertion point between the *n* and the colon at the end of *Admission.*

2 Press SPACE and then type **price**
After looking at it, however, you decide that *Admission* by itself is clear and decide to delete *price.*

3 Press BACKSPACE once.
The insertion point moves one character to the left, erasing the *e* at the end of *price.*

4 Press (BACKSPACE) five more times to remove the remaining characters in *price* and restore the flyer to its original form.

Now, assume you want to remove *Streets* from the flyer.

To make corrections using (DEL):

1 Position the insertion point immediately after the *n* in *Western.*

2 Press (DEL) once.
The character to the right of the insertion point (the space) is erased.

3 Press (DEL) seven more times to remove *Streets.*

Now assume you want to see how the flyer looks with the label *Science Fiction* in front of the heading.

To make corrections using Word's Undo and Redo features:

1 Position the insertion point at the beginning of the document (in front of *Film*).

2 Type `Science Fiction` and press (SPACE)

Once you see it on the screen, however, you can tell that the label isn't really necessary and distracts from the festival title, so you decide to delete it. You can use the Undo button, shown in Figure 1.5, to reverse most word processing operations.

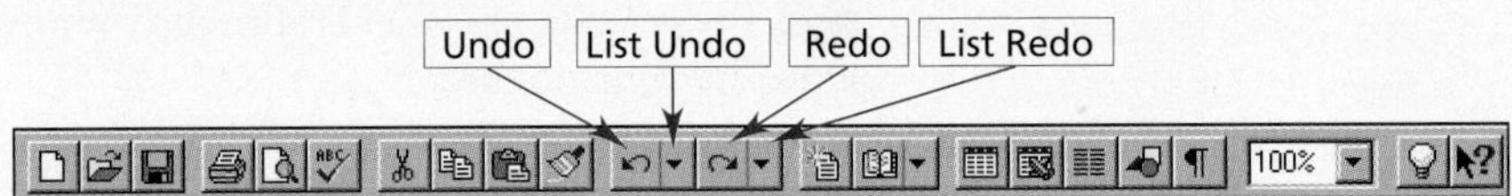

Figure 1.5

3 Select the Undo button on the Standard toolbar.
All the characters you typed are removed, and the text has been restored to its original form. Assume, however, that you're not sure about the heading and want to see it in place again.

4 Select the Redo button (see Figure 1.5) on the Standard toolbar.
This reverses the undo and restores the text. Now you decide finally that *Science Fiction* really isn't needed.

5 Select the Undo button again to remove the text.

Assume that you also decide to restore *Streets,* deleted before you added *Science Fiction* at the beginning of the flyer.

6 Select the Undo button a second time to restore Streets.

The Undo command can usually reverse any changes you have made since the last time you saved your document and does so in reverse order of the one in which you made the changes. The Undo command will reverse most (but not all) Word for Windows operations. The number of steps you can undo or redo depends on the complexity of the steps and the configuration of the computer. To see a list of operations that can be undone or redone, click the List Undo button or the List Redo button on the Standard toolbar shown in Figure 1.5.

CHECKING SPELLING AS YOU TYPE

Word monitors your input as you type and checks words against its built-in dictionary. If it can't find a word in the dictionary, it flags that word with a wavy red underline and changes the spelling icon in the lower-right corner of the screen. When Word has not detected spelling errors, the icon contains a check mark. When Word discovers what appear to be spelling errors, the icon contains a red X. To correct spelling errors, you can click the wavy underline using the right mouse button and make a selection from a list of possible corrections.

To check spelling automatically:

1 Position the insertion point on the blank line at the end of the document.

2 Type **June 15** and press TAB

3 Type **The Blob** and press ENTER

4 Type **Paramount, USA, 1958. It's teenagers vs. ravenous Jello, as a gelatinous mass from space begins devouring small-town inhabitants.** and press ENTER

If Word's AutoCorrect feature is on, the word processor will automatically capitalize *Ravenous* because it follows a period, even though the period is not at the end of a sentence.

5 Select the *R* in *ravenous* and change it to a lowercase *r.*
If Word's automatic spell checking feature is turned on, a wavy red underline will appear under *Jello.* The spelling icon in the lower-right corner of the screen will have a red X to indicate that Word has discovered what appear to be spelling errors.

6 Position the mouse pointer over *Jello,* and click the right (not left) mouse button.
A pop-up menu will appear, displaying a list of possible corrections, as shown in Figure 1.6. The correct spelling is Jell-O, a trademarked commercial name. (This spelling may look odd, but check the shelves at the grocery store next time you're shopping.)

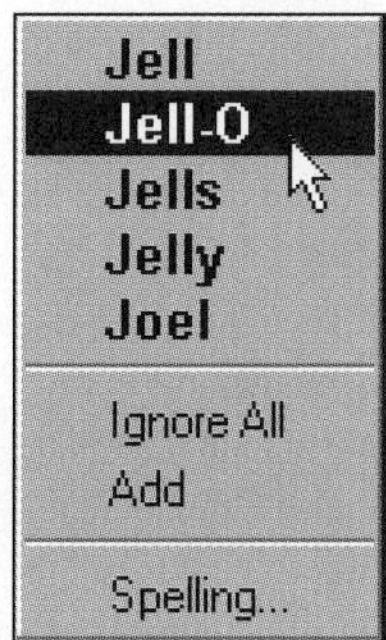

Figure 1.6

7 Select Jell-O from the list.
The correction is made automatically. Jell-O is a proper name contained in Word's online dictionary, probably because it's an unusual word and commonly misspelled. Many proper names, however, are not in the dictionary and will be flagged as misspelled even when perfectly correct. That might include your own name, the names of people you write or refer to frequently, or the name of your town or city. If you use those words often enough, you will probably want to add them to your own personal dictionary that supplements Word's main dictionary. If you are using your own computer, Word will already be configured to store a custom dictionary where it can find and use it again, and you can skip the next set of numbered steps. However, if you are using a lab computer, you will probably need to save your custom dictionary on a floppy disk that you can take with you. The following steps show how to do that.

To save a custom dictionary on a floppy disk:

1 Select Options from the Tools menu to open the Options dialog box.

2 Select the Spelling tab if it is not already on top.

3 Select the Custom Dictionaries button.
The Custom Dictionaries dialog box will appear, as shown in Figure 1.7.

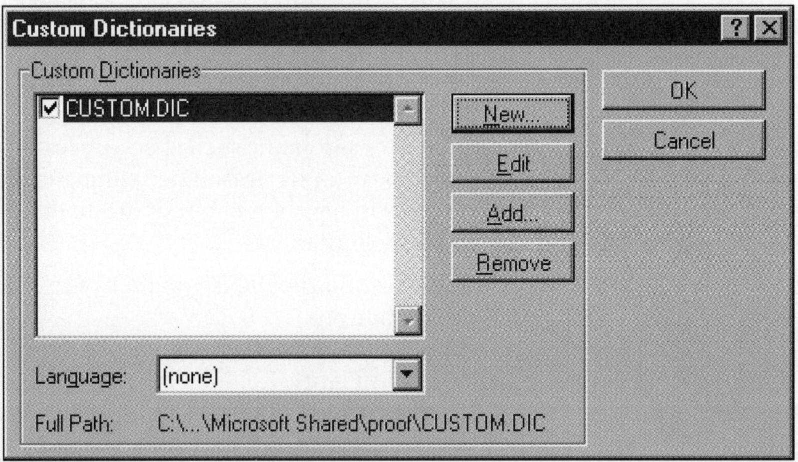

Figure 1.7

4 Select the New button.

5 Select the Save in box, and select the drive where you want to store the dictionary (probably A: or B:).

6 Select the File name box, and type in the name of your dictionary with the suffix dic, for instance, **`Lee's Dictionary.dic`**

7 Select Save.

8 Make sure your new dictionary is active (has a check mark to the left of it).

9 Select OK to close the Custom Dictionaries dialog box.

10 Select OK to close the Options dialog box.

When you want to use the dictionary at a subsequent word processing session, you will need to tell Word where to find your custom dictionary using the Custom Dictionaries dialog box, but selecting the Add button rather than the New button.

To add a word to the online dictionary:

1 Position the insertion point on the blank line at the end of the document.

2 Type **June 22** and press TAB

3 Type **Godzilla, King of the Monsters** and press ENTER
Godzilla is flagged as a misspelled word because it does not appear in Word's dictionary. You can add the word to the active custom dictionary so that Word will not report it as misspelled in the future.

4 Position the pointer over *Godzilla,* and click the right (not the left) mouse button to make the pop-up menu appear as before.

5 Select Add.

If you don't want red wavy lines on your screen but don't want to add a word to your custom dictionary, you can have Word ignore that word, at least during this word processing session.

To ignore a word that does not appear in the dictionary:

1 Position the insertion point on the blank line at the end of the document.

2 Type **Toho, Japan, 1954.**
Toho is the name of the Japanese film studio that produces the Godzilla movies, and because the name does not appear in Word's dictionary, it will be marked with a wavy red underline.

3 Position the pointer over *Toho,* and click the right mouse button to make the pop-up spelling menu appear.

4 Select Ignore All.
Word will now ignore all instances of the word *Toho* during the current word processing session.

COMPOSING PARAGRAPHS

Entering text in Word for Windows is a lot like typing on a typewriter—with one notable exception. You should press ENTER, the equivalent of the carriage return on a typewriter, only at the end of a paragraph, not at the end of every line within the paragraph. Like most word processors, Word for Windows contains a feature called ***word wrap,*** which allows it to determine where line endings need to fall. Word wrap allows you to type on your keyboard without having to worry about when to break a line. If you add or delete text from a paragraph, Word for Windows will recast the lines accordingly. If you change the margins in your document so that the lines are shorter or longer, Word for Windows will again automatically revise the line endings.

As you type, text fills the line and continues to the next line automatically. Word moves the insertion point to the beginning of the next line. Further, the program moves the last word of one line to the next line if the word does not fit. At the end of a paragraph, you will press ENTER which inserts a paragraph mark (¶). Only the last line of each paragraph should end with a paragraph mark. To insert a blank line, you would press ENTER again.

Check that the beginning lines of the flyer shown in Figure 1.8 are on the screen.

Film·Festival¶
50's·Creature·Features¶
Show·Times:·8·p.m.·and·10·p.m.,·Bijou·Theater,·Main·and·Western·Streets → Admission:·$2¶
June·15→The·Blob¶
Paramount,·USA,·1958.·It's·teenagers·vs.·ravenous·Jell-O,·as·a·gelatinous·mass·from·space·begins·devouring·small-town·inhabitants.¶
June·22→Godzilla,·King·of·the·Monsters¶
Toho,·Japan,·1954.¶

Figure 1.8

To enter more of the flyer:

1 Position the insertion point after the period following *inhabitants,* on the third from the last line of the document.

2 Press SPACE and type **The film was one of Steve McQueen's first roles and became synonymous with bad film making despite its relative popularity, a sequel, and a remake.**

3 Move the insertion point to the very end of the document, after the period following *1954.*

4 Press SPACE and type the remainder of this portion of the film flyer, as shown in Figure 1.9.

At this point, information for the flyer is incomplete. Other members of your publicity committee will be giving you more information later. If you make a mistake, keep typing. You will be able to correct mistakes later when you edit the document. Press TAB to produce the tab character (→) shown in Figure 1.9. Remember not to press ENTER at the end of a line unless it is the end of a paragraph or the end of a short line or unless you want to insert a blank line.

Tab character

```
Film Festival¶
50's Creature Features¶
Show Times: 8 p.m. and 10 p.m., Bijou Theater, Main and Western Streets
 R  Admission: $2
June 15 R The Blob¶
Paramount, USA, 1958. It's teenagers vs. ravenous Jell-O, as a
gelatinous mass from space begins devouring small-town inhabitants. The
film was one of Steve McQueen's first roles and became synonymous with
bad film making despite its relative popularity, a sequel, and a
remake.¶
June 22 R Godzilla, King of the Monsters¶
Toho, Japan, 1954. One critic called the monster a 400-foot-high plucked
chicken. Perhaps, but he started an industry. Raymond Burr stars
opposite the chicken in this recut US release.¶
June 29 R I Married a Monster from Outer Space¶
Paramount, USA, 1958. Despite the title this is a well-made film about a
woman who marries an alien masquerading as her husband. (It happens!)
Shot in eight days on a budget of $350,000.¶
July 6 R The Beast From 20,000 Fathoms¶
Warner Bros., USA, 1953. In a culture fascinated by Einstein's equation,
this was the first of the prehistoric-monster-unearthed-by-an-atomic-
explosion genre.¶
July 13 R The Creature from the Black Lagoon¶
July 20 R The Brain Eaters¶
American International, USA, 1958. The parasites have been described as
"hamburgers equipped with tiny handlebars" and as "bunny slippers." Ray
Bradbury was not amused. He sued the studio for plagiarizing The Puppet
Masters. Leonard Nimoy plays the bearded spokesman for the parasites.¶
```

Figure 1.9

Correct any misspellings in your typing, but note that *recut* is a legitimate word and that *McQueen, Bradbury,* and *Nimoy* are all proper names, none of which appear in Word's online dictionary. You can choose to add them to your custom dictionary or simply have Word ignore them.

The content of your flyer should be the same as that of the document shown in Figure 1.9. However, the distribution of the text on each line may be different. For example, different margin settings might be in effect or a special type font (print style and number of characters per inch) may be set for the printer.

Tip If you learned to type on a typewriter, you may have picked up some habits that don't mix well with word processing. You've already seen that you should press ENTER only at the end of a paragraph, not at the end of each line as you would on a typewriter. Here are some other differences:

- The letter O and the numeral 0 are different keys—and different characters—on a computer.
- The letter l and the numeral 1 are also different.
- You should type only one space following a period.
- Don't use underlining to emphasize text except in manuscripts. Use italic instead. You'll see how to do that in Project 3.
- Use tabs, not spaces, to align text. You already know how to enter tab characters, and you'll see how to set tabs in Project 4.

Saving a New Document

Normally, you will want to save your work, with all changes, to disk. The ability to save a document is the real power of word processing or any computer program. Once a file has been saved to disk, you can call your document back to the screen, change the document, and save it again. Word for Windows provides several ways to save your document: choosing the Save or Save As options from the File menu or selecting the Save button on the Standard toolbar.

You must provide a storage location and file name for any document you wish to save. Windows 95 allows long file names. The file name plus drive designator and folder path can be up to 255 characters. The name cannot include certain special characters, such as ? or : or *. Word for Windows will automatically add the file name extension .doc to your document files. (You can also add your own file name extension, but it makes retrieving documents more awkward.) The instructions in this module assume you are saving your documents to a floppy disk in drive A:. If needed, you can modify the location specification from drive A: to the appropriate disk drive and directory as necessary for the computer system.

***To save your document under the file name* Film Flyer:**

1 Select the Save button on the Standard toolbar.
The Save As dialog box should appear, as shown in Figure 1.10.

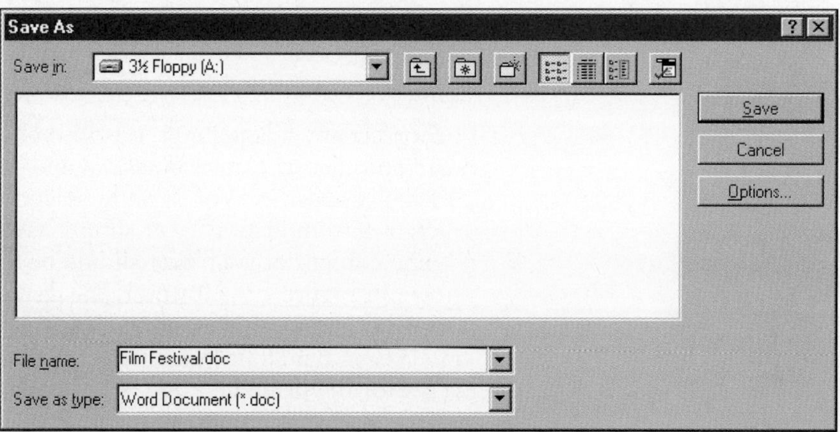

Figure 1.10

2 Type `Film Flyer` in the File name box, but do not press ENTER yet.

3 Click the Save in box to open a menu of drive choices.

4 Select the A: option.

5 Select Save.

If you get an error message, it's probably because you don't have a formatted disk in the drive you specified.

Notice that as soon as you save your file to disk, a message at the left of the status bar (at the very bottom of the screen) displays the file name, and a bar chart shows the progress of the save operation. Notice also that the title bar at the very top of the screen now indicates the new file name, with the file name extension .doc attached.

To add text to the film flyer:

1 Position the insertion point at the end of the line for the July 13 film.

2 Press ENTER and type the partial description of this film shown in Figure 1.11.

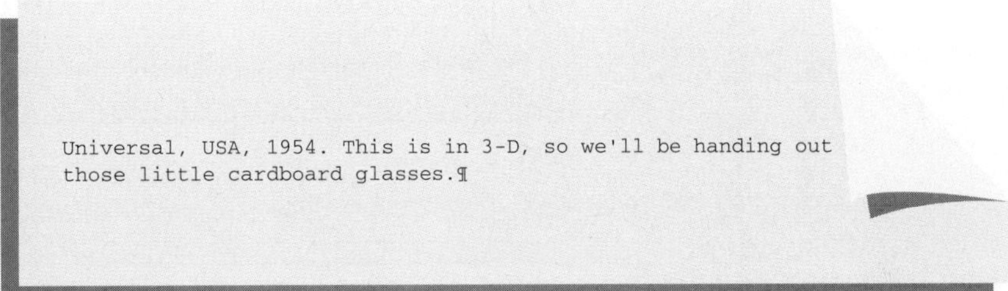

Universal, USA, 1954. This is in 3-D, so we'll be handing out
those little cardboard glasses.¶

Figure 1.11

To save changes in an existing document:

1 Select the Save button on the Standard toolbar.

This time, Word for Windows 95 will not ask you the name of the file. Word assumes you want to save the file under the existing name, thus overwriting the previous version of your document. That way, you'll keep only one copy of the file and your disk won't be cluttered with different versions of the same document. In general, this is a good policy, but it's good insurance to keep one extra copy of your document on disk just in case something goes wrong, such as a scratch on the disk or a power interruption that makes the file unusable.

Word for Windows can make automatic backup copies for you so that you always have the most recent and next most recent versions of your document saved to disk. Then every time you save your document, the existing file is renamed to begin with *Backup of* and the file name extension is changed from .doc to .wbk, while the new version of the file is saved with the file name extension .doc. If something goes wrong with the original file, you can open the backup copy and work with it.

To have Word for Windows make automatic backup copies:

1 Choose Options from the Tools menu.

2 Select the Save tab if it is not already on top.

3 Select the Always Create Backup Copy box so that a check mark appears in the box to the left, as shown in Figure 1.12.

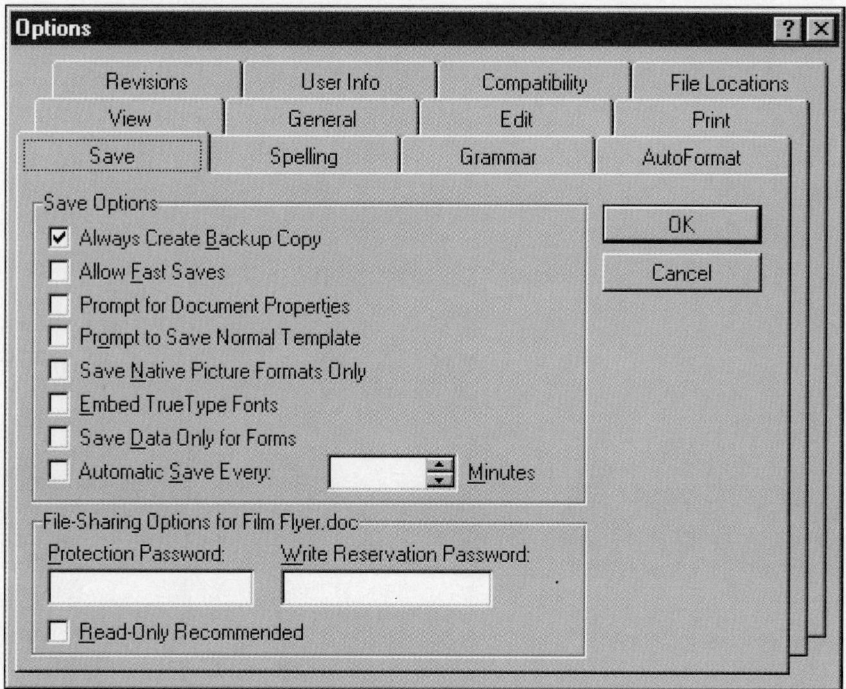

Figure 1.12

4 Select OK in the Options Save dialog box.

You can also use the Save tab of the Options dialog box to have Word save documents automatically every few minutes if you want added insurance against data loss.

Tip Be sure to save your document regularly. You're probably aware that when you turn off the computer, everything that hasn't been saved to disk is lost. You can lose hours of work in microseconds. Obviously, you should save your work every time you plan to shut off the computer. You also should save every time you take a break or every time you've typed a few paragraphs—every 10 to 15 minutes at least. You never know when a voltage spike, a power outage, or someone tripping over a power cord will unravel all those electrons that represent your efforts.

Adding a Graphic to the Film Flyer

To add more visual interest to the film flyer, you will add a small picture at the top of the page. Word for Windows 95 normally includes a collection of clipart files. If those have not been installed on your computer, ask your instructor or lab assistant how to proceed.

To insert a graphic:

1 Position the insertion point at the very beginning of the flyer, in front of *Film*.

2 Select Picture from the Insert menu.

3 Select the file Film.wmf in the Insert Picture dialog box, as shown in Figure 1.13.

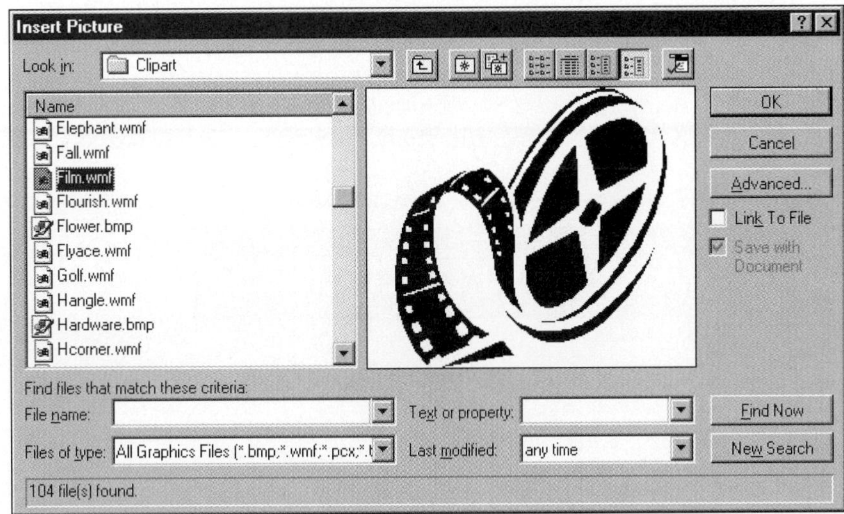

Figure 1.13

4 Select OK.

5 Save your document file.

Exiting Word for Windows

To quit Word for Windows and return to the Windows desktop:

1 Choose Exit from the File menu (or click the Close button, marked with an X, in the upper-right corner).
If you've made changes in your document since you last saved it, you'll get a warning message asking if you want to save changes (Yes) or discard changes (No).

2 If you get the warning message, choose Yes to save changes.
Word should return you to the Windows desktop.

THE NEXT STEP

A flyer, of course, is only one of the kinds of documents you can prepare using a word processor. The possibilities are virtually limitless. Anything that involves words can be prepared with a word processor, from simple letters or memos to complex reports or books.

All writing involves selecting that first word. The power of a word processor is that you can easily change that word, add to it, move it, delete it, save it, retrieve it, or print it. The same techniques you used to begin this flyer will also work for a news release for the film festival, for a letter, a lab report, or a term paper.

This concludes Project 1. You can either exit Word or go on to work the Study Questions, Review Exercises, and Assignments.

SUMMARY AND EXERCISES

Summary

- You can set Word to display or hide nonprinting characters such as paragraph marks (¶), spaces (·), and tabs (→).
- You can move the insertion point one or more characters at a time by using different combinations of arrow keys and command keys or by moving the pointer and clicking.
- Word allows you to undo, and subsequently redo, several previous word processing operations, including typing or deleting text.
- Word automatically spell checks your document as you work, marking any words it cannot find in its online dictionary with a wavy red line.
- In Word, text automatically "wraps" from the end of one line to the beginning of the next. You need to press ENTER (the equivalent of a carriage return on a typewriter) only at the end of a paragraph.
- To insert a blank line, press ENTER at the beginning of the line.
- When you save your document, you can choose the drive and directory where you want to store the file. Word uses the same conventions as Windows 95 does for naming files.
- You can set Word to automatically create a backup file for you each time you save a document.
- Remember to save your files frequently. You can save your document quickly by selecting the Save button on the Standard toolbar.

Key Terms and Operations

Key Terms	**Operations**
end-of-document mark (end mark)	Save a file
insertion point	Create a new file
nonprinting characters	Redo a command
paragraph mark	Undo a command
templates	
wizards	
word wrap	

Study Questions

Multiple Choice

1. The end of a paragraph is indicated by which of these symbols?
   a. ·
   b. |
   c. →
   d. ¶

2. Which of the following is not a nonprinting character?
   a. #
   b. ·
   c. →
   d. ¶

3. Which of the following key commands moves the insertion point to the beginning of a line?
   a. CTRL+←
   b. ← +←
   c. END
   d. HOME

4. When typing text in Word for Windows, you should press ENTER at the end of a:
   a. line.
   b. paragraph.
   c. page.
   d. document.

5. Word for Windows uses which of the following as a file name extension for document files?
   a. .txt
   b. .doc
   c. .wp
   d. .wbk

6. You can toggle nonprinting characters on and off by selecting:
   a. the selection bar at the left of the text.
   b. the Hide option from the View menu.
   c. the Show/Hide ¶ button on the Standard toolbar.
   d. the Print button on the Standard toolbar.

7. The Save button on the Standard toolbar looks like:
   a. a file folder.
   b. a floppy disk.
   c. two sheets of paper.
   d. an envelope.

8. The end of your document is indicated by:
   a. a ¶ mark.
   b. a → mark.
   c. a vertical bar (|).
   d. a short horizontal bar (__).

9. Which of the following key commands will take you to the end of your document?
   a. CTRL+↓
   b. END
   c. CTRL+PGDN
   d. CTRL+END

10. To delete the character to the right of the insertion point, you would press:
    a. →
    b. BACKSPACE
    c. DEL
    d. TAB+BACKSPACE

Short Answer

1. When you type, characters appear at the spot in the text marked by the __________.

2. You can erase text using either the __________ key or the __________ key.

3. Word can keep your next-most-recent version of a document as a __________ copy.

4. ________ is a word processing feature that automatically breaks a paragraph into individual lines.
5. You can position the insertion point using either the ________ or the ________.
6. Pressing ENTER inserts a ________ mark into your document.
7. Pressing CTRL + → moves the insertion point to the ________ in your document.
8. The → symbol within your document is a nonprinting character that designates a ________.
9. The file name for your document is displayed in the ________.
10. To move immediately to the beginning of your document, press ________.

For Discussion

1. What does the Undo command do? What does the Redo command do?
2. How is a word processor different from a typewriter?
3. What are the rules for naming a file in Word?
4. What is a backup copy of a document? Why is a backup copy useful?

Review Exercises

Creating a Cover Letter

You want to have a cover letter to use when you distribute the film flyers to merchants and ask them to post the flyer or keep a small supply on hand to give out.

1. Write the cover letter shown in Figure 1.14 that will be given out to merchants.

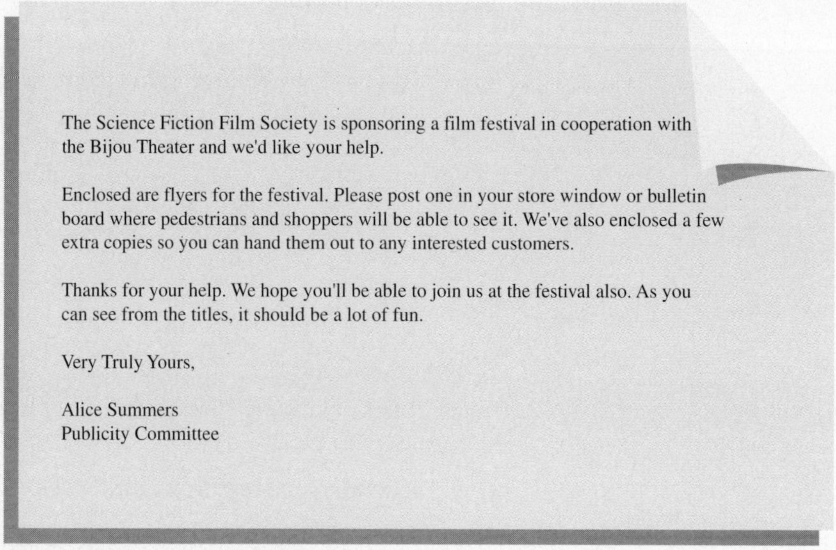

The Science Fiction Film Society is sponsoring a film festival in cooperation with the Bijou Theater and we'd like your help.

Enclosed are flyers for the festival. Please post one in your store window or bulletin board where pedestrians and shoppers will be able to see it. We've also enclosed a few extra copies so you can hand them out to any interested customers.

Thanks for your help. We hope you'll be able to join us at the festival also. As you can see from the titles, it should be a lot of fun.

Very Truly Yours,

Alice Summers
Publicity Committee

Figure 1.14

2. Add the current date to the top of the cover letter.
3. Add a salutation, *Dear Merchant:*
4. Add a sentence to the third paragraph that says to get more flyers they should call (123) 555-7890.
5. Change *Very truly yours* to *Sincerely yours.*
6. Save the cover letter under the file name *Flyer cover letter.*

Using a Wizard to Create a Letter

Word comes with a handful of preformatted and prewritten letters. All you have to do is direct the Letter Wizard to the type of letter you want, and it will do the rest. You may or may not find these letters useful, but the following process demonstrates how Word's wizards work. Wizards are not always installed. Ask your instructor or lab assistant what to do if you cannot find the wizards.

1. Select New from the File menu.
2. Select the Letters & Faxes tab.
3. Select the Letter Wizard.
4. Select the prewritten business letter option, then select Next.
5. Select Letter to Mom, then select Next.
6. Select Plain Paper, then select Next.
7. Type in your mom's name and address and your own name and address, then select Next.
8. Select Contemporary, then select Next.
9. Select Just display the letter, then select Finish.
10. Save the letter for the next time you need to write home.

Assignments

Getting Art on the Net

You will find entire galleries full of artwork on the World Wide Web. Whether you can incorporate a given piece of art into a document will depend on the graphics file format and the graphics filters installed for your copy of Word. Graphics files in the TIFF (Tagged Image File Format) format are usually safe. If you check the Benjamin/Cummings URL http://www.aw.com/is/select/word7, you will find some alternative monster movie TIFF files you can use on the film flyer. Download one and substitute it for the clipart at the top of the flyer.

Creating a Telephone List

Enter your personal list of telephone numbers for family, friends, business contacts, emergency services, and so on, using the following format:

```
Last name, first name → Telephone number
```

The list can be in any order. You will sort the list in alphabetical order and print it out in a later project. Save the file under the name *Telephone List.*

PROJECT 2: EDITING A DOCUMENT

Objectives

After completing this project, you should be able to:

- Retrieve documents
- Insert text
- Select text
- Delete text
- Move text
- Copy text
- Work with two documents at the same time
- Save documents under different names
- Preview and print documents

In this project, you will make changes in the film festival flyer you created in Project 1, save the file under a new name, and print the document. The changes will involve inserting, selecting, deleting, copying, and moving text. In the days of the typewriter, you would have made these changes with a pair of scissors in one hand and a jar of paste in the other. Then you would have had to retype the entire document, probably more than once. With Word, you'll be able to make all changes on the screen, preview the result, and print out the flyer when you're satisfied.

CASE STUDY

You created a flyer in Project 1 that should look like Figure 2.1.

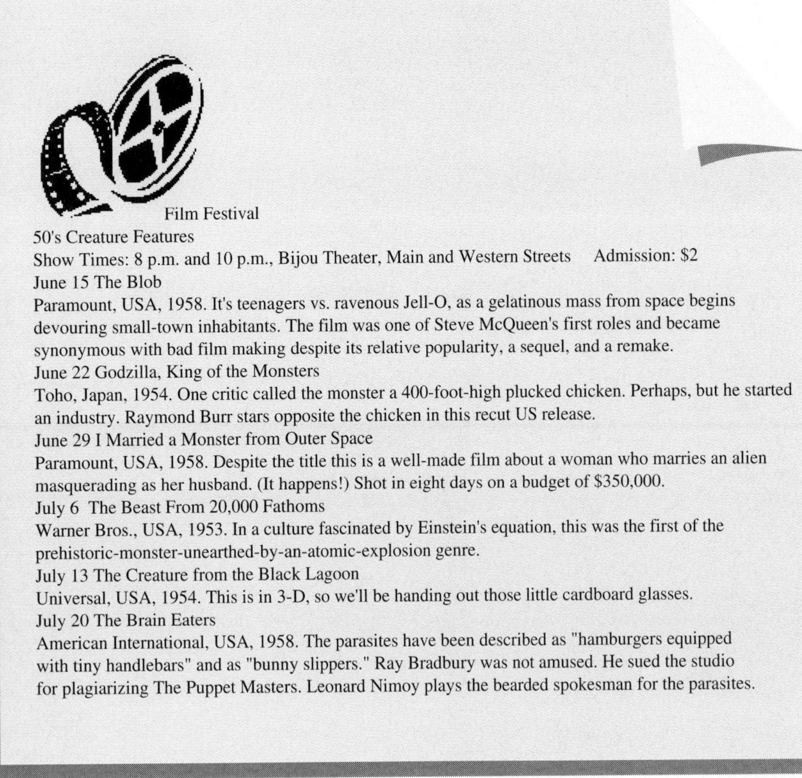
Film Festival
50's Creature Features
Show Times: 8 p.m. and 10 p.m., Bijou Theater, Main and Western Streets Admission: $2
June 15 The Blob
Paramount, USA, 1958. It's teenagers vs. ravenous Jell-O, as a gelatinous mass from space begins devouring small-town inhabitants. The film was one of Steve McQueen's first roles and became synonymous with bad film making despite its relative popularity, a sequel, and a remake.
June 22 Godzilla, King of the Monsters
Toho, Japan, 1954. One critic called the monster a 400-foot-high plucked chicken. Perhaps, but he started an industry. Raymond Burr stars opposite the chicken in this recut US release.
June 29 I Married a Monster from Outer Space
Paramount, USA, 1958. Despite the title this is a well-made film about a woman who marries an alien masquerading as her husband. (It happens!) Shot in eight days on a budget of $350,000.
July 6 The Beast From 20,000 Fathoms
Warner Bros., USA, 1953. In a culture fascinated by Einstein's equation, this was the first of the prehistoric-monster-unearthed-by-an-atomic-explosion genre.
July 13 The Creature from the Black Lagoon
Universal, USA, 1954. This is in 3-D, so we'll be handing out those little cardboard glasses.
July 20 The Brain Eaters
American International, USA, 1958. The parasites have been described as "hamburgers equipped with tiny handlebars" and as "bunny slippers." Ray Bradbury was not amused. He sued the studio for plagiarizing The Puppet Masters. Leonard Nimoy plays the bearded spokesman for the parasites.

Figure 2.1

At this point, the flyer is a first draft. As with many documents that are shaped by a committee and driven by scheduling realities, the flyer will evolve over time. Your word processor will help in this evolution by giving you something concrete to share with others and by making it easy to make alterations.

Designing the Solution

In real-life projects, things always seem to change. Schedules change. People change their minds. Opportunities arise. Challenges crop up. As the film series evolves, you will need to alter the flyer to correspond with these changes.

In this project, you'll use some of Word's editing tools to rearrange and adjust the flyer. Because you saved your file from Project 1, you'll be able to do all this with a minimum of retyping. At the end of this project, you'll preview and print out a copy of the film flyer.

RETRIEVING A DOCUMENT

One of the major advantages of a word processing program is its ability to store documents on disk, allowing you to open documents later for revision and printing. That way you don't have to retype an entire document if you want to make changes or corrections. To open a file you've saved before, call up the Open dialog box and indicate the file you want to retrieve.

To retrieve the document Film Flyer:

1 Start Word and then choose Open from the File menu, or select the Open button on the Standard toolbar.

The Open dialog box, shown in Figure 2.2, will appear on the screen. If this dialog box looks familiar, it's because this box is very similar to the Save As dialog box you used at the end of Project 1.

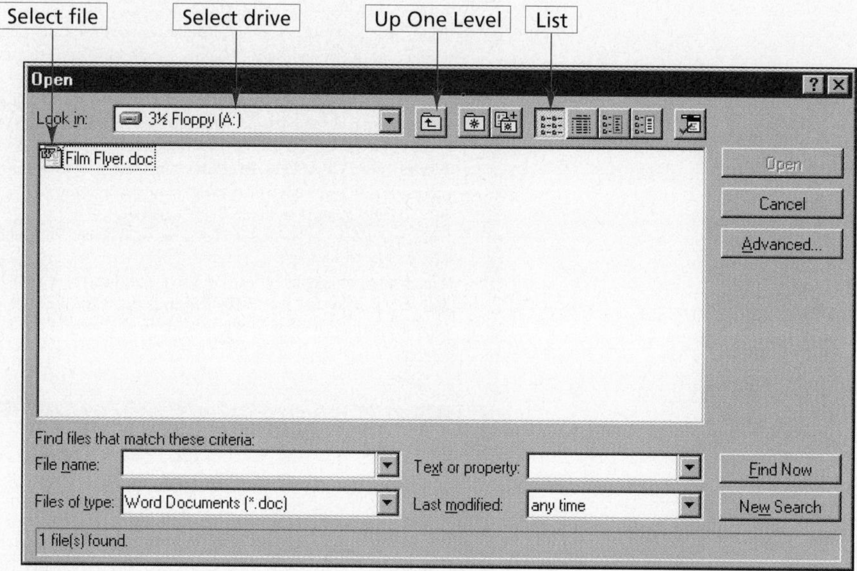

Figure 2.2

2 Select the List button.

3 If needed, change the drives shown in the Look in box to the drive where you saved the document file in Project 1.

4 In the box beneath the Look in box, select the folder containing the document file.

5 Make sure the Files of type box contains Word Documents (*.doc). If it doesn't, use the pull-down menu to change the setting so that document files will be listed.

6 Select *Film Flyer.doc* in the box beneath the Look in box.

7 Select Open.

The flyer you started in Project 1 should appear on the screen.

Tip If you want to return to exactly where you left off with a file when you were last working with it, press SHIFT + F5 before you do anything else. Word will return the insertion point to its last location.

INSERTING TEXT

Word normally operates in ***insert mode,*** which means characters you type on the keyboard are inserted into whatever text already exists in your document. You can switch to ***overtype mode,*** in which characters you type replace existing characters. If Word is in overtype mode, OVR appears darkened in the status bar at the bottom of the screen.

To toggle between insert and overtype mode:

1 Double-click OVR in the status bar at the bottom of the screen, or press INS
OVR appears darkened in the status bar, as shown in Figure 2.3. (If you're using the keyboard and OVR does not appear darkened, INS has probably been assigned another function. See the next Tip for instructions on how to reset it.)

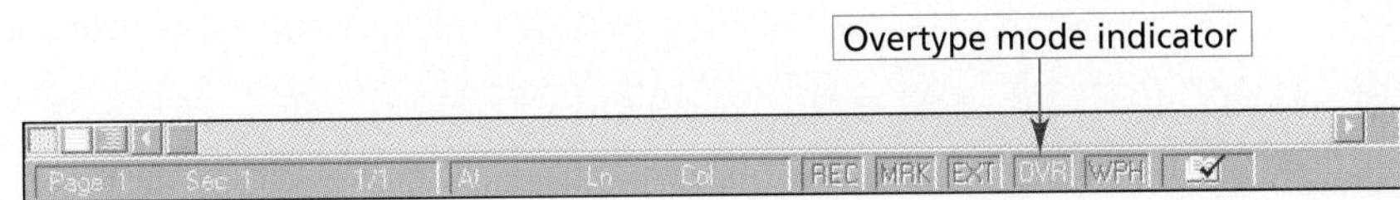

Figure 2.3

2 Double-click OVR in the status bar again, or press INS again.
Overtype mode will be cleared, and OVR will be dimmed in the status bar. Word will be in insert mode again.

> ***Tip*** The INS key can be assigned another function in Word. It can be used to paste in text that has been moved to the clipboard. You'll see how to use the clipboard later in this project, but for now you may need to change what INS is used for so that you will be able to do the preceding steps. To change the INS key assignment, first choose Options from the Tools menu. Second, select the tab labeled *Edit.* Then turn off the check mark in the box beside the line *Use the INS Key for Paste.* (You can also turn overtype mode on or off using the line just below that one, which is labeled *Overtype Mode.*) Select OK to close the Option dialog box.

Assume that your committee has just discovered that in order to break even on the film festival, it will need to charge $2.50 admission. You will have to amend the flyer accordingly. Be sure that Word is in insert mode (OVR should be dimmed in the status bar).

To insert text into your letter:

1 Position the insertion point immediately after *$2* at the end of the line in the third paragraph.

2 Type a period and **50**
Word inserts each character as you type it, moving existing text ahead to make room for the new characters. Assume your committee is given a

correction. The shooting budget for *I Married a Monster from Outer Space* was $175,000, not $350,000 as you were originally told.

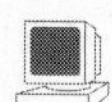

To type over text in your letter:

1 Position the insertion point immediately in front of the *3* in *350,000.*

2 Switch to overtype mode so that OVR appears darkened in the status bar.

3 Type **175** to correct the cost.
The characters you type replace those already on the screen.

4 Switch back to insert mode so that OVR is again dimmed in the status bar.

Tip Although Word gives you a choice, it's usually best to work in insert mode (where OVR is dimmed). Overtyping destroys text, making it easy to accidentally wipe out valuable text or formatting information. Although using insert mode exclusively sometimes results in extra unwanted text, it's not difficult to delete such text, as you'll see shortly.

If necessary, you can save your file, exit Word now, and continue this project later.

SELECTING TEXT

The general rule when using Word is "select, and then do." Many operations in Word involve selecting a block of text and then doing something with that selection. A selection can be a single character, a word, a sentence, a paragraph, or your entire document. Once you've selected a text block, you can move the block, copy it, delete it, or change the way it looks. As with many other operations, Word gives you several ways to select text. In the steps that follow, you will try different ways to select text although you won't do anything with the text blocks just yet. You'll see how to select text first with the mouse and then with the keyboard.

To select text by dragging:

1 If necessary, start Word, open the Film Flyer document, and position the pointer somewhere inside the word *Married* in the June 29 movie title.

2 Press the left mouse button and hold it down.

3 Without releasing the mouse button, move the pointer to a different part of the screen.
As you drag the pointer, the text you drag over appears highlighted (white letters on a black background), and your selection is anchored at the point where you initially pressed the mouse button. Notice also that you can select individual characters while you stay within the word *Married,* but that once the selection expands to include other words, Word automatically "rounds off" the selection to include whole words only (and the space that follows the word).

4 Still holding down the mouse button, position the pointer somewhere within *Space,* at the end of the line.

5 Release the mouse button to select the highlighted text. Your selection should match the block shown in Figure 2.4.

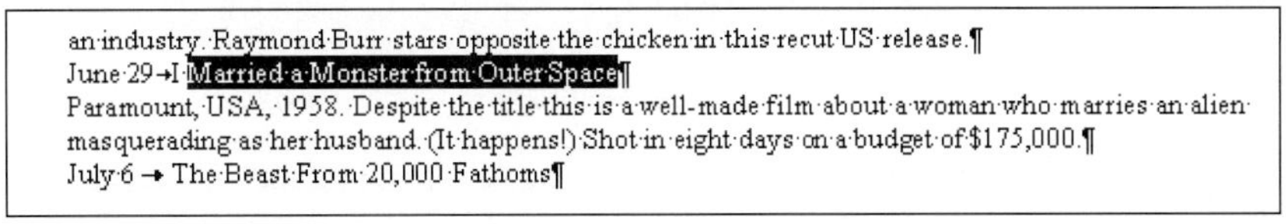

an·industry.·Raymond·Burr·stars·opposite·the·chicken·in·this·recut·US·release.¶
June·29→I·Married·a·Monster·from·Outer·Space¶
Paramount,·USA,·1958.·Despite·the·title·this·is·a·well-made·film·about·a·woman·who·marries·an·alien·masquerading·as·her·husband.·(It·happens!)·Shot·in·eight·days·on·a·budget·of·$175,000.¶
July·6 → The·Beast·From·20,000·Fathoms¶

Figure 2.4

If you want to cancel a text selection, you can simply click once or press one of the arrow keys.

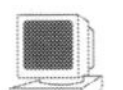

To cancel a text selection:

1 Click once or press one of the arrow keys.

You can also select parts of your text using the mouse within the selection bar, the area within the document window just to the left of the text. When the pointer is in the selection bar, it changes from an I-beam shape into an arrow that points upward and to the right.

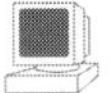

To select a line of text using the selection bar:

1 Move the pointer into the selection bar just to the left of the July 6 title line, as shown in Figure 2.5.

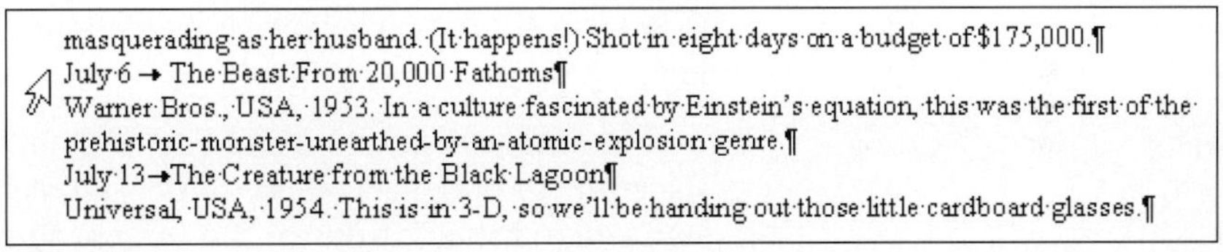

masquerading·as·her·husband.·(It·happens!)·Shot·in·eight·days·on·a·budget·of·$175,000.¶
July·6 → The·Beast·From·20,000·Fathoms¶
Warner·Bros.,·USA,·1953.·In·a·culture·fascinated·by·Einstein's·equation,·this·was·the·first·of·the·prehistoric-monster-unearthed-by-an-atomic-explosion·genre.¶
July·13→The·Creature·from·the·Black·Lagoon¶
Universal,·USA,·1954.·This·is·in·3-D,·so·we'll·be·handing·out·those·little·cardboard·glasses.¶

Figure 2.5

The shape of the pointer changes to an arrow.

2 Click to select one line, as shown in Figure 2.6.

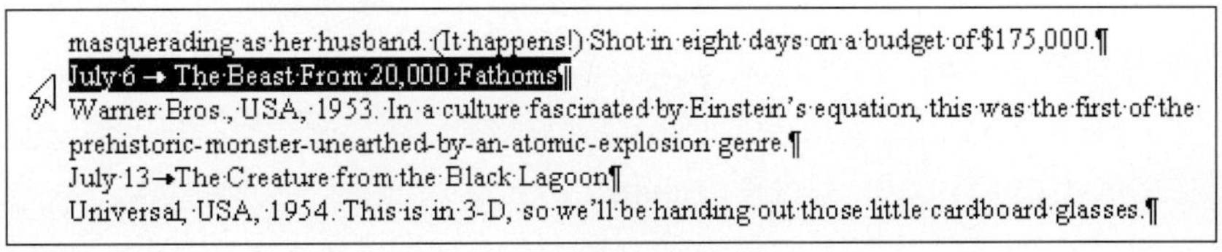

masquerading·as·her·husband.·(It·happens!)·Shot·in·eight·days·on·a·budget·of·$175,000.¶
July·6 → The·Beast·From·20,000·Fathoms¶
Warner·Bros.,·USA,·1953.·In·a·culture·fascinated·by·Einstein's·equation,·this·was·the·first·of·the·prehistoric-monster-unearthed-by-an-atomic-explosion·genre.¶
July·13→The·Creature·from·the·Black·Lagoon¶
Universal,·USA,·1954.·This·is·in·3-D,·so·we'll·be·handing·out·those·little·cardboard·glasses.¶

Figure 2.6

To select several lines, click and drag the pointer up or down in the selection bar. Table 2.1 describes other ways of selecting text using the mouse.

Table 2.1

Selection	Action
Word	Double-click the word.
Sentence	Hold down CTRL and click anywhere within the sentence.
Paragraph	Double-click in the selection bar next to the paragraph, or triple-click anywhere within the paragraph.
Entire document	Hold down CTRL and click in the selection bar, or triple-click in the selection bar.

Sometimes it's faster or more convenient to select text using the keyboard. The simplest way is to use the arrow keys in combination with the SHIFT key.

To select text using SHIFT and the arrow keys:

1 Use the arrow keys to position the insertion point immediately in front of *Godzilla* on the June 22 film entry line.

2 Hold down SHIFT and press → several times.
Notice that this works like dragging. As the insertion point moves, the text is highlighted, always anchored where you began the selection. Unlike when you drag the mouse, however, Word does not round off to whole words if the selection includes more than one word.

3 With SHIFT still pressed, press ↑ several times.

4 Continuing to hold down SHIFT use the arrow keys to move the insertion point so that the selection includes the *s* in *Monsters* at the end of the line.

5 Release SHIFT to complete the selection.

6 Cancel the text selection by clicking or by pressing one of the arrow keys.

The F8 key is the Extend key. When you press F8 once, it anchors the selection and begins extend mode, signaled by the EXT indicator in the status bar at the bottom of the screen, shown in Figure 2.7. You can extend the selection using the mouse or arrow keys, or you can press F8 a second time to select a word, a third time to select a sentence, a fourth time to select a paragraph, and a fifth time to select the entire document. To cancel a selection, you must first turn off extend mode. To turn off extend mode, press ESC or double-click the EXT indicator in the status bar.

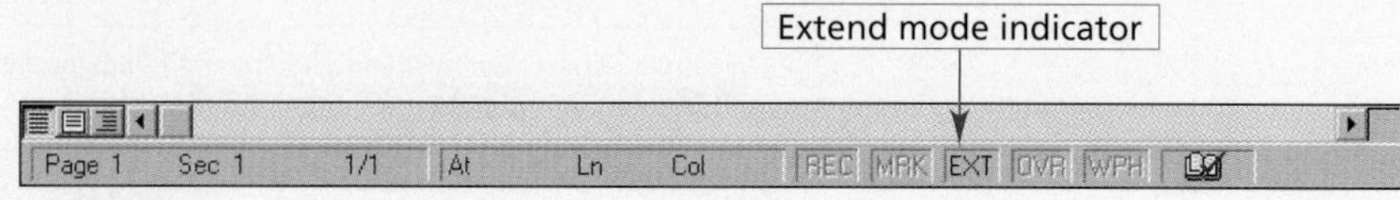

Figure 2.7

You can also extend a selection by using SHIFT in combination with keys that you might use to move the insertion point to different locations within your document, as summarized in Table 2.2.

Table 2.2

To Extend a Selection	Action
To the end of a word	CTRL + SHIFT + →
To the beginning of a word	CTRL + SHIFT + ←
To the end of a line	SHIFT + END
To the beginning of a line	SHIFT + HOME
To the end of a paragraph	CTRL + SHIFT + ↓
To the beginning of a paragraph	CTRL + SHIFT + ↑
To the end of a document	CTRL + SHIFT + END
To the beginning of a document	CTRL + SHIFT + HOME
To the whole document	CTRL + A

Deleting Text

Once you've selected text, one of the things you can do with that text is delete it. You can delete text permanently, or you can remove it from your document and place it in a temporary storage location called the ***clipboard.*** Later you can retrieve that text from the clipboard and place it somewhere else in your document or in some other Windows application (such as a spreadsheet or database program).

To delete a word permanently:

1 Select the word *Streets,* as shown in Figure 2.8.

Tip Recall that the easiest way to select a single word is to double-click the word.

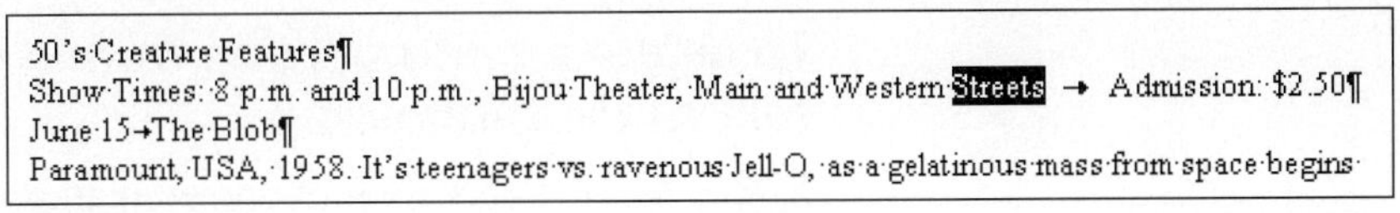

50's·Creature·Features¶
Show·Times:·8·p.m.·and·10·p.m.,·Bijou·Theater,·Main·and·Western·Streets → Admission:·$2.50¶
June·15→The·Blob¶
Paramount,·USA,·1958.·It's·teenagers·vs.·ravenous·Jell-O,·as·a·gelatinous·mass·from·space·begins·

Figure 2.8

2 Press either DEL or BACKSPACE

The word is deleted, and the remaining text closes up to fill in the space where the word used to be. If necessary, the word wrap feature resets the line endings for the entire paragraph. The word you deleted is gone forever—well, almost. You can still reverse the deletion with Word's Undo feature.

To undo a deletion:

1 Select the Undo button on the Standard toolbar.

Note that *Streets* is restored.

2 Select the Redo button to delete *Streets.*

Remember that you can undo several of the most recent operations in Word in reverse order. So even if you deleted text and went on to perform other word processing operations, you would probably still be able to retrieve that deleted text by repeating the undo operation as many times as needed.

If you have a text block selected and then begin typing on the keyboard, Word ordinarily replaces the selected text with the new text.

To replace parasites *with* bunny slippers:

1 Select *parasites* at the end of the description of the July 20 film, as shown in Figure 2.9.

July·20→The·Brain·Eaters¶
American·International,·USA,·1958.·The·parasites·have·been·described·as·"hamburgers·equipped·with·tiny·handlebars"·and·as·"bunny·slippers."·Ray·Bradbury·was·not·amused.·He·sued·the·studio·for·plagiarizing·The·Puppet·Masters.·Leonard·Nimoy·plays·the·bearded·spokesman·for·the·parasites.¶

Figure 2.9

2 Type **b**

As soon as you type the new character, the selected text is deleted and the new text begins to replace it.

3 Finish typing *bunny slippers* to complete the replacement.

> ***Tip*** Ordinarily it's very convenient to have revised text replace selected text, but like anything that deletes text, this method can be dangerous. If you don't want Word to treat selected text this way, you can set the word processor to insert new text in front of the selection rather than replacing selected text. To do this, choose Options from the Tools menu. In the dialog box, select the Edit tab, and then set the Typing Replaces Selection box to off (clear the check mark from the box) and select OK.

To delete a text selection from a document and move the text to the clipboard:

1 Select the July 13 film entry, including the description following the movie title.

The screen should resemble Figure 2.10.

Warner·Bros.,·USA,·1953.·In·a·culture·fascinated·by·Einstein's·equation,·this·was·the·first·of·the·prehistoric-monster-unearthed-by-an-atomic-explosion·genre.¶
July·13→The·Creature·from·the·Black·Lagoon¶
Universal,·USA,·1954.·This·is·in·3-D,·so·we'll·be·handing·out·those·little·cardboard·glasses.¶
July·20→The·Brain·Eaters¶
American·International,·USA,·1958.·The·parasites·have·been·described·as·"hamburgers·equipped·with·

Figure 2.10

2 Choose Cut from the Edit menu (or select the Cut button on the Standard toolbar, or press CTRL+**X**).

The text has been removed from your document, but a copy of it is temporarily stored in the clipboard. The text will remain in the clipboard until you copy something else into the clipboard or until you quit Windows 95. The clipboard is part of Windows and is available to any Windows application, such as a spreadsheet or database. You can use the clipboard to transfer information back and forth between one Word document and another, or between Word and another Windows application.

Tip After you have selected the text to be cut, click the right mouse button, and then select Cut.

MOVING TEXT

By deleting text to the clipboard in the preceding steps, you've actually performed the first half of a text-block move operation. You moved text from the document into the clipboard. All that remains is to move that text from the clipboard to some other part of your document. Assume that your publicity committee has just found that, because of a booking problem, the film you had scheduled for July 13 will be available only on July 6, so you need to change the order of the films on the flyer.

To insert text from the clipboard:

1 Position the insertion point immediately in front of *July* in July 6, as shown in Figure 2.11.

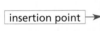

insertion point

masquerading·as·her·husband.·(It·happens!)·Shot·in·eight·days·on·a·budget·of·$175,000.¶
July·6 → The·Beast·From·20,000·Fathoms¶
Warner·Bros.,·USA,·1953.·In·a·culture·fascinated·by·Einstein's·equation,·this·was·the·first·of·the·prehistoric-monster-unearthed-by-an-atomic-explosion·genre.¶

Figure 2.11

2 Choose Paste from the Edit menu (or select the Paste button on the Standard toolbar, or press CTRL + **V** or click the *right* mouse button and select Paste).

Your screen should resemble Figure 2.12. Note that the film entries have been reordered. The dates are reversed, but you will fix that shortly by moving the dates themselves.

masquerading·as·her·husband.·(It·happens!)·Shot·in·eight·days·on·a·budget·of·$175,000.¶
July·13→The·Creature·from·the·Black·Lagoon¶
Universal,·USA,·1954.·This·is·in·3-D,·so·we'll·be·handing·out·those·little·cardboard·glasses.¶
July·6 → The·Beast·From·20,000·Fathoms¶
Warner·Bros.,·USA,·1953.·In·a·culture·fascinated·by·Einstein's·equation,·this·was·the·first·of·the·prehistoric-monster-unearthed-by-an-atomic-explosion·genre.¶
July·20→The·Brain·Eaters¶
American·International,·USA,·1958.·The·parasites·have·been·described·as·"hamburgers·equipped·with·

Figure 2.12

Tip The clipboard, as you know, still contains the text you just inserted, and you could insert that same text somewhere else if you wanted. If you have to repeat text, you can use this feature of the clipboard to expedite your work.

Word also allows you to move text using the F2 key. This type of text move doesn't involve the clipboard, so whatever text is already in the clipboard won't be disturbed. To move text with F2, you would first select the text you want to move, press F2 to begin the move, position the insertion point where you want the text to appear, and press ENTER to complete the move. You will use F2 to move the July 6 date to its correct place in the listing.

To move the July 6 date using F2

1 Select *July 6* but not the tab character following.
Your screen should resemble Figure 2.13.

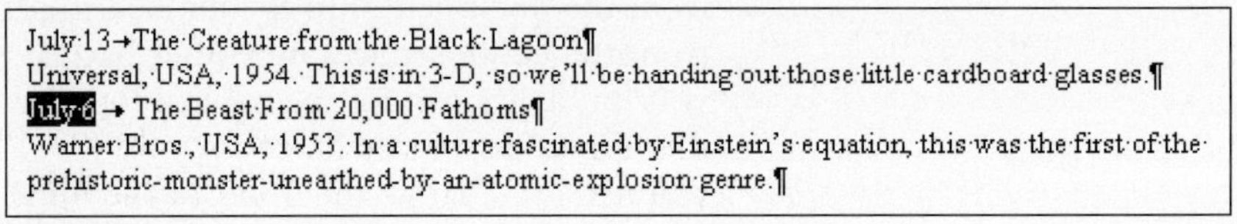

July·13→The·Creature·from·the·Black·Lagoon¶
Universal,·USA,·1954.·This·is·in·3-D,·so·we'll·be·handing·out·those·little·cardboard·glasses.¶
July·6 → The·Beast·From·20,000·Fathoms¶
Warner·Bros.,·USA,·1953.·In·a·culture·fascinated·by·Einstein's·equation,·this·was·the·first·of·the·prehistoric-monster-unearthed-by-an-atomic-explosion·genre.¶

Figure 2.13

2 Press F2
The status bar at the bottom of the screen now prompts you for the next step in the move operation, as shown in Figure 2.14.

Figure 2.14

3 Position the insertion point—now a dotted vertical line—at the destination for the move, just in front of *July 13,* as shown in Figure 2.15.

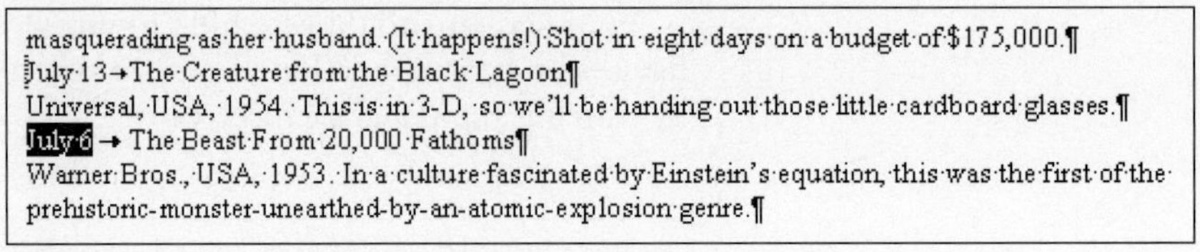

masquerading·as·her·husband.·(It·happens!)·Shot·in·eight·days·on·a·budget·of·$175,000.¶
July·13→The·Creature·from·the·Black·Lagoon¶
Universal,·USA,·1954.·This·is·in·3-D,·so·we'll·be·handing·out·those·little·cardboard·glasses.¶
July·6 → The·Beast·From·20,000·Fathoms¶
Warner·Bros.,·USA,·1953.·In·a·culture·fascinated·by·Einstein's·equation,·this·was·the·first·of·the·prehistoric-monster-unearthed-by-an-atomic-explosion·genre.¶

Figure 2.15

4 Press ENTER
The date *July 6* should now appear just before the *July 13* date, as shown in Figure 2.16. *The Beast From 20,000 Fathoms* movie entry is now undated.

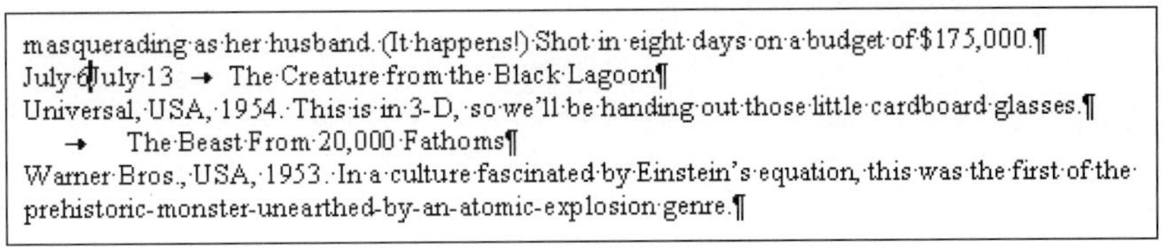

masquerading·as·her·husband.·(It·happens!)·Shot·in·eight·days·on·a·budget·of·$175,000.¶
July·6July·13 → The·Creature·from·the·Black·Lagoon¶
Universal,·USA,·1954.·This·is·in·3-D,·so·we'll·be·handing·out·those·little·cardboard·glasses.¶
→ The·Beast·From·20,000·Fathoms¶
Warner·Bros.,·USA,·1953.·In·a·culture·fascinated·by·Einstein's·equation,·this·was·the·first·of·the·prehistoric-monster-unearthed-by-an-atomic-explosion·genre.¶

Figure 2.16

Word also allows you to move selected text quickly by dragging it from one spot and dropping it in another using the mouse. This operation is called ***drag and drop.***

To move the July 13 *date using drag and drop:*

1 Select *July 13,* as shown in Figure 2.17.

Tip Recall that you can select individual characters using (SHIFT) plus the arrow keys.

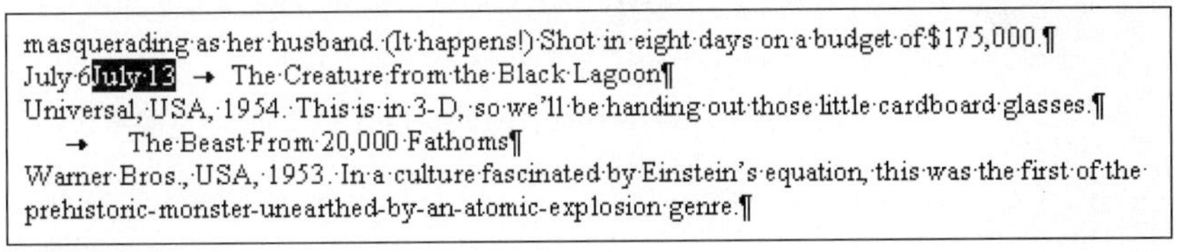

masquerading·as·her·husband.·(It·happens!)·Shot·in·eight·days·on·a·budget·of·$175,000.¶
July·6July·13 → The·Creature·from·the·Black·Lagoon¶
Universal,·USA,·1954.·This·is·in·3-D,·so·we'll·be·handing·out·those·little·cardboard·glasses.¶
→ The·Beast·From·20,000·Fathoms¶
Warner·Bros.,·USA,·1953.·In·a·culture·fascinated·by·Einstein's·equation,·this·was·the·first·of·the·prehistoric-monster-unearthed-by-an-atomic-explosion·genre.¶

Figure 2.17

2 Position the pointer somewhere within the selection to change the shape of the pointer to an arrow. Press and hold down the mouse button to "grab" the selected text block, as shown in Figure 2.18.

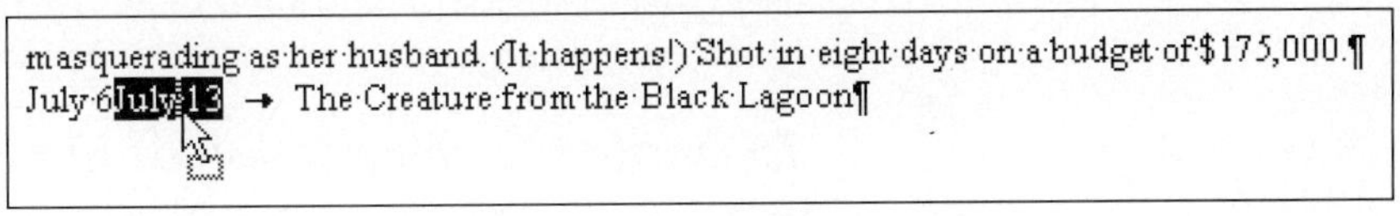

masquerading·as·her·husband.·(It·happens!)·Shot·in·eight·days·on·a·budget·of·$175,000.¶
July·6July·13 → The·Creature·from·the·Black·Lagoon¶

Figure 2.18

Note that the pointer has a small rectangle attached to it, which signifies the block of text you are moving. Note also that you can use the pointer to move the insertion point, which has changed from an I-beam to a dotted vertical bar.

3 Continuing to hold down the mouse button, move the pointer so that the dotted insertion point is positioned just in front of the tab character preceding *The Beast From 20,000 Fathoms,* as shown in Figure 2.19.

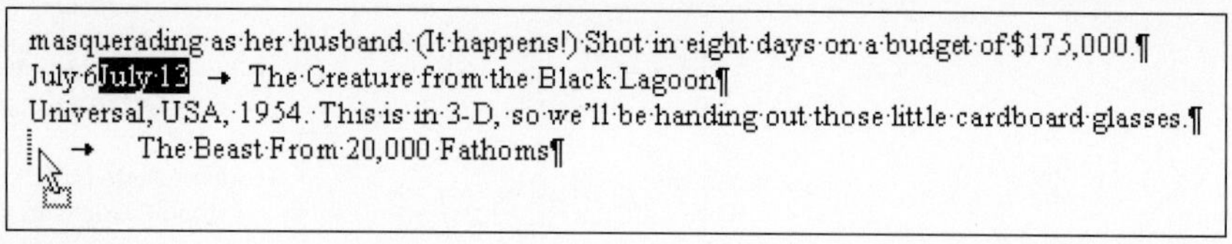

masquerading as her husband. (It happens!) Shot in eight days on a budget of $175,000.¶
July 6July 13 → The Creature from the Black Lagoon¶
Universal, USA, 1954. This is in 3-D, so we'll be handing out those little cardboard glasses.¶
→ The Beast From 20,000 Fathoms¶

Figure 2.19

4 Release the mouse button.
The two dates should be correctly positioned, as shown in Figure 2.20.

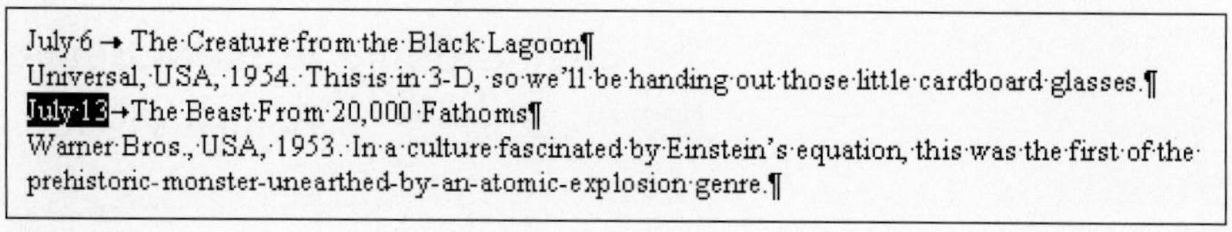

July 6 → The Creature from the Black Lagoon¶
Universal, USA, 1954. This is in 3-D, so we'll be handing out those little cardboard glasses.¶
July 13→The Beast From 20,000 Fathoms¶
Warner Bros., USA, 1953. In a culture fascinated by Einstein's equation, this was the first of the prehistoric-monster-unearthed-by-an-atomic-explosion genre.¶

Figure 2.20

5 Save your file but do not close it.

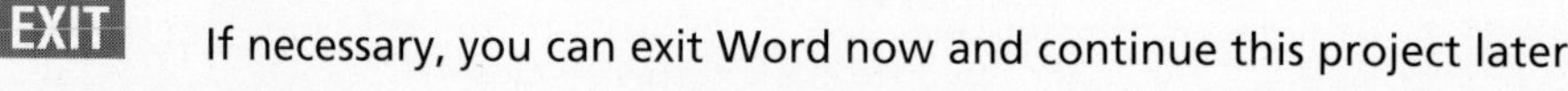

If necessary, you can exit Word now and continue this project later.

WORKING WITH TWO DOCUMENTS AT ONCE

Assume that you've been asked to send names and descriptions of three of the movies listed in the film flyer to one of the people on your publicity committee, and you want to send the information in the form of a memo. Rather than retype all of the descriptive information, you can set up the basic memo structure and then copy the rest of the information from the film flyer document.

To create the top portion of the memo:

1 Select the New button on the Standard toolbar (do not close the film flyer document).

2 Type in the memo heading information as shown in Figure 2.21, substituting the current date for the date shown.

Reminder The arrow symbols shown on screen represent tabs.

Science·Fiction·Film·Society¶
¶
¶
MEMO¶
¶
¶
To: → Alice·Summers¶
¶
From: → Paul·Kettering¶
¶
Date: → March·14,·1999¶
¶
Subject:→Film·descriptions·as·requested¶
¶
¶
¶

Figure 2.21

3 Save the memo using the file name *Publicity Memo.*

The basic memo structure is complete. Now you need to copy the movie descriptions from the film flyer to the body of the memo. This will involve working with two documents at once, a relatively simple task with Word.

Word allows you to have several documents open at the same time and to switch from one to another easily. You can view the documents one at a time in a single document window, switching from one to another using the Window menu. Alternatively, you can have several document windows open simultaneously. You'll use both techniques as you copy information from the film flyer to the memo.

The publicity memo is now the active document—the one visible in the document window and the one you are able to edit. Both the memo and the flyer are open documents, however, and you can switch from one to the other using the Window menu.

To switch between the flyer and the memo:

1 Select *Film Flyer.doc* from the Window menu, as shown in Figure 2.22, to make the flyer the active document.

Figure 2.22

2 Select *Publicity Memo.doc* from the Window menu to make the memo the active document.

COPYING TEXT

Copying text is very much like moving text. The difference is that the originally selected text is not deleted when a copy of it is inserted elsewhere. As with moving, you can copy by using the clipboard, by using the function keys, or by dragging and dropping. You'll try out all three methods in the following series of steps.

In completing the memo, rather than retyping the descriptions, you can pull them directly from the rough draft of the flyer and move them to the memo.

To copy text using the clipboard:

1 Make the film flyer the active document.

2 Select the title and description of the July 6 film, including the paragraph mark at the end of the description. Do not include the date or the tab character, however.
The selection should look like Figure 2.23.

masquerading·as·her·husband.·(It·happens!)·Shot·in·eight·days·on·a·budget·of·$175,000.¶
July·6 → The·Creature·from·the·Black·Lagoon¶
Universal,·USA,·1954.·This·is·in·3-D,·so·we'll·be·handing·out·those·little·cardboard·glasses.¶
July·13→The·Beast·From·20,000·Fathoms¶

Figure 2.23

3 Choose Copy from the Edit menu (or select the Copy button on the Standard toolbar, or press (CTRL)+**C** or click the right mouse button and select Copy) to copy the selection to the clipboard.
Notice that the film flyer remains unchanged.

4 Select Publicity Memo.doc from the Window menu to make the memo the active document.

5 Position the insertion point on the last (blank) line of the memo.

6 Choose Paste from the Edit menu (or select the Paste button on the Standard toolbar, or press (CTRL)+**V** or click the right mouse button and select Paste).

7 Press (ENTER) to leave a blank line.
Your document should resemble Figure 2.24, with the film title and description appearing in the body of the memo.

Science·Fiction·Film·Society¶
¶
¶
MEMO¶
¶
¶
To: → Alice·Summers¶
¶
From: → Paul·Kettering¶
¶
Date: → March·14,·1999¶
¶
Subject:→Film·descriptions·as·requested¶
¶
¶
The·Creature·from·the·Black·Lagoon¶
Universal,·USA,·1954.·This·is·in·3-D,·so·we'll·be·handing·out·those·little·cardboard·glasses.¶
¶
¶

Figure 2.24

To copy text using (SHIFT)+(F2)

1 Make the flyer the active document (select Film Flyer.doc from the Window menu).

2 Select the title and description of the July 13 film, including the paragraph mark following the description, but excluding the date and the tab character.

3 Press (SHIFT)+(F2)
A Copy to where? prompt appears in the status bar at the bottom of the screen.

4 Make the publicity memo the active document.

5 Click in the document and position the dotted insertion point on the blank line at the bottom of the memo.

6 Press (ENTER) to complete the copy.

7 Press (ENTER) again to leave a blank line.

You can copy text between two documents using drag and drop, but you will need to have both document windows visible on the screen at the same time.

To make two document windows:

1 Check the list of open documents using the Window menu. Close all documents except the memo and the flyer.
The Window menu should resemble Figure 2.25.

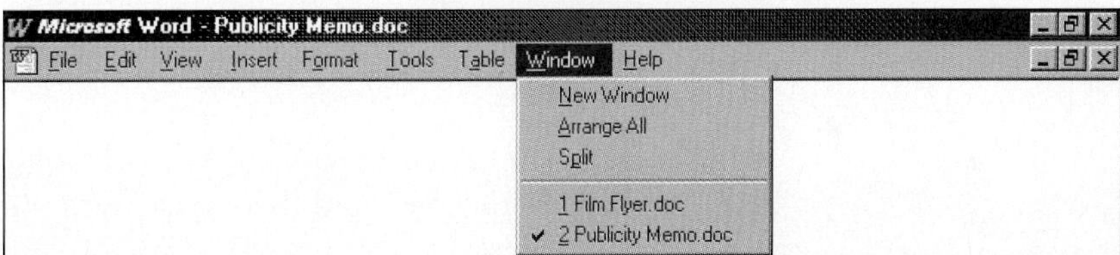

Figure 2.25

2 Select Arrange All from the Window menu.

3 Scroll each window so that you can see the film description for the June 22 movie in the film flyer window and so that you can see the bottom of the text of the memo in the publicity memo window. The screen should appear as shown in Figure 2.26.

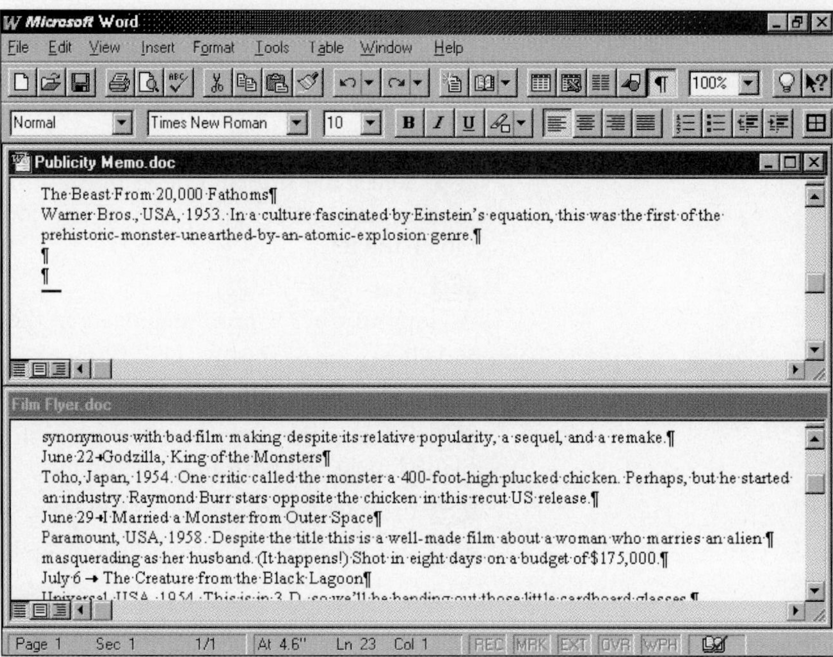

Figure 2.26

To copy text by dragging and dropping:

1 Select the title and description of the June 22 movie in the film flyer window. As before, include the paragraph mark at the end of the description, but exclude the date and tab character.

2 Move the pointer inside the selection so that the pointer turns into an arrow.

3 Hold down CTRL and press the mouse button. Continue to hold down both CTRL and the mouse button until you're ready to paste the copied text.
Note that the pointer has a small dotted rectangle attached to it and that a dotted insertion point appears beside the rectangle. The pointer includes a plus sign to indicate that this is a copy, not a move, operation.

4 Move the dotted insertion point to the last line of the memo in the other window.

5 Release both the mouse button and CTRL to insert the text in the memo.

6 Click the maximize button at the top of the publicity memo window to return to one document window.

Reminder Word allows great flexibility in selecting, moving, and copying text. Sometimes it might seem as if there are so many different ways to accomplish the same thing that you can't remember any of them. Recall that you can get a list of keyboard or mouse commands at any time through the Help facility. You will quickly develop your own preferences for working with text.

Saving a Document Under a Different Name

Saving a file under a new name creates a new file. The new file becomes the active file, which is the file currently being edited. The old file stored under the previous name will remain unchanged unless you deliberately open that file and alter it. You can use this feature to save intermediate drafts of a document. For instance, it is usually a good idea to save an extra copy of a document under a different name if you are about to undertake an extensive revision. That gives you a version to fall back on if you get mixed up in the middle of the revision or make a mistake and turn all of your hard work into electronic garbage.

To save an existing document under a new name:

1 Make the film flyer the active document.

2 Open the Save As dialog box by choosing Save As (*not* Save) from the File menu.

> ***Warning*** If you choose Save, Word will immediately save the file under its current name and defeat the purpose of separately saving the second draft of the film flyer.

3 In the File name box, type `Revised Film Flyer,` the new name for the document.

4 If needed, change the drive and directory in the Save in box.

5 Select Save.
The title bar at the top of the screen now shows the new file name.

6 Make the publicity memo the active document.

Previewing and Printing a Document

The end result of a word processing effort is usually a printed document: something you can mail, give to someone else to read, or mark up for further revision. Before you commit your document to paper, however, Word can prepare a preview on the screen. The preview shows just how the printed document will look: where page breaks will fall, where page numbers will appear, how headings and margins will look, and so on.

The Print Preview screen looks like Figure 2.27, with the Print Preview toolbar at the top just above the miniature page. You can edit your document in print-preview mode while you check margins, page breaks, heading positions, and so on, to be sure the page will look just as you want it to. The Print button prints the file immediately. The Magnifier button toggles between edit mode (with the usual I-beam pointer) and zoom mode (with a magnifying-glass pointer). When in zoom mode, you can click to switch back and forth between a full-page view and a close-up view. The One Page button displays a single page of your document, and the Multiple Pages button allows you to view several miniature pages at once. The Zoom control box allows you to set the magnification of the preview page. The View Ruler button toggles the ruler on and off. The Shrink to Fit button may be able to eliminate the last page of your document if that page contains only a few lines of text. The Full Screen button toggles to a preview display containing only your document and the Print Preview toolbar. The Close button turns off print-preview mode and returns to the display mode you were using before. The Help button can be used to obtain more information about any of these features.

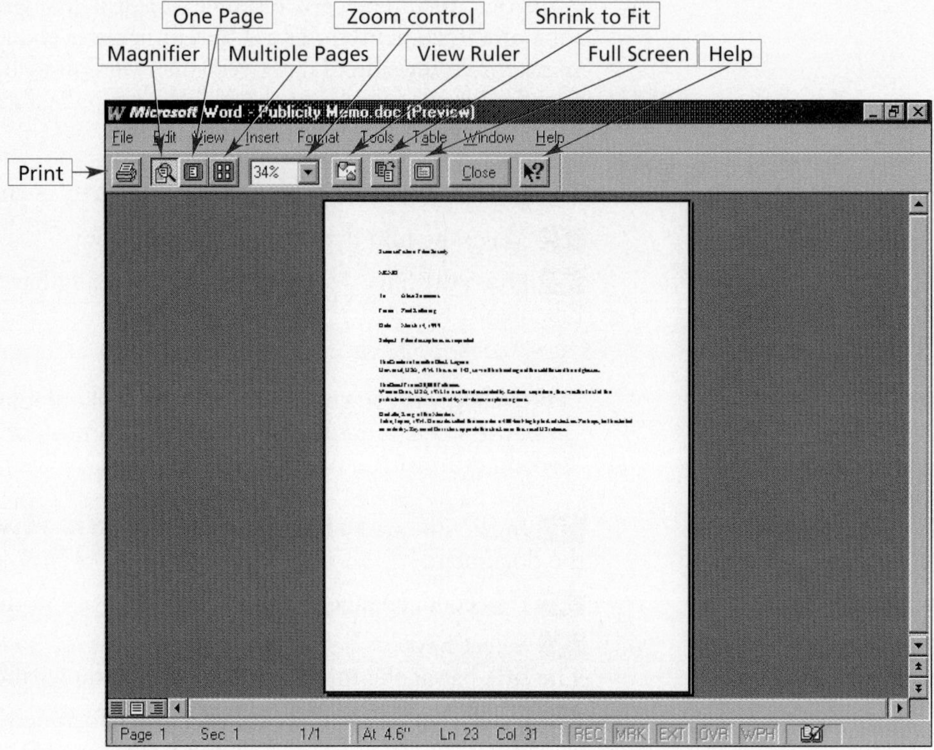

Figure 2.27

To preview and print the document:

1 Select the Print Preview button on the Standard toolbar.

2 Choose Print from the File menu (or press CTRL + **P**).

The Print dialog box will appear, as shown in Figure 2.28. The printer for the system will be listed in the Name box. The print settings default to printing one copy of your entire document. You can change the number of copies and you can set the range of pages you want if you don't need to print the entire document.

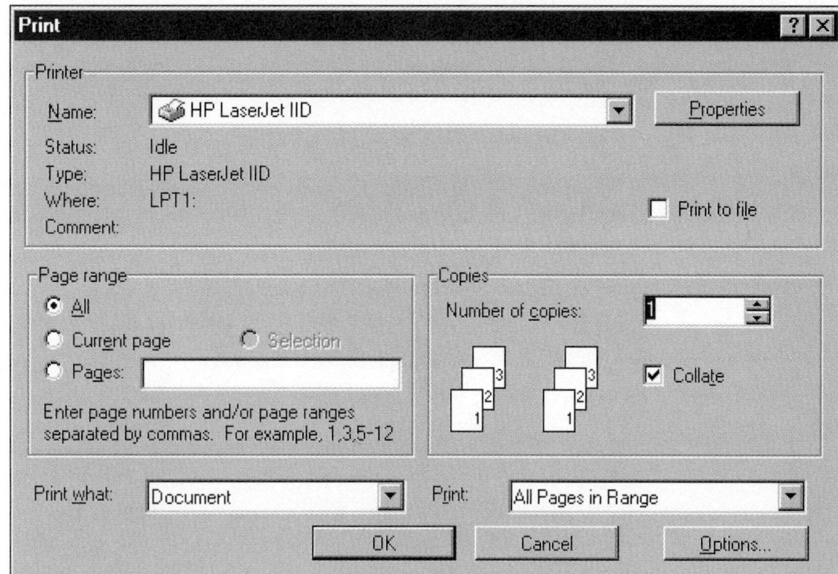

Figure 2.28

3 Select OK in the Print dialog box.
A brief message appears telling you that Word is preparing the document for printing and transmitting information to the printer.

4 Compare your printed copy to the print-preview display for your document.

5 Select the Close button on the Print Preview toolbar to exit the print-preview mode.

6 Save the memo file and close it.

If you already know that your document is formatted correctly, you can bypass the preview before printing. You can open the Print dialog box by choosing Print from the File menu, setting the defaults as needed, and then selecting OK. To really expedite printing, you can simply accept whatever defaults are in effect and print by using the Print button on the Standard toolbar. This is the approach you will use to print the revised film flyer.

To print using the Print button:

1 Make the revised film flyer the active document if it is not already.

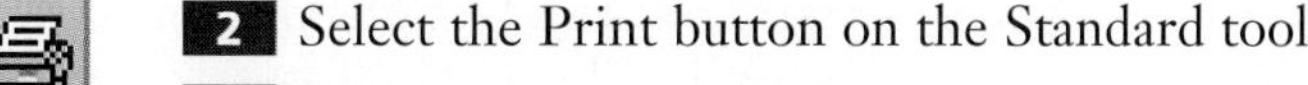

2 Select the Print button on the Standard toolbar.

3 Close the revised film flyer.

The Next Step

The ability to move, copy, and edit text makes it relatively easy to assemble new documents from existing ones without retyping. You could take your own résumé, for example, and modify it for a specific internship or job opening, customizing the text to speak to the requirements of that particular position.

You could take a similar approach for a cover letter. By changing the name and address of the person you're writing to, and perhaps making other alterations in the text of the letter, you can quickly produce a personalized letter.

This concludes Project 2. You can either exit Word or go on to work the Study Questions, Review Exercises, and Assignments.

Summary and Exercises

Summary

- You can retrieve documents you've stored to disk by choosing Open from the File menu or by selecting the Open button on the Standard toolbar.
- You can switch between insert mode and overtype mode by pressing INS or by double-clicking OVR in the status bar. It is safest to work in insert mode.
- The general strategy when working in Word is "select, and then do," which means first select a block of text, and then do something with it.
- You can select blocks of text in a variety of ways: dragging with the mouse, using SHIFT with the arrow keys, clicking in the selection bar, or using F8
- You can delete text permanently by using DEL or BACKSPACE You can delete text to the clipboard by choosing Cut from the Edit menu, by pressing CTRL+X or by selecting the Cut button on the Standard toolbar.
- If you type something while a text block is selected, the typed text replaces the selected text.
- You can move text in three ways: you can delete text to the clipboard and then copy it from the clipboard back into your document; you can use F2; and you can drag and drop text selections.
- Copying text is like moving text, except you don't delete the text from its original location. You can copy text to the clipboard, you can use SHIFT+F2, or you can drag and drop using the mouse with CTRL
- Document templates, which are preformatted for various kinds of written materials, can be opened in the New dialog box.
- You can work with more than one open document at once in Word, switching among them using the Window menu.
- You can save separate drafts of a document by changing the file name when you save the file. To do that, select Save As from the File menu.
- Word will preview your printed document on the screen so that you can check page breaks, margins, and so on before you actually print the file.

Key Terms and Operations

Key Terms
clipboard
drag and drop
insert mode
overtype mode

Operations
Copy text
Cut text
Delete text
Paste text
Preview and print a document
Select text

Study Questions

Multiple Choice

1. When you copy a block of text, it is temporarily stored in the:
   a. buffer.
   b. clipboard.
   c. status bar.
   d. block file.

2. Which of the following will not select text?
   a. holding down SHIFT and pressing one of the arrow keys
   b. clicking in the selection bar
   c. holding down CTRL and clicking
   d. clicking at the end of a line

3. Which of the following inserts text from the clipboard?
   a. CTRL + **X**
   b. CTRL + **C**
   c. CTRL + **I**
   d. CTRL + **V**

4. If Word is in overtype mode:
   a. OVR appears in the status bar.
   b. The pointer changes to an X shape.
   c. The title bar blinks as a warning.
   d. The insertion point becomes a dotted line.

5. To select a single word:
   a. Press F8 three times.
   b. Press CTRL and click the word.
   c. Press CTRL + **W**
   d. Double-click the word.

6. If you delete a text block with DEL, you can retrieve the text block:
   a. by pressing CTRL + **V**
   b. by choosing Paste from the Edit menu.
   c. with the Undo command.
   d. by pressing F2

7. To select an entire document:
   a. Hold down CTRL and press F8
   b. Hold down CTRL and click in the selection bar.
   c. Double-click in the selection bar.
   d. Choose Entire from the Select menu.

8. The Copy button on the Standard toolbar looks like:
   a. a pair of scissors.
   b. two sheets of paper.
   c. a sheet of paper and a clipboard.
   d. a printer.

9. If you save a document under a new name:
   a. The old name and associated file are deleted.
   b. The old file gets the new name, and the old name is deleted.
   c. The file you are editing retains the old name.
   d. Both the old and the new files will be saved to disk.
10. When it is in the selection bar, the pointer:
    a. has a small rectangle attached to it.
    b. is shaped like an I-beam.
    c. is a vertical blinking line.
    d. becomes an arrow pointing up and to the right.

Short Answer

1. To toggle between insert mode and overtype mode, press __________.
2. The general rule in using Word is "__________, and then do."
3. To cancel a text selection, click or press one of the __________ keys.
4. The Extend key is the __________ key.
5. The Move key is the __________ key.
6. After you copy text from the clipboard, the clipboard still contains __________.
7. To copy a text selection using the mouse, you must hold down the __________ key while dragging the selection.
8. To select text using the keyboard, you can hold down the __________ key and then press one of the arrow keys.
9. You can delete a block of text using either the __________ or __________ keys.
10. When you exit Windows, the contents of the clipboard are __________.

For Discussion

1. Why is it usually better to use insert mode than overtype mode?
2. What is the difference between deleting text using DEL or BACKSPACE and deleting text using CTRL+X?
3. Word allows you to move text blocks in several different ways, using both the mouse and the keyboard. What are the advantages and disadvantages of each?

Review Exercises

Correcting a Rough Draft

1. Type a rough draft of the memo shown in Figure 2.29 (without making the corrections yet).

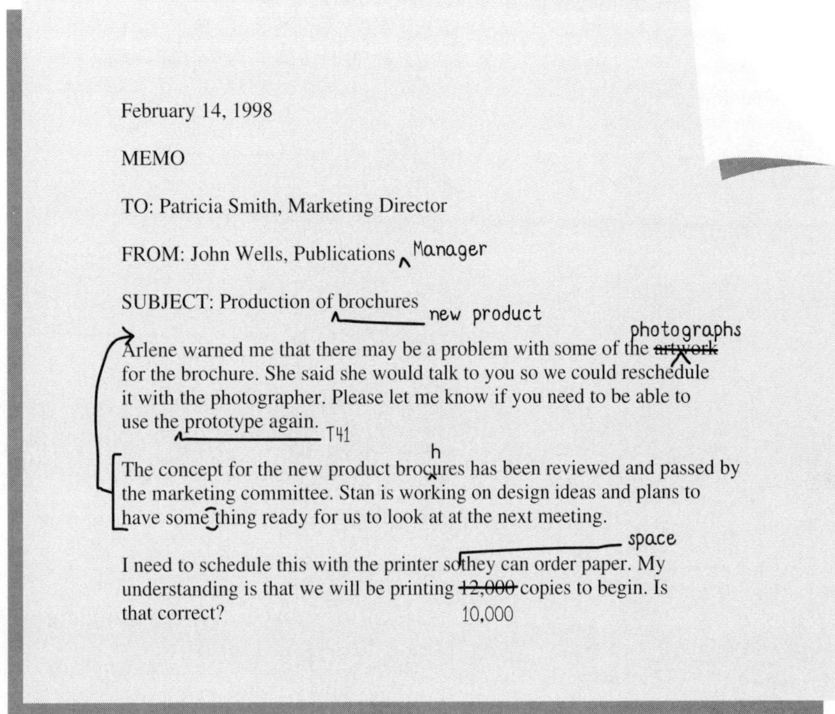

February 14, 1998

MEMO

TO: Patricia Smith, Marketing Director

FROM: John Wells, Publications Manager

SUBJECT: Production of brochures new product

Arlene warned me that there may be a problem with some of the artwork photographs for the brochure. She said she would talk to you so we could reschedule it with the photographer. Please let me know if you need to be able to use the prototype again. T41

The concept for the new product brocures h has been reviewed and passed by the marketing committee. Stan is working on design ideas and plans to have some thing ready for us to look at at the next meeting.

I need to schedule this with the printer sothey space can order paper. My understanding is that we will be printing 12,000 10,000 copies to begin. Is that correct?

Figure 2.29

2. Make the corrections noted.
3. Save the file under the file name *Brochure Memo,* and print the file.

Creating a Meeting Agenda

1. Type the meeting agenda items shown in Figure 2.30. Use TAB to indent the agenda items.

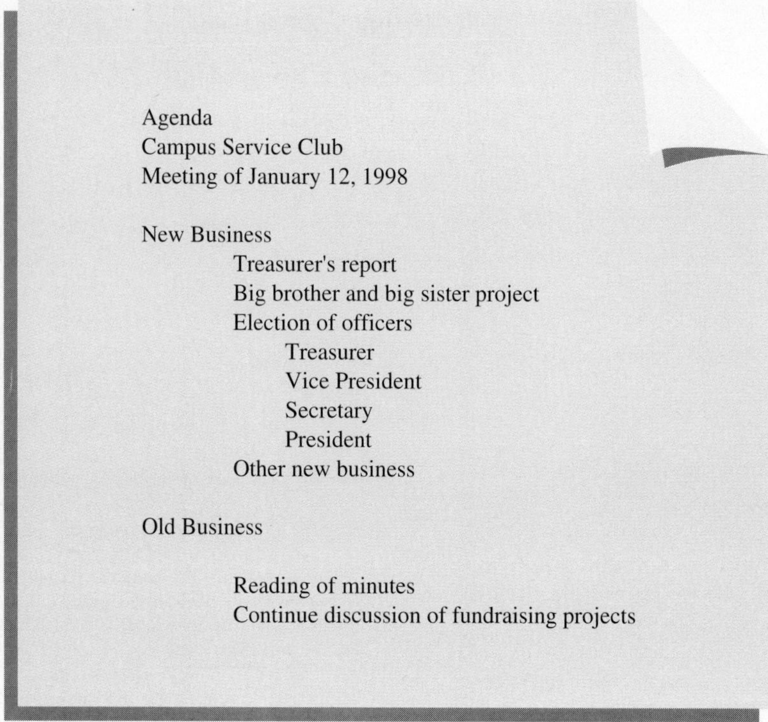
Agenda
Campus Service Club
Meeting of January 12, 1998

New Business
Treasurer's report
Big brother and big sister project
Election of officers
Treasurer
Vice President
Secretary
President
Other new business

Old Business

Reading of minutes
Continue discussion of fundraising projects

Figure 2.30

2. Substitute today's date for the date in Figure 2.30.
3. Move the *Old Business* heading and the items under it so that this section appears before the *New Business* section.
4. Move the *Election of officers* and positions listed under that heading so that this section is the first item under *New Business.*
5. Reorganize the list of officers so that it is more logical.
6. Save the revised agenda under the file name *Meeting Agenda.*
7. Print a copy of the agenda.

Assignments

Copying Web Information

In Windows 95, you can use the clipboard to move text from one application to another. Find information on the Web about a movie that interests you, and compile a set of research notes. Check the Benjamin/Cummings URL http://www.aw.com/is/select/word7 for links to movie databases on the Web. Copy information about the movie from your Web browser into a blank Word document. Find other information about the same movie, and copy it into the same document. Save your movie research notes in a file, and print a copy.

Modifying a Telephone List

Retrieve the telephone list you saved under the file name Telephone List at the end of Project 1. Reorganize the first five items on your list as follows (you'll reorganize the rest of the list using a faster method in a later project). Select what should be the first line alphabetically by clicking alongside it in the selection bar. Drag and drop that line at the top of the list. Then select what should be the second line and move it under the first. Continue until the first five lines of your list are in alphabetical order. Put a title at the top of the list if you haven't already. Save the list, and print a copy of it.

PROJECT 3: CHARACTER FORMATTING

Objectives

After completing this project, you should be able to:

- Apply character styles such as boldface, italic, and underline
- Change type styles and sizes
- Create subscripts and superscripts
- Repeat and copy character formats
- Insert special characters

In this project, you will begin to polish the appearance of the flyer using character formatting: type styles and sizes, character emphasis, and special characters. You'll begin by formatting the entire flyer so that it no longer looks like a draft. You'll add boldface headings in a different type style to set off the headings and help organize the page visually. And you'll add some special typographic characters to give the flyer a more polished and professional look. All this is a first step into desktop publishing.

CASE STUDY: POLISHING THE FLYER

Printed documents communicate not only by what they say, but also by how they look—by their form and appearance. Even though we're warned not to judge a book by its cover, most of us do exactly that. An attractive book, magazine, or brochure is more likely to be read and will probably have more credibility than one that looks sloppy, hastily put together, or unattractive. The same is true of smaller documents such as flyers, reports, and letters.

Word allows you to control the appearance of whatever document you're preparing in a variety of ways. You can select different typefaces and type sizes. You can make the type boldface or italic. You can use special characters such as foreign-language characters or mathematical symbols. With these capabilities, you can transform a rough draft into a document that looks polished and professional.

The flyer you began in the first project is complete and well organized at this point, but it lacks polish. It looks like the draft that it is. You probably wouldn't expect it to attract attention if you posted it on bulletin boards around campus. Dressing up the flyer requires the use of Word's extensive character-formatting capabilities.

Designing the Solution

A good rule of thumb in designing any document is summed up in the widely used KISS formula: keep it simple, stupid. Smart designers usually try to keep it simple by, for example:

- Using a minimum number of typefaces
- Grouping material that belongs together into blocks
- Making one element (probably an illustration or headline) stand out for emphasis
- Setting tabs and indentations so that type blocks line up and the page looks better organized

In this project, you'll format the flyer using typefaces that are professional and polished. You'll provide emphasis and clarity by making the title and headings stand out. You'll use italics and special characters to make the text conform better to common style conventions, thus raising its credibility.

At the end of this project, the flyer should look like Figure 3.1.

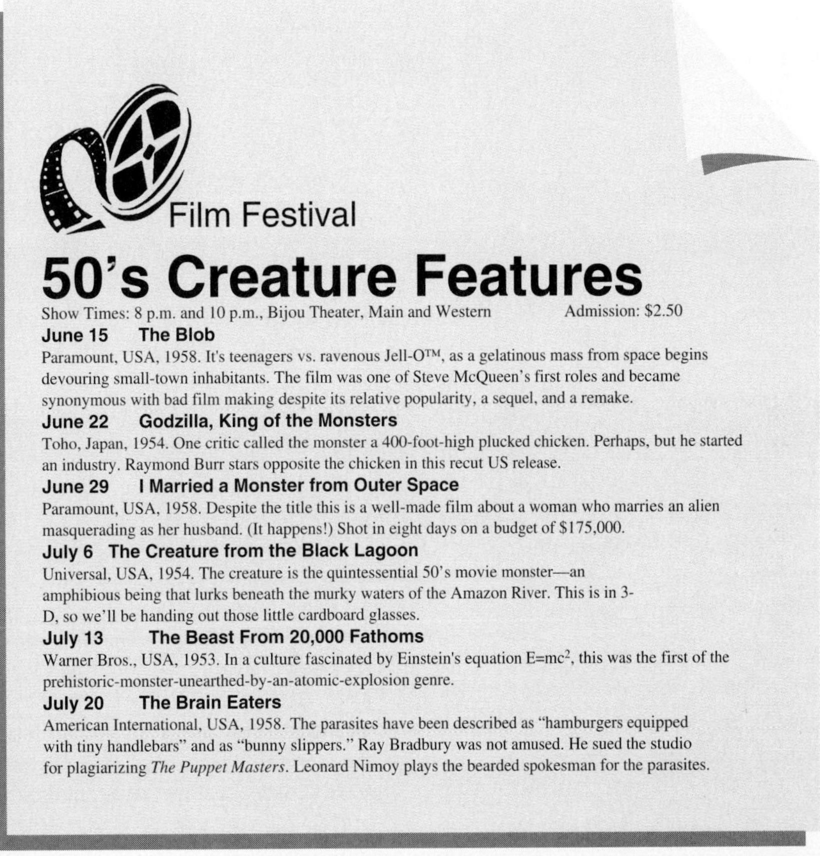

Film Festival

50's Creature Features

Show Times: 8 p.m. and 10 p.m., Bijou Theater, Main and Western   Admission: $2.50

June 15 The Blob

Paramount, USA, 1958. It's teenagers vs. ravenous Jell-O™, as a gelatinous mass from space begins devouring small-town inhabitants. The film was one of Steve McQueen's first roles and became synonymous with bad film making despite its relative popularity, a sequel, and a remake.

June 22 Godzilla, King of the Monsters

Toho, Japan, 1954. One critic called the monster a 400-foot-high plucked chicken. Perhaps, but he started an industry. Raymond Burr stars opposite the chicken in this recut US release.

June 29 I Married a Monster from Outer Space

Paramount, USA, 1958. Despite the title this is a well-made film about a woman who marries an alien masquerading as her husband. (It happens!) Shot in eight days on a budget of $175,000.

July 6 The Creature from the Black Lagoon

Universal, USA, 1954. The creature is the quintessential 50's movie monster—an amphibious being that lurks beneath the murky waters of the Amazon River. This is in 3-D, so we'll be handing out those little cardboard glasses.

July 13 The Beast From 20,000 Fathoms

Warner Bros., USA, 1953. In a culture fascinated by Einstein's equation $E=mc^2$, this was the first of the prehistoric-monster-unearthed-by-an-atomic-explosion genre.

July 20 The Brain Eaters

American International, USA, 1958. The parasites have been described as "hamburgers equipped with tiny handlebars" and as "bunny slippers." Ray Bradbury was not amused. He sued the studio for plagiarizing *The Puppet Masters*. Leonard Nimoy plays the bearded spokesman for the parasites.

Figure 3.1

CHARACTERS, PARAGRAPHS, AND SECTIONS

Word recognizes three types of building blocks that make up a document: characters, paragraphs, and sections. Each one of these building blocks has specific characteristics and can be formatted in different ways. For instance, characters can be bold or italic, paragraphs can be indented or double spaced, and sections can be page numbered or printed sideways.

As usual in Word, the general rule is "select, and then do." First you select the part of your document you want to format, and then you apply the formatting. If you want to underline text, you first select the characters you want to underline, and then you tell Word to underline them. If you want to boldface text, you select the text and then tell Word to boldface it.

Characters can have a variety of formats, as shown in Figure 3.2.

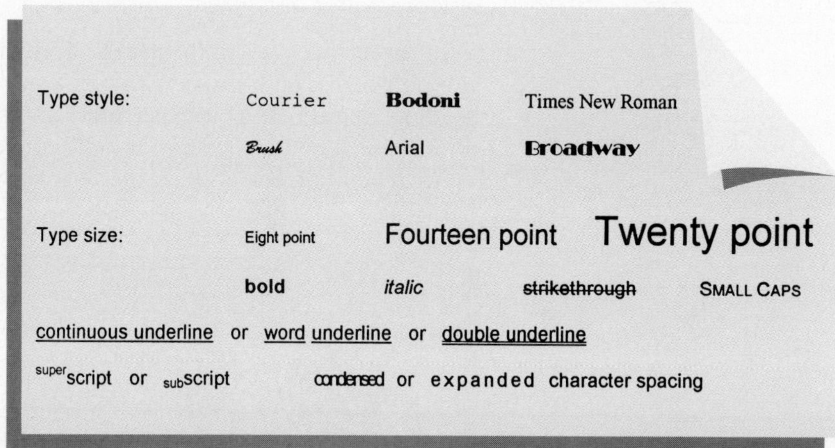

Figure 3.2

How you format your documents will affect the legibility and appearance of those documents, and probably influence the documents' credibility and attractiveness to readers. You can use character formats to establish the tone and structure of your document, to provide emphasis, and to produce special effects to gain attention.

Applying Character Formats

Once you've selected the text you want to format, you can apply character formats in any of three ways: by using the Font dialog box, the keyboard, or the Formatting toolbar. You'll learn all three in the steps that follow, working with the sample flyer from Projects 1 and 2.

The appearance of your flyer is obviously important. It must attract attention and look credible. Its precise final appearance will depend heavily on the type of printer you're using, but you can do a lot to dress up the flyer regardless. You will begin by retrieving the last version of the flyer, saved as Revised Film Flyer.doc in Project 2.

To retrieve the flyer file:

1. Start Word and click the Open button in the Standard toolbar.
2. Adjust the Look in box and box beneath as needed to locate the file.
3. Select *Revised Film Flyer.*
4. Select Open.

5 Select the Show/Hide ¶ button if needed to make nonprinting characters visible.
Your document should resemble Figure 3.3.

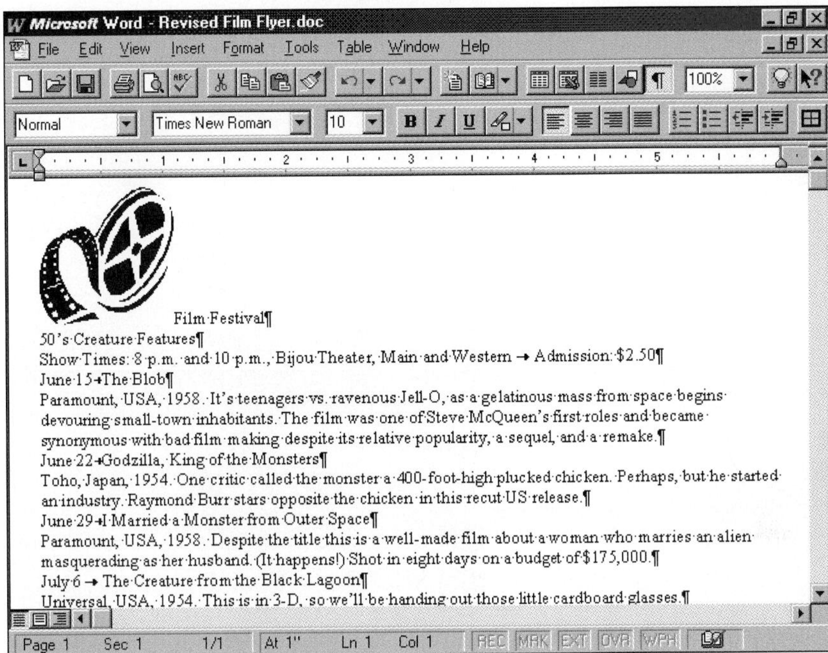

Figure 3.3

In standard style, the names of newspapers, magazines, books, and so on are normally italicized. You'll begin formatting the flyer by italicizing *The Puppet Masters,* the title of the book mentioned in the description of the July 20 film.

To italicize text using the Font dialog box:

1 Select the title of the book so that the text appears as shown in Figure 3.4.

July·20→The·Brain·Eaters¶
American·International,·USA,·1958.·The·parasites·have·been·described·as·"hamburgers·equipped·with·tiny·handlebars"·and·as·"bunny·slippers."·Ray·Bradbury·was·not·amused.·He·sued·the·studio·for·plagiarizing·The·Puppet·Masters.·Leonard·Nimoy·plays·the·bearded·spokesman·for·the·bunny·slippers.¶

Figure 3.4

2 Choose Font from the Format menu.
The Font dialog box, shown in Figure 3.5, will appear.

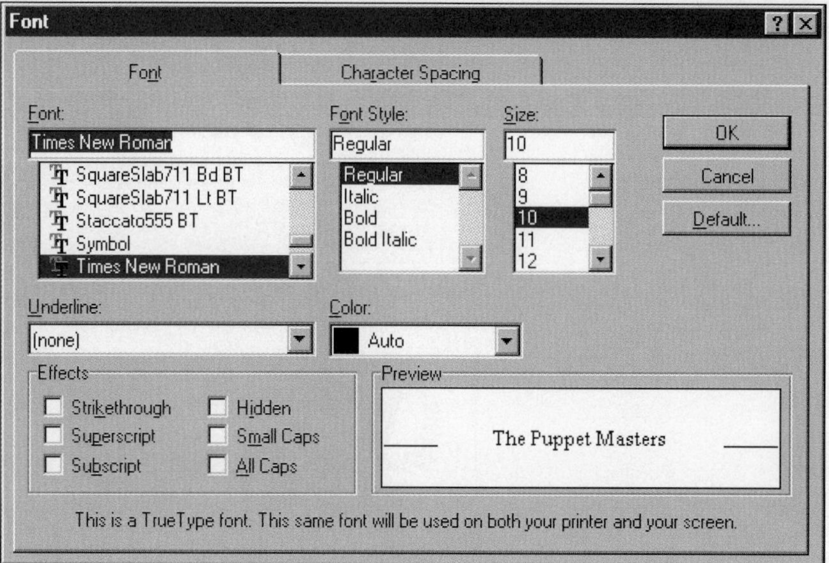

Figure 3.5

3 Select the Font tab if it is not already on top.

4 Select Italic from the Font Style box.
Note that the Preview box in the lower-right corner shows how the text will look with the italic style applied.

5 Select OK.
The title of the book now appears in italics. (Cancel the text selection if necessary to see the formatting clearly.)

To remove the italics using the Font dialog box:

1 Select the title of the book again.

2 Choose Font from the Format menu.

3 Select Regular from the Font Style box.

4 Select OK.
Normal characters have replaced the italics.

> ***Tip*** For quick access to the Font dialog box after you have selected characters to be formatted, place the pointer over the selected text, click the right mouse button, and then select Font.

The Font dialog box is the most powerful character formatting tool you have in Word. You can use it to apply or clear any character formats in any combination. But if you have frequent need for simple character formats, using the dialog box will begin to seem awkward and time consuming. Word therefore provides two shortcuts: the Formatting toolbar and keyboard formatting commands. The ***Formatting toolbar*** appears near the top of the screen and allows you to use a mouse to make quick changes in common character and paragraph formats.

To italicize text using the Formatting toolbar:

1 If the Formatting toolbar, shown in Figure 3.6, does not appear near the top of the screen, choose Toolbars from the View menu, select Formatting, and then select OK.

Figure 3.6

2 If necessary, select the title of the book again so that *The Puppet Masters* is highlighted once more.

3 Select the Italic button in the Formatting toolbar.

4 Select the button again to clear the italic formatting.

Each click on the button toggles back and forth between italic and nonitalic formatting. The Formatting toolbar also provides two other buttons for quick character formatting: one for boldface and one for underlining.

To italicize text using the keyboard:

1 Select the name of the book title once more so that *The Puppet Masters* is highlighted.

2 Press CTRL+**I** to apply italic.

3 Press CTRL+**I** a second time to remove the formatting.

4 Press CTRL+**I** a third time to reapply italic.

Word makes available a series of keyboard shortcuts to format characters, as shown in Table 3.1.

Table 3.1

Keyboard Shortcut	Character Style
CTRL+SHIFT+**A**	All caps
CTRL+**B**	Bold
CTRL+SHIFT+**D**	Double underline
CTRL+SHIFT+**H**	Hidden text
CTRL+**I**	Italic
CTRL+SHIFT+**K**	Small caps
CTRL+**U**	Continuous underline
CTRL+SHIFT+**W**	Word underline
CTRL+=	Subscript
CTRL+SHIFT+=	Superscript

EXIT If necessary, you can save your file, exit now, and continue this project later.

Changing Typeface and Type Size

The terminology that Word uses for type styles and sizes is the same as that used for more than two centuries by commercial printers, book publishers, and newspapers. A particular style of type is known as a ***font.*** By most classification systems, there are only a few very general categories of type styles; these categories are shown in Figure 3.7.

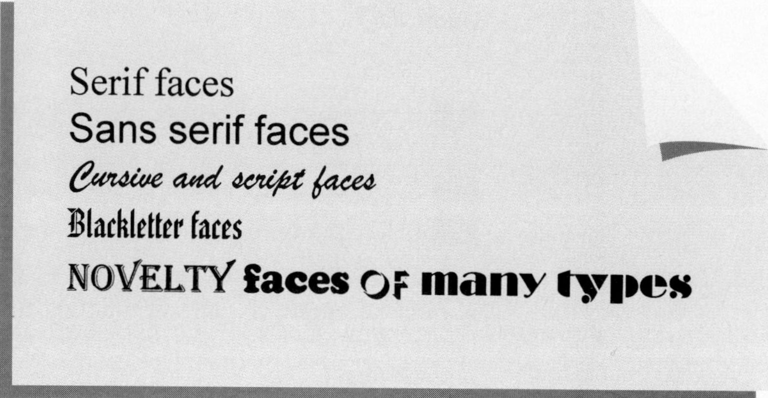

Serif faces
Sans serif faces
Cursive and script faces
Blackletter faces
NOVELTY faces OF many types

Figure 3.7

Within these general categories are thousands of type styles or fonts. Which fonts you have available in Word will depend on the printer and what fonts have been installed in Windows on the computer. A typewriter font, such as Courier New, is a ***fixed-space font,*** which means all letters have equal width and letters line up in columns. A fixed-space font is a good choice for manuscripts or other materials in draft form. Most typefaces are ***proportionally spaced,*** which means some letters are wider than others. A lowercase *i* is much thinner than an uppercase *W,* for instance, in a proportionally spaced font. ***Serif fonts*** have small crosslines, called serifs, at the end of the main letter strokes. A serif font such as Times New Roman is a good choice for ***body text***—the main reading material in reports, letters, and so on. ***Sans serif fonts,*** such as Helvetica or Arial, lack those crosslines. Sans serif fonts are slightly difficult to read for large amounts of text, but they are an excellent choice for headings, especially when bold. Cursive, blackletter, and novelty fonts should be avoided except where they are obviously appropriate, such as cursive type for a formal invitation or a particular novelty font for a poster.

Most type fonts are available in different styles, such as bold or italic. You can use styles for emphasis or to provide variation in your document. You might boldface a heading to make it stand out more clearly. Or you might italicize the title of a document to make it distinct from other information on the page.

Tip It's wonderful to have an assortment of type styles and sizes to work with in your documents. Unfortunately, it's tempting to want to use them all. Avoid the temptation because it leads to a hodgepodge of type styles that looks as though it was clipped from old magazines and pasted on paper like a ransom note.

A good rule of thumb is to avoid using more than two different typefaces in any one document. You could use a sans serif face such as Arial or Helvetica (in different styles and sizes) for the headings and a serif face such as Times New Roman (also in various styles and sizes) for body text. The result will be a cleaner, more tightly integrated document, but with enough variety that it doesn't look plain or uninteresting.

Printers measure type size in ***points.*** A point is 1/72 of an inch, so 72-point type is 1 inch high. Most books are printed using 9- to 11-point type. Most of the headings in this module are in 22-point type. Average newspaper headlines are about 30 to 40 points. Word is capable of producing type sizes from 4 to 127 points in 1/2-point increments. Whether that full range of sizes is actually available to you will depend on the font you're using and on the printer.

The steps in the pages that follow assume you have at least a few different type fonts and sizes to work with although you may not be able to match the exact fonts used in the examples. You will begin by formatting the entire flyer in 12-point Times Roman, then changing the heading lines to a sans serif font. The most common such font is Arial, which is used in the following examples. If Arial isn't available, substitute Helvetica or the closest sans serif font you have.

To change typeface and size using the Formatting toolbar:

1 Select the entire document (triple-click in the selection bar or press CTRL + **A**).

2 Click the down arrow button to the right of the Font size box in the Formatting toolbar, as shown in Figure 3.8.

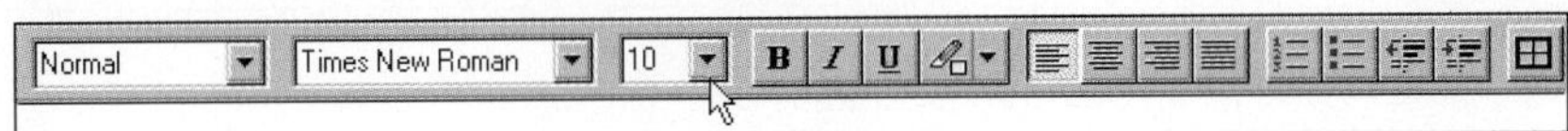

Figure 3.8

3 Select 12.

Your flyer is probably already formatted as Times New Roman, the default typeface for Word's Normal template. In that case, you can skip to step 6. If it is formatted with some other typeface, steps 4 and 5 will convert it to Times New Roman.

4 Click the down arrow button to the right of the Font box in the Formatting toolbar.

5 Select Times New Roman (or some equivalent serif text face).

6 Select the text on the top line of the flyer: *Film Festival.*

7 Click the down arrow button to the right of the Font box in the Formatting toolbar.

8 Select Arial (or some equivalent sans serif face).

9 Use the Font size box to format the selected text as 24 point.

Changing fonts and point sizes with the Font dialog box works the same way as using the Formatting toolbar. The difference is that although the dialog box isn't as easily accessible, you can change other character attributes at the same time if you need to.

To change font size and character style using the Font dialog box:

1 Select the second line of the flyer: *50's Creature Features.*

2 Choose Font from the Format menu to open the Font dialog box.

3 Select the Font tab if it is not on top already.

4 Select Arial in the Font box.

5 Select Bold in the Font Style box.

6 Select 36 in the Size box.

7 Select OK.

8 Click anywhere in the text to cancel the selection.

The top of your document should resemble Figure 3.9.

Film·Festival¶

50's·Creature·Features¶

Show·Times:·8·p.m.·and·10·p.m.,·Bijou·Theater,·Main·and·Western·Admission:·$2.50¶
June·15 → The·Blob¶
Paramount,·USA,·1958.·It's·teenagers·vs.·ravenous·Jell-O,·as·a·gelatinous·mass·from·space·begins·devouring·small-town·inhabitants.·The·film·was·one·of·Steve·McQueen's·first·roles·and·became·synonymous·with·bad·film-making·despite·its·relative·popularity,·a·sequel,·and·a·remake.¶

Figure 3.9

Tip When word processors that could use various type fonts in various sizes were first developed, writing instructors noticed an interesting phenomenon. Students using the older word processors, which limited them to one set of characters, seemed to write better than students using the newer, more flexible machines. The problem, apparently, was that students using the newer word processors were being mesmerized by all the formatting options and distracted from the content of their writing. As a result, the quality of their writing suffered.

The solution, of course, is not to get rid of the formatting flexibility—the design and format of a document are part of the way the document communicates. On the other hand, it's not very wise to expect a dazzling design to cover up bad writing. In the end, it's probably best to make writing and design two distinct issues and focus on them separately. Word can help you do this with the Draft font. To use this font, you would choose Options from the Tools menu, select the View tab, and select Draft Font. Your entire document will be displayed in a single type font and size. This option makes it easier to focus on the words themselves. Then, when you are ready to address character-formatting issues, go back to the View tab in the Options dialog box and clear the Draft Font selection.

Using Subscripts and Superscripts

Subscripts and superscripts are useful for footnote references, chemical formulas, or mathematical notation. A ***subscript*** appears slightly below the normal baseline for the text (H_2O); a ***superscript*** appears slightly above the baseline ($c^2 = a^2 + b^2$). Word will automatically reduce the size of the character so that it fits as a superscript or subscript.

To format a superscript using the Font dialog box:

1 In the July 13 film description, position the insertion point between *equation* and the comma that follows.

2 Press (SPACE) then type **E=mc2**

3 Select the single character *2* in *E=mc2*.

4 Choose Font from the Format menu to open the Font dialog box.

5 Select the Font tab if it is not already on top.

6 Select Superscript in the Effects area (so that a check mark appears in the box beside it), as shown in Figure 3.10.

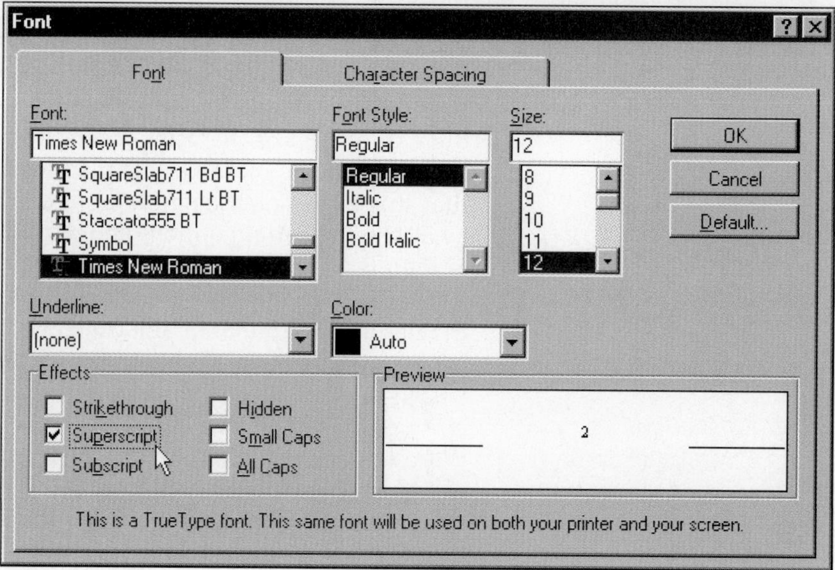

Figure 3.10

7 Select OK.
Your screen should look like Figure 3.11.

July·13→The·Beast·From·20,000·Fathoms¶
Warner·Bros.,·USA,·1953.·In·a·culture·fascinated·by·Einstein's·equation·E=mc²,·this·was·the·first·of·the·prehistoric-monster-unearthed-by-an-atomic-explosion·genre.¶

Figure 3.11

If necessary, you can save your file, exit now, and continue this project later.

Repeating and Copying Character Formats

To polish the flyer more, it would help to have the film dates and titles appear more distinctly, in a boldface sans serif font. You could format the date and title lines by selecting each one, then applying the needed format, and then going on to the next date and title line. Obviously, the more complex the format, the longer this procedure will take. Word provides shortcuts to make this type of operation easier and faster. Repeating character formats is useful if you've just formatted one block of text and want to apply the same format to a series of other blocks. Copying character formats allows you to "borrow" the existing format information from one block of text and apply it to another block.

To repeat a character format:

1 Select the date and title line of the June 15 film. (Recall that the easiest way to select a single line is to click in the selection bar to the left of the line.)

2 Choose Font from the Format menu to open the Font dialog box.

3 Select the Font tab if it is not already on top.

4 Select the same sans serif face that you selected for the name in the top line of the document (probably Arial).

5 Select Bold in the Font Style box.

6 Select OK to complete the format choice.
Check to see that the heading is now displayed in boldface sans serif.

7 Select the date and title line for the June 22 film.

8 Choose Repeat Font Formatting from the Edit menu (or press CTRL + **Y**) to repeat the formatting operation.

The Repeat Font Formatting command works well as long as you do all the formatting operations at the same time. If you want to copy existing character formatting in the middle of performing other operations, however, Word allows you to borrow formatting information without copying the content itself. This is a two-step operation that uses the Format Painter button in the Standard toolbar. First you "dip the paintbrush" in the formatting that you want to copy. Then you "brush" across the text you want to format.

To copy a character format using the Format Painter button:

1 Position the insertion point somewhere within one of the two date and film title lines you've already formatted in boldface sans serif.

2 Select the Format Painter button in the Standard toolbar.
Note that the pointer now has a small paintbrush attached to it.

3 Drag the paintbrush pointer to select the date and title line for the June 29 film.
As soon as you release the mouse button to complete the text selection, the format information, but not the content, is transferred from the already formatted date and title line to the one you selected.

4 Use the same procedure to format the other three date and title lines in the flyer.

INSERTING SPECIAL CHARACTERS

A font of type normally contains many characters that don't appear on the keyboard, such as foreign-language characters, mathematical symbols, and publishing symbols. In addition, special fonts are available that consist entirely of special characters. Word allows you easy access to both through the Insert Symbol command.

Assume that one of the members of your publicity committee reminds you that Jell-O is a trademarked name and should be identified as such in the flyer by the trademark sign (™).

To insert a special publishing character:

1 Position the insertion point between *Jell-O* and the comma that follows it in the description of the June 15 film.

2 Choose Symbol from the Insert menu to open the Symbol dialog box.

3 Select the Symbols tab if it is not already on top.

4 Select *(normal text)* in the Font box if it isn't selected already.

5 Select the ™ symbol, as shown in Figure 3.12.

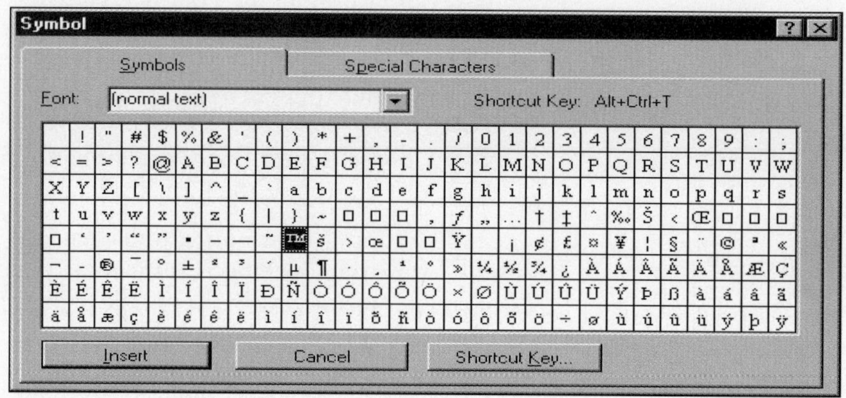

Figure 3.12

Note that the shortcut keystroke combination for this special character (ALT+CTRL+T) appears at the top of the dialog box. If you use a special symbol frequently, it would probably be faster to remember and use its keystroke combination.

6 Select Insert to insert the trademark symbol.

7 Select Close to close the Symbol dialog box.

You can also use Word's ***AutoCorrect*** feature to insert special characters, including the trademark symbol. As its name suggests, AutoCorrect is designed to automatically correct typing errors, so if you type *adn,* it will automatically substitute *and.* AutoCorrect can also substitute symbols for their typed abbreviations. If you type *(tm),* Word will substitute ™. If you type *(c),* Word will substitute ©. If you type two hyphens *(--),* Word will substitute a dash. Assume you need to add another sentence to the description of the July 6 movie.

To use AutoCorrect to create a dash character:

1 Position the insertion point immediately in front of *This* following the year of release of the July 13 movie.

2 Type **`The creature is the quintessential 50's movie monster`** (with no space following).

3 Type two hyphens, one immediately following the other and with no spaces before or after.

4 Type **`an amphibious being that lurks beneath the murky waters of the Amazon River.`**

5 Press (SPACE)
Word substitutes a single dash character for the two hyphens you typed.

To save and print your document:

1 Save your document.

2 Print a copy of the flyer.

The Next Step

Explore what other special characters are available on the computer system you are using. In addition to the special characters available in the Normal Text font, many systems have a Symbol font, containing the Greek alphabet and a variety of mathematical symbols, and a Wingdings font, containing different sorts of arrows, highlighted numbers, astrological signs, and so on.

Through these special characters and character formats, the personal computer has brought a new look to all kinds of documents, from business letters, to reports, to newsletters. The widespread availability of different typefaces in different sizes has made it straightforward and inexpensive to do what only commercial printers used to do at relatively high prices. These capabilities are part of the basis of the desktop publishing revolution.

Unfortunately, having the equipment to use typefaces doesn't teach you how to use them. Start collecting examples of documents you think are well designed, particularly documents of a type that are of special interest to you. You can adapt those design ideas to your own work. Watch also for documents you think are poorly designed, and note what it would take to transform these documents into an effective format.

Summary and Exercises

Summary

- Word distinguishes three types of building blocks in a document: characters, paragraphs, and sections. Each has its own set of formatting characteristics.
- Characters can be normal, bold, italic, underlined, or a number of other styles. They can be superscripted or subscripted. They can be different fonts or point sizes. They can have expanded or condensed character spacing.
- You can format blocks of characters by first selecting the characters and then applying the format.
- You can apply character formats by using the Font dialog box, the Formatting toolbar, or keyboard commands.
- Type styles are known as fonts. Type sizes are measured in points (1/72 of an inch).
- You can repeat formatting operations by choosing Repeat from the Edit menu (or pressing (CTRL)+**Y**).

- You can copy character formats by using the Format Painter button in the Standard toolbar.
- You can insert special characters using the Insert Symbol command and Word's AutoCorrect feature. Most systems have special fonts containing nothing but special characters and symbols.

Key Terms and Operations

Key Terms
AutoCorrect
body text
fixed-space font
font
Formatting toolbar
points
proportionally spaced font
sans serif font
serif font
subscript
superscript

Operations
Change type font and size
Copy character formats
Insert special characters

Study Questions

Multiple Choice

1. Word recognizes three types of document building blocks. Which of the following is *not* one of them?
   a. characters
   b. words
   c. paragraphs
   d. sections
2. Which of the following key combinations formats selected text as bold?
   a. SHIFT + **B**
   b. ALT + **B**
   c. CTRL + **B**
   d. SHIFT + CTRL + **B**
3. A point, the measurement system for type size, is equivalent to:
   a. 1/8 inch
   b. 1/35 inch
   c. 1/72 inch
   d. 1/100 inch
4. Which of the following type styles is generally best for large amounts of reading matter?
   a. serif
   b. sans serif
   c. cursive
   d. novelty
5. Which of the following includes a superscript?
   a. CO_2
   b. Español
   c. $A = \pi r^2$
   d. Française
6. To repeat a formatting operation, press:
   a. CTRL + **R**
   b. CTRL + **Y**
   c. CTRL + **X**
   d. CTRL + **O**
7. Which of the following is not a character attribute (a character format that can be changed in the Font dialog box)?
   a. double spacing
   b. underlining
   c. font
   d. color
8. You are most likely to find Greek characters such as π or δ in:
   a. the Times Roman font.
   b. the Wingdings font.
   c. the Helvetica font.
   d. the Symbol font.

9. Which of the following character formats is not available in the Formatting toolbar?
   a. bold
   b. font changes
   c. superscript
   d. underline

10. Foreign-language accents and other special symbols are available through which of these menus?
    a. File
    b. Edit
    c. Format
    d. Insert

Short Answer

1. To format selected text as italic, press ________.
2. To format selected text as bold, press ________.
3. The ________ allows you to set type style, type size, bold, italic, or underline with a few clicks.
4. A particular style of type is called a ________.
5. A line of 18-point type is about ________-inch tall.
6. The name of a serif typeface available on your system is ________.
7. To select a single word prior to italicizing it, place the pointer somewhere within the word and ________.
8. To remove underlining from a word, first select the word and then click ________ in the Formatting toolbar.
9. You can copy format information by using the ________ button in the Formatting toolbar.
10. If you want type that is 1 inch tall for a poster, you should select the text block and set the size to ________ points.

For Discussion

1. How can you copy character formats using the mouse?
2. How can you avoid typographical monotony if you use only two fonts in a document?
3. Take an advertisement from a magazine and classify the fonts used in it according to the following system: serif, sans serif, cursive, blackletter, and novelty.

Review Exercises

Formatting a Memo

1. Retrieve the memo you corrected at the end of Project 2, named *Brochure Memo.*
2. Format all the text in a serif face like Times New Roman.
3. Make all the characters 11 point.
4. Make the *MEMO* heading 14 point in a sans serif face (such as Arial or Helvetica).
5. Boldface the headings *To, From,* and *Subject.*
6. Save the file, and print a copy of it.

Formatting a Meeting Agenda

1. Retrieve the agenda you saved under the name *Meeting Agenda* at the end of Project 2.
2. Format all the text as 12-point Times New Roman (or a similar serif face).
3. Format the *Agenda* title line as 24-point Arial or Helvetica, in bold.
4. Format the name of the club and the date line as 14-point Arial or Helvetica.
5. Make the *Old Business* and *New Business* headings bold.
6. Save the revised memo, and print a copy of the document.

Creating a News Release

Word's templates must be installed on your system in order to work this exercise. Ask your professor if you do not find them on your system.

1. Open a new document based on the Professional Press Release template (located under the Publications tab in the New dialog box).
2. Change the name of the company to the *SciFi Film Society.*
3. Change the address and telephone information to your own. (Make up a fax number if necessary.) Change the name of the contact person to your name.
4. Change the release time to *For Immediate Release*
5. Change the main heading to *50's Creature Features Film Festival Scheduled for Summer*
6. Change the size of the main heading to 14 point so that it will all fit on one line. Delete the subheading.
7. Change the date line from San Francisco to your town. Change the date to the current date.
8. Change the body of the release to:

   Six 1950's movie monsters will invade the screen again this summer in a film festival sponsored by the SciFi Film Society and the Bijou Theater.

   ''We picked the movies to have some fun and to take a look at how movie monsters developed after King Kong was re-released in the early 1950s,'' said Paul Kettering, president of the film society.

   The festival will feature *The Beast From 20,000 Fathoms*, based on a Ray Bradbury short story, and the first of the Godzilla movies, released in the United States in 1954. Also included will be *The Blob*, one of Steve McQueen's first films and thought by some to be one of the worst films ever made.

9. Save the file as *Film Festival News Release,* and print a copy of it.

Assignments

Finding Fonts on the Web

When type was cast in metal, type foundries required complex and expensive equipment. Each type style and size required a separate set of molds to manufacture the type. As a result, relatively few type fonts were available. Computerized fonts, however, are just electronic patterns—much easier to design and manufacture. Check the B/C URL http://www.aw.com/is/select/word7 and explore the links to electronic type foundries. Some may even have samples you can download and try for yourself.

Formatting the Telephone List

Typefaces have personalities. Some are conservative, whereas others are flashy. Some are easygoing; others are forceful. Retrieve the telephone list you saved under the file name *Telephone List.* Just for fun, create a new version of the list under the file name *Silly Fone List* (you'll need to use the Save As option).

Pick a name on your list, and select the line it's on (by clicking once in the selection bar). Format that line with a typeface that matches as closely as possible the personality of the person whose name appears there. Pick a bold, conservative face if that fits, or an elegant, italic face if that fits. Repeat for each of the people on your list. Save the list and print a copy.

Now, retrieve the original version from the file *Telephone List.* Format it in a way that makes the list easy to read and use. Consider font and size. You may want to boldface names so that they stand out better. Format the heading to separate it from the names and addresses. When you're finished, save the list again under the file name *Telephone List,* and print a copy.

PROJECT 4: PARAGRAPH FORMATTING

Objectives

After completing this project, you should be able to:

- Set the alignment of lines in a paragraph
- Change paragraph shading
- Create paragraph indentations
- Set tab stops
- Set paragraph spacing
- Copy paragraph formats
- Create and apply simple styles

In this project, you will continue to polish the appearance of the film flyer using paragraph formatting. You will use paragraph indentation and tab stops to make the separate movie titles and descriptions stand out more clearly. You will use a typographic reverse (white type on a black background) to make the title more dominant. You will create your own custom indentation style and use it to create consistently formatted paragraphs within the flyer.

CASE STUDY: STRUCTURING THE FLYER

In the last project, you began to polish the flyer by using professional-looking type fonts, by adding bold and italics for emphasis, and by using special characters for precision and accuracy. The flyer still looks somewhat jumbled, however. It lacks a visible typographic structure that clearly displays its underlying organization. You can use paragraph indentations and tab stop settings to align blocks of text in a way that makes the organization of the flyer apparent at a glance.

Designing the Solution

To make the individual dates and movie titles stand out, you can indent the descriptions and put extra space between them. That will structure the flyer more like a calendar and make it much easier to comprehend. To make the main heading bolder and create typographic contrast on the flyer, you can make it white against black. To give the heading information a more interesting shape, you can move the top label to the right, center the main heading, and force the subheading to fill out the line.

When you finish, the top portion of the flyer should look like Figure 4.1.

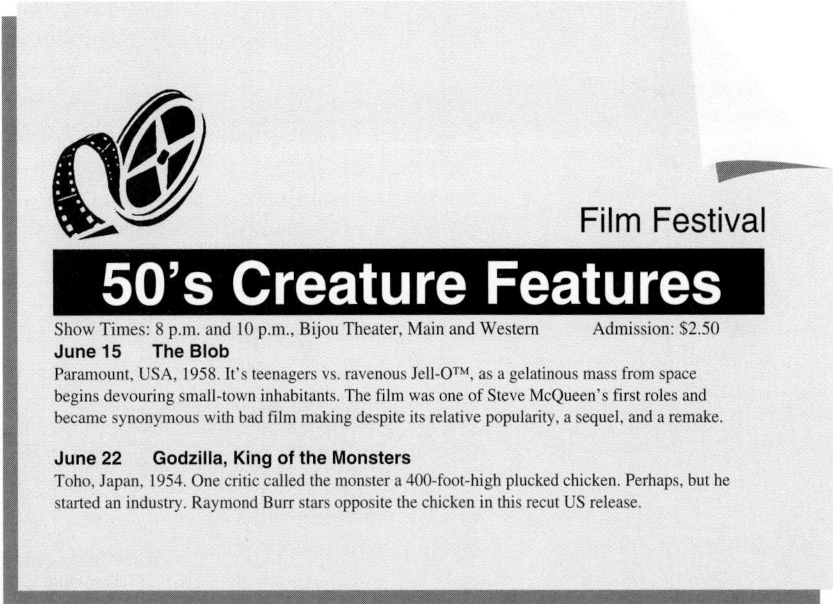

Figure 4.1

Choosing Paragraph Format Options

Webster's Dictionary says a paragraph is "a distinct section or subdivision of a written or printed composition that consists of from one to many sentences, forms a rhetorical unit, and is indicated by beginning on a new, usually indented, line."

Word's operating definition is simpler and shorter: a paragraph begins after a paragraph mark (¶) and ends with the next paragraph mark. In Word, strictly speaking, paragraphs have to do with formatting, not grammar although there is often an obvious parallel.

You can format paragraphs in Word to change the alignment of lines, how lines are indented, tab stops, line spacing, spacing between paragraphs, how the paragraph will be treated at a page break, and borders and shading. It will probably come as no surprise that you format paragraphs by first selecting them and then applying the formatting. A paragraph is considered selected in Word when the insertion point is anywhere within the paragraph or when the current selection includes some part of the paragraph. If you want to format a single paragraph, you can just position the insertion point somewhere inside that paragraph. If you want to format more than one paragraph, you can create a selection block that includes at least some part of each paragraph to be formatted.

As with character styles, you can apply paragraph formatting in any of three ways: by using the Paragraph dialog box, the keyboard, or the Formatting toolbar. You can do almost all common paragraph formatting using your mouse and the Formatting toolbar.

Line Alignment

One of the most basic paragraph formats is line alignment. Word can create four kinds of paragraph line alignment: aligned left, centered, aligned right, or justified (see Figure 4.2). For most work, ***aligned left*** is appropriate and more legible. ***Centered alignment*** works well for some headings and for small amounts of text that need a formal presentation. ***Aligned right*** formatting should be avoided except for a very few lines of text, such as a figure caption or short heading. Text with ***justified alignment*** has an even margin on both left and right sides and usually looks best with multicolumn formats such as newsletters.

The Brain Eaters (aligned left)
American International, USA, 1958. The parasites have been described as "hamburgers equipped with tiny handlebars" and as "bunny slippers." Ray Bradbury was not amused. He sued the studio for plagiarizing *The Puppet Masters*. Leonard Nimoy plays the bearded spokesman for the bunny slippers.

The Brain Eaters (centered)
American International, USA, 1958. The parasites have been described as "hamburgers equipped with tiny handlebars" and as "bunny slippers." Ray Bradbury was not amused. He sued the studio for plagiarizing *The Puppet Masters*. Leonard Nimoy plays the bearded spokesman for the bunny slippers.

The Brain Eaters (aligned right)
American International, USA, 1958. The parasites have been described as "hamburgers equipped with tiny handlebars" and as "bunny slippers." Ray Bradbury was not amused. He sued the studio for plagiarizing *The Puppet Masters*. Leonard Nimoy plays the bearded spokesman for the bunny slippers.

The Brain Eaters (justified)
American International, USA, 1958. The parasites have been described as "hamburgers equipped with tiny handlebars" and as "bunny slippers." Ray Bradbury was not amused. He sued the studio for plagiarizing *The Puppet Masters*. Leonard Nimoy plays the bearded spokesman for the bunny slippers.

Figure 4.2

The flyer that you've begun is currently all aligned left, the default line alignment in Word. You will realign some of the heading lines to give the top of the film flyer a stronger structure.

Tip Formatting paragraphs is easier when it's clear where they begin and end. If paragraph marks are not displayed on the screen, select the Show/Hide ¶ button in the Standard toolbar to display them.

To align the heading using the Paragraph dialog box:

1 If the flyer is not in the document window, retrieve it now. The screen should resemble Figure 4.3.

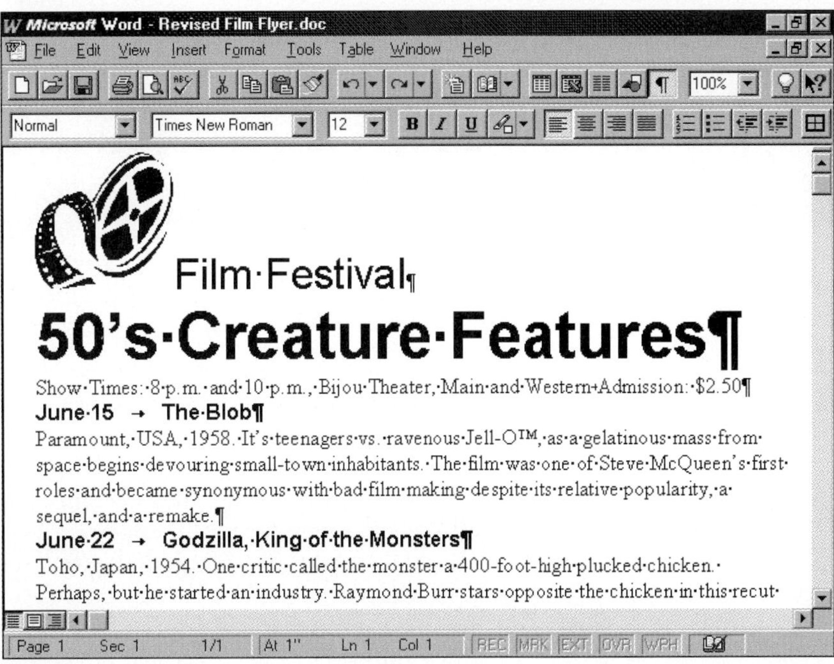

Figure 4.3

2 Position the insertion point somewhere within the title, *50's Creature Features.*

3 Choose Paragraph from the Format menu to open the Paragraph dialog box.

4 Select the Indents and Spacing tab if it is not already on top.

5 Select the Alignment pull-down list box so that the four alignment options are revealed, as shown in Figure 4.4.

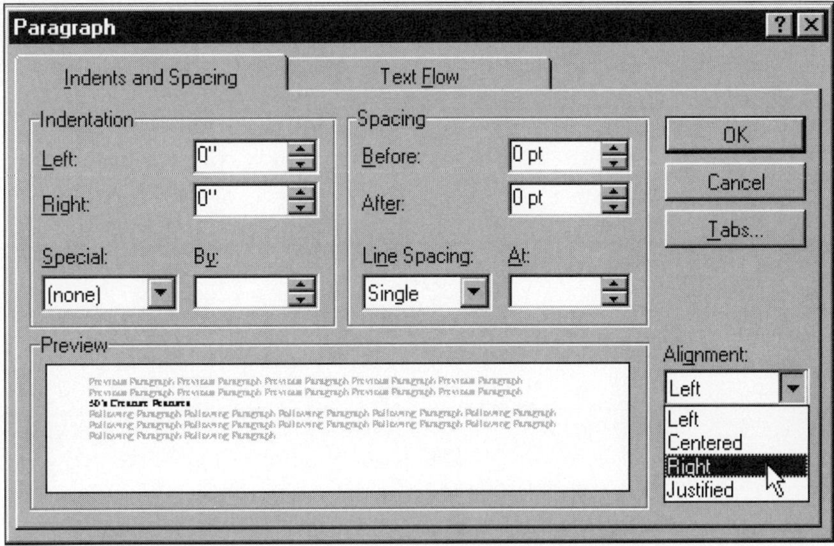

Figure 4.4

6 Select the Right option.
The bold paragraph in the Preview box changes shape to show how selected paragraphs will look after the formatting is applied.

7 Select OK to complete the formatting choice.

Note the appearance of the heading on the page. If there were many lines, or if the lines were longer, they would be very difficult to read. It's for that reason that right-aligned paragraphs are rarely used. You will be changing the heading in the following steps.

Tip For quick access to the Paragraph dialog box, position the pointer on the paragraph you want to format, click the right mouse button, and then select Paragraph.

The Paragraph dialog box is comprehensive: it gives you access to nearly all the paragraph formats available in Word. But you'll rarely use all the formats, and the Paragraph dialog box requires several keystrokes or mouse operations to use. To speed up the process, Word allows you to use the Formatting toolbar and keyboard for the more common paragraph formatting options.

To align the heading of the flyer using the Formatting toolbar:

1 Select the heading as before (position the insertion point somewhere within *50's Creature Features*).

2 Select the Center button in the Formatting toolbar, as shown in Figure 4.5.

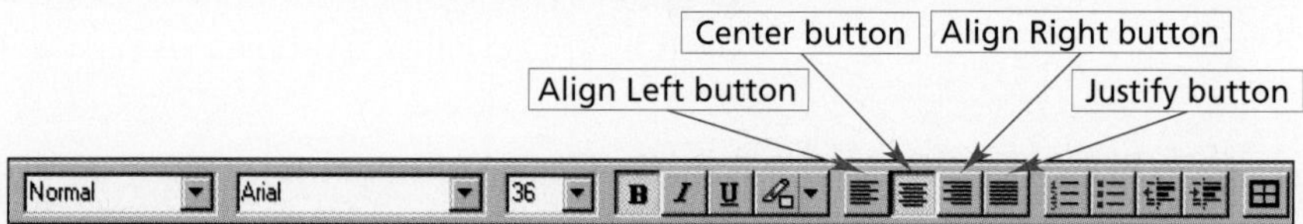

Figure 4.5

3 Select the other three alignment buttons to see how they affect the heading.
The justified alignment will look like the left alignment because the heading is only one line long.

4 Click the Align Left button to leave the heading aligned left.

Word also provides simple keyboard shortcuts for aligning paragraphs. These shortcuts are summarized in Table 4.1.

Table 4.1

Keyboard Shortcut	Paragraph Alignment
CTRL + L	Aligned left
CTRL + E	Centered
CTRL + R	Aligned right
CTRL + J	Justified

To center the heading using the keyboard:

1 Select the heading as before.

2 Press CTRL + E to center the heading.

CHANGING PARAGRAPH SHADING

To make the flyer more visible and commanding, it would be useful to make the title of the film series—*50's Creature Features*—more prominent. A simple way to do this is to use a typographic ***reverse,*** in which white letters appear against a black background. This type of treatment is one of the borders and shadings options available using Word's ***Borders toolbar.***

To reverse the film series title:

1 Be sure the insertion point is positioned somewhere within the film series title line: *50's Creature Features.*

2 Click the Borders button at the right end of the Formatting toolbar to make the Borders toolbar appear, shown in Figure 4.6.

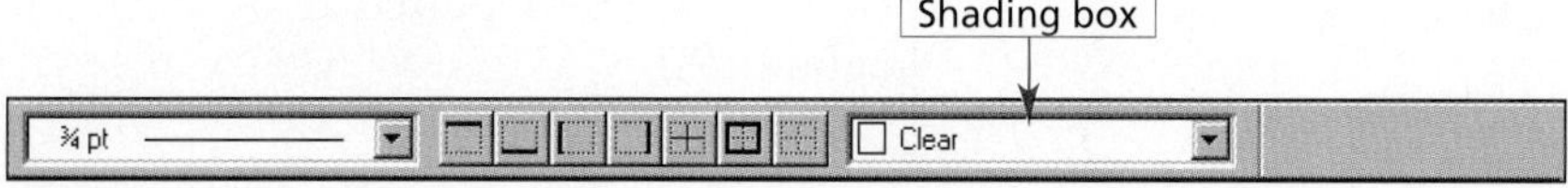

Figure 4.6

3 Click the down arrow to the right of the Shading box on the Borders toolbar.

4 Select Solid (100%) to apply the reverse.

5 Click the Borders button on the Formatting toolbar again to close the Borders toolbar.

The Borders toolbar also allows you to put gray shading or patterns behind a paragraph, to put lines above or below, or to put boxes around the paragraph. Used sparingly, these effects can be very useful in emphasizing headings or singling a paragraph out for particular emphasis.

INDENTING PARAGRAPHS

Word allows you to indent a paragraph from the left and right margins and to indent the first line independently on the left. You could, for instance, indent from both left and right margins to indicate a block of quoted material, or you could indent the first line alone to make paragraph breaks more obvious. You also could leave the first line unindented and indent only the subsequent lines in the paragraph, which is called a ***hanging indentation.***

To make the flyer easier to read and make the dates more obvious, you will format most of the paragraphs so that the movie descriptions are indented and line up with the film titles. The dates will appear to the left of each film title.

Table 4.2 shows several keyboard commands you can use to establish paragraph indentations.

Table 4.2

Keyboard Shortcut	Paragraph Indentation
CTRL+M	Indent to next tab
CTRL+SHIFT+M	Decrease indentation by one tab
CTRL+T	Hanging indentation to next tab
CTRL+SHIFT+T	Reduce hanging indentation by one tab

To establish an indentation using the keyboard:

1 Position the insertion point somewhere within the description section of the June 15 film. Do not include the date and film title line.

2 Press CTRL+M

The lines in the description paragraph are all indented to the first default tab stop, which is located at 1/2 inch. The date and film title line remain unindented.

Tip You can use the Increase Indent button on the Formatting toolbar to indent selected text to the next tab stop. The Decrease Indent button will move the indentation leftward to the preceding tab stop.

You can use a mouse to set or modify indentations and tab stops on Word's ruler, which is shown in Figure 4.7. The three triangular ***indent markers*** are used to set indentations. You can "grab" each indent marker with the mouse pointer and slide the marker to the left or right to adjust the indentation. (To grab a marker, position the pointer over it and then click and hold down the mouse button; the marker will move with the pointer.) The top-left indent marker sets the amount of indentation for the first line. The bottom-left indent marker sets the amount of indentation for the remaining lines in the paragraph; this indentation determines the paragraph's left edge. The indent marker at the right sets the amount of indentation from the right edge. You'll be moving the left indent markers to increase the amount of indentation to 3/4 inch so as to leave adequate space for all the dates.

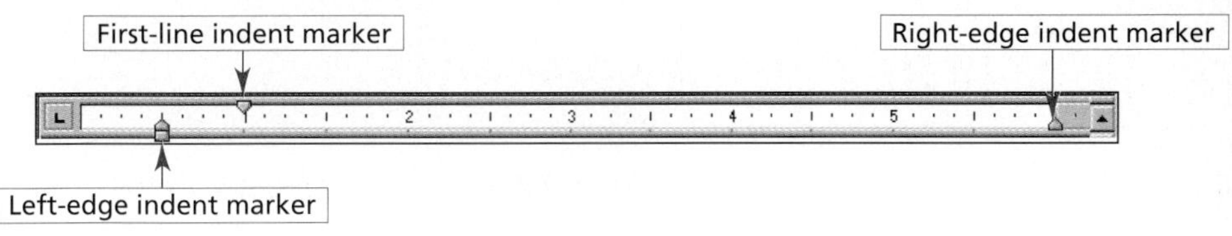

Figure 4.7

Caution In doing the following series of numbered steps, be sure to grab the box that moves both the first-line and left-edge indent markers in tandem. If you grab only the lower triangle, which represents the left-edge indent marker, you will change only the left-edge indentation and create a hanging indent.

To set indentations with the ruler indent markers:

1 Make sure the ruler is visible on the screen. If not, choose Ruler from the View menu.

2 Make sure the insertion point is positioned somewhere inside the paragraph describing the June 15 film.

3 Position the pointer on the small box below the left-edge indent marker.

4 Press and hold down the mouse button to grab the first-line and left-edge indent markers.

5 Move the indent markers to the right so that they are positioned at the ¾-inch mark on the ruler, as shown in Figure 4.8.

6 Release the mouse button.

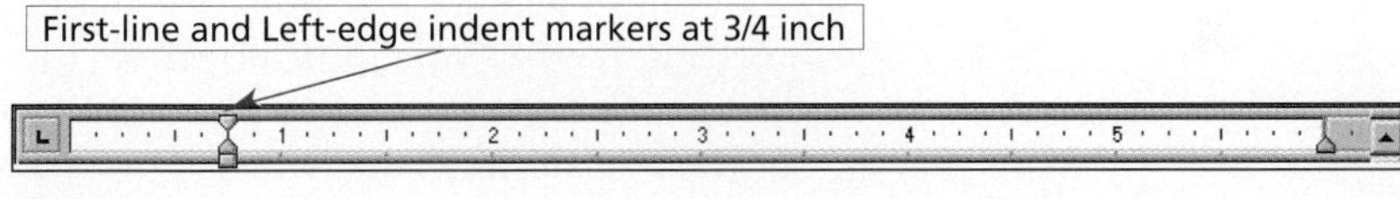

Figure 4.8

If necessary, you can save your file, exit Word now, and continue this project later.

SETTING TAB STOPS

The default tab stops in Word are normally set at ½-inch intervals. They are marked on the ruler with very small hash marks just below the ruler itself, as shown in Figure 4.9. The default settings are often satisfactory, but frequently you'll want to customize the settings to give your material optimum presentation. You can set not only the location of the tab stop, but also its style.

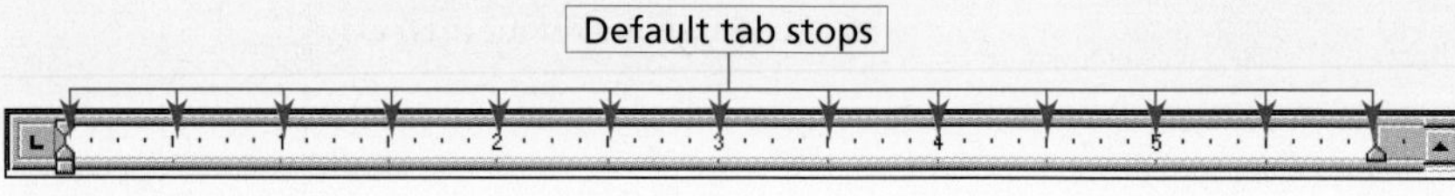

Figure 4.9

Word implements four styles of tab stops: left, center, right, and decimal. The ***left tab stop*** aligns the text on the left side under the tab stop. The ***center tab stop*** centers text on the tab stop. The ***right tab stop*** aligns text on the right side under the tab stop. The ***decimal tab stop*** aligns text (or, more commonly, numbers) on the decimal point under the tab stop. Figure 4.10 shows examples of each style of tab and the ruler line above, which indicates the tab stop settings.

Left tab	Center tab	Right tab	Decimal tab
will align	will	will align	195.33
along the	center	along the	1.23
left edge	lines	right edge	1,234.56

Figure 4.10

Each of the four styles of tab stops is indicated on the ruler by a different symbol and is set using the Tab Alignment button at the left edge of the ruler. You will select the Tab Alignment button until the style of tab stop you want appears. Then you will click the ruler where you want to set the tab stop. A tab stop of the style you selected will be inserted on the ruler. You can set additional tab stops by clicking at other points on the ruler. If you need to, you can grab the tab stops with the pointer and slide the markers from side to side to adjust the tab settings on the ruler. If you want to delete a tab stop, you can grab the marker with the pointer and drag the marker up or down off the ruler so that the tab marker disappears. Remember that tab stop settings are a paragraph format, so you must select all the text where you want the tab stops to be in effect before you set the tabs.

To unify the heading lines typographically, you will move the *Film Festival* heading and the admission price to the far right using tab stops. This treatment will create an overall block shape for the heading lines.

To move the Film Festival heading and admission price to the right margin:

1 Insert a tab character between the graphic and *Film Festival* in the first line of the flyer.

Be sure the insertion point is positioned somewhere within the first line.

2 Select the Tab Alignment button on the ruler until the right tab style appears, indicated by the symbol shown in Figure 4.11.

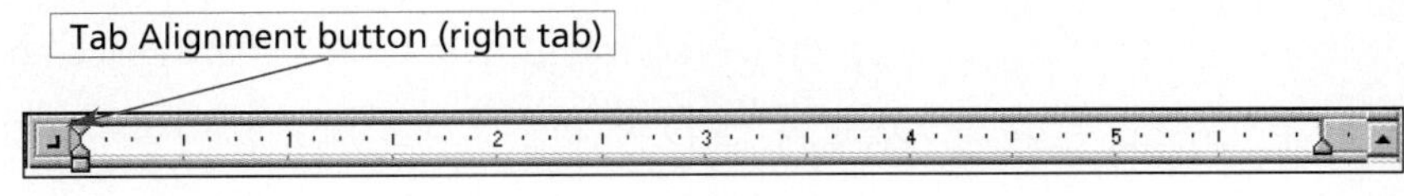

Figure 4.11

The tab actually needs to be positioned at the 6-inch mark, but Word will not allow you to set a tab stop on the margin. You can, however, set the tab stop close to the margin and then adjust it so that it is positioned correctly.

3 Click at the 5½-inch mark on the ruler to set the tab.

4 Grab the tab marker with the pointer and slide it to the right so that it is positioned at the 6-inch mark.

5 Position the insertion point somewhere on the third line of the flyer, listing the show times, theater location, and admission price.

6 Select Repeat Formatting from the Edit menu (or press CTRL + **Y**).

When you indented the description paragraph for the June 15 film earlier, you injected white space to the left of the description paragraph and helped separate one film listing from another. To make the organization neater, however, the film title should line up with the left edge of the film's description.

To set the tab stop for the film title line:

1 Position the insertion point somewhere within the date and title line for the June 15 film.

2 Select the Tab Alignment button on the ruler until the left tab style appears, indicated by the L-shaped symbol, as shown in Figure 4.12.

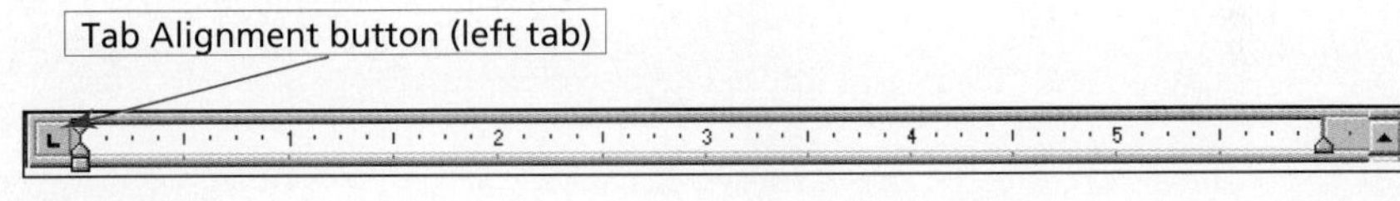

Figure 4.12

3 Click at the ¾-inch mark on the ruler to set the tab. Adjust the tab stop if needed by grabbing the marker with the pointer and sliding the marker from side to side.
The listing for the June 15 film should resemble Figure 4.13.

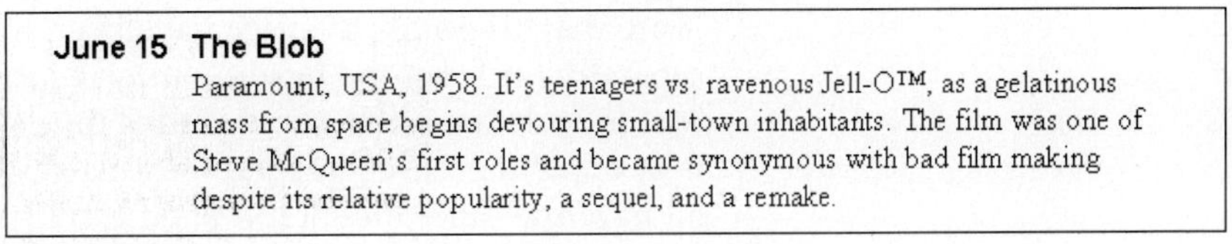

June 15 The Blob
Paramount, USA, 1958. It's teenagers vs. ravenous Jell-O™, as a gelatinous mass from space begins devouring small-town inhabitants. The film was one of Steve McQueen's first roles and became synonymous with bad film making despite its relative popularity, a sequel, and a remake.

Figure 4.13

The listing for the June 15 film is now much more clearly organized as a visual unit on the page. To complete the organization of the listing, however, it will help to add some space above the film title to separate it from the text above it.

Setting Paragraph Spacing

Paragraph spacing is a paragraph format in Word. You can set the spacing between lines in a paragraph (sometimes called ***leading*** because printers used to space lines apart using metal strips made of lead). You can also add extra space before or after a paragraph. To separate the film listing from typographic matter above it, you will add 10 points of space before the date and title paragraph.

To add space before a paragraph:

1 Using the *right* mouse button, click somewhere within the date and title line of the June 15 film.

2 Select Paragraph from the pull-down menu to open the Paragraph dialog box.

3 Type **`10`** in the Spacing Before box, as shown in Figure 4.14.

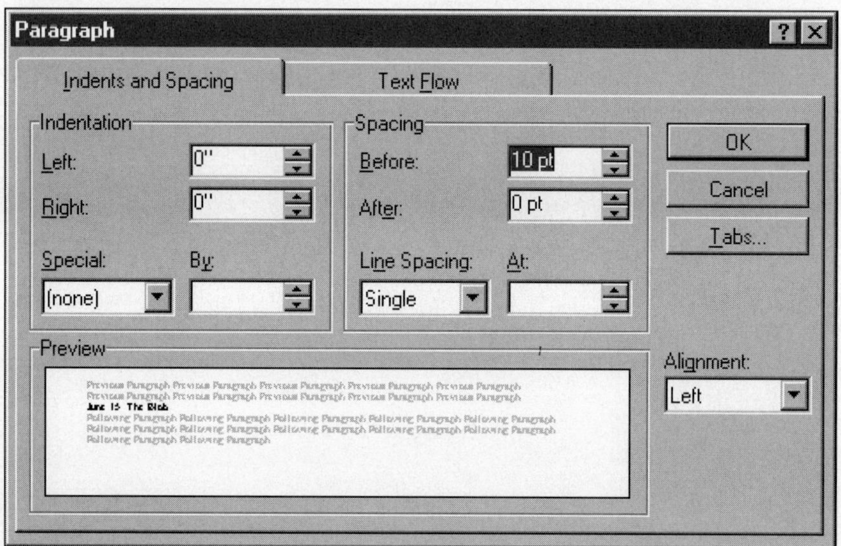

Figure 4.14

4 Select OK.

Note that 10 points of space have been inserted above the film title line, separating it from the heading information. The June 15 film listing now stands apart from the others and is much easier to read. What remains is to apply the same paragraph formatting to the other film listings so that all have the same indentation and extra spacing.

Tip If you want a quick look at font and paragraph formats, select the Help button at the right end of the Standard toolbar. The pointer will change into an arrow with a question mark attached to it. Then click anywhere in the text to get a listing of formatting information. When you are done, press ESC to cancel Help.

COPYING PARAGRAPH FORMATS

The formatting information for a paragraph is stored in the paragraph mark (¶) at the end of the paragraph. If you delete the paragraph mark, the formatting information for that paragraph disappears and the paragraph takes on the formatting of the paragraph it is joined with. On the other hand, if the insertion point is inside a paragraph and you press ENTER to begin a new paragraph, the new paragraph takes on the formatting of the previous one.

Perform the following steps to learn how Word's paragraph formatting information is copied from one paragraph to another.

To create an additional indented paragraph:

1 Be sure paragraph marks (¶) are visible to make it clear where paragraphs are located in your document.

2 Position the insertion point at the beginning of the description of the June 15 film, immediately in front of *Paramount.*

3 Press ENTER to start a new paragraph.
The new paragraph is indented just like the one where the insertion point was located. Anything you typed on this new line would be indented, just like the lines that follow it.

4 Press BACKSPACE to delete the new paragraph you just added.

To create an additional nonindented paragraph:

1 Position the insertion point at the end of the date and title line for the June 15 film, following *Blob.*

2 Press ENTER to start a new paragraph.
The new paragraph is not indented and has extra space before it, just like the line above it.

3 Press BACKSPACE to remove the new paragraph.

When you create a new paragraph from an old one, the new one receives the same formatting attributes as the old. That's helpful when you're adding text to an existing document. But it doesn't help when you want to copy formatting information from one paragraph to an already existing paragraph.

Using Styles

To complete formatting the film listings in the flyer, you need to copy formatting from one paragraph to another existing paragraph. You have formatted the June 15 film listing by indenting the description, setting tabs, and adding extra spacing above the film title line, but the other film listings are still unformatted. It's possible, of course, to format the remaining listings individually—selecting each one in turn, then applying the indent format, adjusting the indent, adding a tab stop and the extra space—but that approach would result in a lot of repetitive work and the possibility of errors and inconsistencies. Word provides an easier way: creating your own paragraph styles and then applying them to other paragraphs.

In Word, a ***style*** is a collection of formatting characteristics that is given a name and is accessible from the Style box in the Formatting toolbar. A particular style includes formatting information about the type font and size as well as about line alignment, indentations, and all other paragraph characteristics.

You have been using Word's default Normal style all along in preparing the film flyer. The style for the current selection appears in the Style box at the far left of the Formatting toolbar, as shown in Figure 4.15.

Figure 4.15

Word has a number of built-in styles such as Normal, but it also allows you to define your own styles. In the following set of steps, you will be creating two new styles, called Date & Title and Description, based on the paragraph formatting you have already applied to the listing for the June 15 film.

To create the Date & Title style:

1 Position the insertion point within the date and title line for the already formatted June 15 film.

2 Select the Style box at the left end of the Formatting toolbar.

3 Type `Date & Title` in the Style box.

4 Press (ENTER) to complete the style definition.

You have defined a new style named Date & Title that sets the tab stop and adds extra space above the line. Now you can apply the new style to date and title lines in the flyer.

To apply the Date & Title style to the June 22 film:

1 Position the insertion point somewhere within the date and title line for the June 22 film.

2 Select the down arrow to the right of the Style box.
The new Date & Title style will be in the list, as shown in Figure 4.16.

Figure 4.16

3 Select Date & Title to apply this style.

To apply the Date & Title style to the remainder of the flyer:

1 Position the insertion point within the date and title line for the June 29 film.

2 Select Repeat Style from the Edit menu (or press CTRL+**Y**) to apply the same styling to the selected paragraph.

3 Repeat this process with the other date and title lines.

To create and apply the Description style:

1 Position the insertion point within the description for the already formatted June 15 film.

2 Select the Style box at the left end of the Formatting toolbar.

3 Type `Description` in the Style box.

4 Press ENTER to complete the style definition.

5 Position the insertion point inside the description paragraph for the June 22 film.

6 Select Description from the Style box on the Formatting toolbar.

7 Format the description paragraphs for the other films.

At this point, the flyer is generally organized and visually structured. If you print out a copy of the flyer, or look at it with Word's Print Preview feature, you will notice that the horizontal space between the dates and the film titles is a little too tight. A slight adjustment would improve the appearance of the flyer markedly.

One of the advantages of using styles is that you can modify the style at any time, and Word will automatically apply the modifications to all paragraphs that have that style. In the steps that follow, you will increase the indent of the description paragraphs by ⅛ inch and move the tab stop in the date and title lines to the right by the same amount. But you will need to make the change in only one of the film listings and then redefine the style based on that listing.

To redefine the Date & Title style:

1 Position the insertion point somewhere within the date and title line for the June 22 film.

2 Use the mouse to grab the tab stop located at ¾ inch on the ruler and drag it to the right one mark, to ⅞ inch.

3 Select Date & Title in the Style box and press ENTER
The Reapply Style dialog box will appear. It allows you to redefine the Date & Title style so that the style will have the new ⅞-inch tab stop.

4 Press (ENTER) to redefine the style.

As soon as you redefine the style, Word reformats the other paragraphs that have the Date & Title style so that they also have a ⅞-inch tab stop.

To redefine the Description style:

1 Position the insertion point somewhere within the description paragraph for any one of the film listings.

2 Use the mouse to grab the small box on the ruler that controls the first-line and left-edge indent markers, and move it to the right, to the ⅞-inch mark.

3 Select Description in the Style box, and press (ENTER)

4 Press (ENTER) to redefine the style, which will automatically be applied to the other description paragraphs.

To save and print the flyer:

1 Save the completed flyer.

2 Print a copy of the flyer.

The Next Step

The basic character and paragraph formats you used in the film flyer can be used in almost any document to lend it credibility, emphasize its organization, and create interest. In many cases, Word can give you a head start on formatting if you use one of the many templates included in the New dialog box. You can adapt and modify any template as needed, and you can even save them to create new templates.

Summary and Exercises

Summary

- Word defines a paragraph as any amount of text that ends with a paragraph mark (¶).
- You format a paragraph by first selecting it and then applying the formatting.
- A paragraph is selected in Word when it contains the insertion point or when some portion of the paragraph is in the current selection.
- You can apply paragraph formatting using the Paragraph dialog box, the keyboard, or the Formatting toolbar. Nearly all common paragraph formatting can be accomplished using the Formatting toolbar and the ruler.
- A paragraph in Word can be formatted with different alignments (left, center, right, justified), different indentations, different tab stop settings, different line spacing, and so on.
- The paragraph mark contains the paragraph's formatting information.

When you press (ENTER) at the end of a paragraph, that paragraph's formatting information is copied into the new paragraph.

- You can use the Borders toolbar to create a typographic reverse, to put lines or boxes around paragraphs, or to put the paragraph in a shaded box.
- You can add extra space before or after a paragraph, or between the lines within the paragraph.
- You can create new paragraph styles using the Style box on the Formatting toolbar and then apply those styles to other paragraphs.
- Word uses four styles of tab stops: left, center, right, and decimal. Each paragraph can have its own settings for tab styles and positions.

Key Terms and Operations

Key Terms
aligned left
aligned right
Borders toolbar
centered alignment
center tab stop
decimal tab stop
hanging indentation
indent marker
justified alignment
leading
left tab stop
reverse
right tab stop
style

Operations
Change paragraph alignment
Copy paragraph formats
Define and use styles
Indent paragraphs
Set tab stops

Study Questions

Multiple Choice

1. To select a paragraph, you must:
   a. Select every character within the paragraph, including the paragraph mark (¶).
   b. Just be sure the paragraph mark (¶) is selected.
   c. Make sure that some part of the paragraph is selected or that the insertion point is somewhere inside the paragraph.
   d. Use the selection bar and mouse.

2. The formatting information for a paragraph is stored in:
   a. the paragraph mark (¶) at the beginning of the paragraph.
   b. the paragraph mark (¶) at the end of the paragraph.
   c. an invisible code at the beginning of the paragraph.
   d. the Formatting toolbar.

3. To create a new style based on an existing formatted paragraph:
   a. Use the Paragraph dialog box.
   b. Press (CTRL)+S
   c. Use the ruler.
   d. Use the Style box in the Formatting toolbar.

4. Which of the following is *not* one of the tab styles in Word?
   a. left
   b. center
   c. right
   d. justified

5. Which of the following keyboard commands will center a paragraph?
   a. (CTRL)+H
   b. (CTRL)+I
   c. (CTRL)+E
   d. (CTRL)+L

6. When you change tab settings or indentations on the ruler, they affect:
   a. the entire document.
   b. the paragraph at the top of the screen.
   c. the selected paragraph(s).
   d. all paragraphs after the insertion point.
7. When you press (ENTER) at the end of a paragraph, you create a new paragraph that has the same formatting as:
   a. a left-aligned paragraph.
   b. the paragraph below it.
   c. a Normal paragraph.
   d. the paragraph above it.
8. To establish a new tab, you should click:
   a. the selection bar.
   b. the ruler.
   c. the Formatting toolbar.
   d. the current paragraph.
9. Which of the following *cannot* be set in the Paragraph dialog box?
   a. paragraph alignment
   b. paragraph indentation
   c. extra space above or below the paragraph
   d. type font and size
10. Which of the following cannot be controlled by the indent markers on the ruler?
    a. the first line at left
    b. the right edge of all lines
    c. the left edge of all lines
    d. the right edge of the top line

Short Answer

1. To center a paragraph, select the paragraph and press __________.
2. To adjust paragraph indentations, use the __________ on the ruler.
3. You can set different styles of tab stops on the ruler by clicking first on the __________.
4. To make a paragraph aligned left, press __________.
5. The three triangular indent markers on the ruler give you independent control of the __________, __________, and __________ of a paragraph.
6. If you delete the paragraph mark between two paragraphs, the new combined paragraph will take on the formatting of the __________ paragraph.
7. The tab style that produces proper alignment in a column of figures is called a __________.
8. The paragraph alignment style that produces an even left and right edge is called __________.
9. To delete a tab stop from the ruler using the mouse, you should drag the tab marker __________.
10. You can format paragraphs in Word using the keyboard, the ruler and Formatting toolbar, or the __________.

For Discussion

1. What types of indentations can be established with Word? How is each indentation type used?
2. Describe how to set tabs so that a column of figures in an expense report would line up.
3. You can produce a table organized in columns using multiple tab settings. Would that be a workable approach to formatting the text in a multi-column document such as a newsletter? Why or why not?
4. What is a paragraph in Word?

Review Exercises

Formatting Paragraphs in a Memo

1. Retrieve the file *Brochure Memo.*
2. Select the date line at the top of the memo and format it with right paragraph alignment.
3. Select the *MEMO* heading and center it.
4. Replace the space following the colon (:) in each of the *To, From,* and *Subject* lines with a tab.
5. Select all three lines, and insert a left tab at the 1-inch mark on the ruler.
6. Select the three paragraphs that make up the body of the memo.
7. Use the mouse to adjust the first-line indent marker on the ruler so that the first line of each paragraph is indented ¼ inch.

   The memo should look like Figure 4.17.

February 14, 1998

MEMO

TO: Patricia Smith, Marketing Director

FROM: John Wells, Publications Manager

SUBJECT: Production of new product brochures

The concept for the new product brochures has been reviewed and passed by the marketing committee. Stan is working on design ideas and plans to have something ready for us to look at at the next meeting.

Arlene warned me that there may be a problem with some of the photographs for the brochure. She said she would talk to you so we could reschedule it with the photographer. Please let me know if you need to be able to use the T41 prototype again.

I need to schedule this with the printer so they can order paper. My understanding is that we will be printing 10,000 copies to begin. Is that correct?

Figure 4.17

8. Save the memo, and print a copy.

Formatting Paragraphs in a Meeting Agenda

1. Retrieve the agenda you saved under the name *Meeting Agenda* at the end of Project 3.
2. Center the top three lines.
3. Delete the tab characters (→) in the document.
4. Indent all the items under the *Old Business* and *New Business* sections one level (to the first default tab stop).
5. Indent the office titles under *Election of officers* an extra heading level (to the next default tab stop).
6. Save the revised agenda, and print a copy of it.

Creating an Invoice

1. Type the information for the invoice shown in Figure 4.18. Include tabs as you think appropriate, but don't worry about alignment until steps 7 and 8.

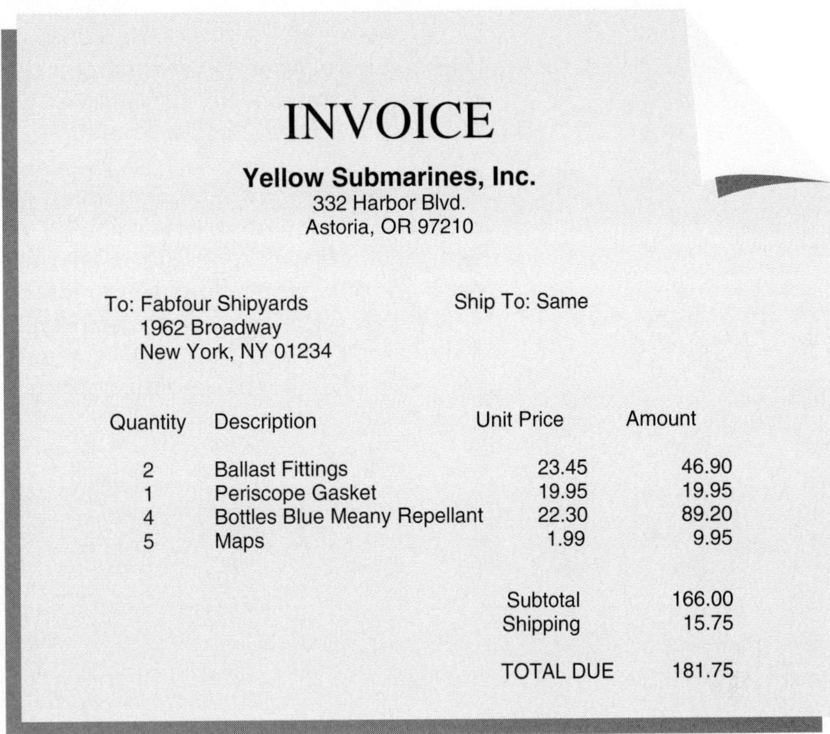

INVOICE

Yellow Submarines, Inc.
332 Harbor Blvd.
Astoria, OR 97210

To: Fabfour Shipyards
1962 Broadway
New York, NY 01234

Ship To: Same

Quantity	Description	Unit Price	Amount
2	Ballast Fittings	23.45	46.90
1	Periscope Gasket	19.95	19.95
4	Bottles Blue Meany Repellant	22.30	89.20
5	Maps	1.99	9.95
		Subtotal	166.00
		Shipping	15.75
		TOTAL DUE	181.75

Figure 4.18

2. Format the entire document in a 12-point sans serif face such as Arial or Helvetica.
3. Center the heading lines.
4. Change the *Invoice* heading to 36-point Times New Roman or a similar serif face, and boldface the heading.
5. Change the formatting of the name of the company to 18-point bold.
6. Change the formatting of the company address lines to 14-point.
7. Select the company name and address lines in the *To* and *Ship To* sections. Insert left tab stops at 3/8 inch, 3 inches, and 3 3/4 inches.
8. Select from the *Quantity/Description/Unit Price/Amount* heading to the bottom of the document. Insert a center tab stop at 1/4 inch. Insert a left tab stop at 1 inch. Insert decimal tab stops at 4 inches and 5 inches.
9. Save your document as *Fabfour Invoice,* and print a copy of it.

Assignments

Visiting Redmond

You can use your Web browser to visit Microsoft at their URL http://www.microsoft.com. Check out the Word for Windows 95 area under Microsoft Office. You'll find free software, drivers, help files, and tips about all kinds of word processing and desktop publishing situations.

Formatting the Telephone List with Leader Tabs

Retrieve the version of your telephone list saved under the file name *Telephone List.* It should be a list of names and telephone numbers separated by tabs. Select all the lines with names and numbers on them, and use the ruler to insert a right tab at about 4 inches (adjust the location of the tab as needed to accommodate the names on your list). The names should now align on the left edge and the numbers, at the 4-inch mark on the right edge.

If the gap between the names and numbers is very wide, it makes it difficult to match numbers with names. Commercial printers use a dotted line, called a leader, to tie the parts of the line together and make the line easier to read. Word allows you to insert leader tabs.

Begin by selecting all the lines (paragraphs) you want to format. Choose Tabs from the Format menu. Select item 2 in the Leader box. As soon as you select OK, the leader will be inserted. Save the list, and print a copy of it.

PROJECT 5: SECTION FORMATTING

Objectives

After completing this project, you should be able to:

- Change paragraph line spacing
- Define and apply styles
- Change margins
- Create bulleted lists
- Add footnotes
- Add headers or footers

In this project, you will begin putting together a short research paper. Like many research papers, this will have footnotes and page numbers in a header. It will have a simple table and a bulleted list. At the end of this project, you'll be able to use basic page formatting and the features of Word that take some of the pain out of preparing reports and papers. Here, you'll create the beginnings of the research paper. In Projects 6 and 7, you'll continue to work with the paper using the tools Word provides for editing and correcting and adding tables.

CASE STUDY: BEGINNING THE RESEARCH PAPER

Assume you are a student in Sociology 415, a course in sociological research. You've been given an assignment to produce a short analytical paper dealing with a social issue and supported by data from a sample study listed in your textbook. Your paper should include relevant references, including the data you have used to support your findings.

Designing the Solution

The overall organization of almost any research paper follows this general pattern:

- Placing the study in context: introductory remarks, possibly a review of work and writings in this area, a statement of your hypothesis
- Description of your study: where your data came from
- Analysis of your study: results, discussion of results, conclusions or recommendations

We'll assume you've done your research, produced a rough draft following this overall organizational pattern, and made revisions. Now you are ready to format the paper. The standard format for a research paper is essentially the same as for a manuscript submitted for publication. The format is designed to be easy to read—and easy to edit, annotate, and revise.

The standard research paper format has been around since the days of the typewriter and is still based on the characteristics of the typewriter. Research papers are nearly always double spaced, which allows more room to mark corrections and make comments. Even with the many type fonts available with modern personal computers, the standard for a research paper remains a typewriter font such as Courier, which facilitates corrections in spelling and word choice. Margins are set wide enough to accommodate more comments, and binding if necessary. Because research papers usually run several pages, you'll want to number the pages for ease of handling. You'll frequently need to quote other people's writing in your own work and then credit these sources in a footnote reference. Some research paper characteristics, footnotes in particular, were difficult and time consuming on a typewriter, but are relatively easy to produce using Word.

You'll begin this project by typing the text for the paper or retrieving it from disk. Then you'll set up and apply the styles for the text and headings. Next you'll set margins and double-space the text. You'll create a bulleted list, add footnotes, and add an indented block quotation. Last, you'll add a header that prints page numbers automatically at the top of each page.

APPLYING AND DEFINING STYLES

The nearly complete draft of the research paper is shown in Figure 5.1. Note that a block quotation and two tables are missing from the draft. You will add those items later.

If the file Gender Roles Paper is available, you will not need to type the text in yourself. If you do need to type the text yourself, the lines in the document window may be longer or shorter, depending on the margin settings on the computer you are using. Don't worry about that; you'll be changing the margins shortly anyway. Note also that there is an intentionally misspelled word—*likelyhood*—that appears several times in the text. It is there to give Word's spelling checker something to do in the next project. If you are typing and make other mistakes, you can leave the mistakes to be corrected later.

Sociology 415
Professor R. Warner
December 6, 1995

Impact of Educational Level on
Views of Gender Roles
by B.J. Mitchell

I am interested in discovering if there is a relationship between educational level and views on gender roles. I believe I will find that as one's level of education increases, the likelyhood of having non-traditional views toward gender roles increases. Examples of non-traditional views include regarding the following as acceptable lifestyle choices: women working in male-dominated fields, men sharing responsibility for work in the home, and women able to hold any job solely on the basis of qualification.
I think there will be a positive connection between higher education and non-traditional views toward gender roles for a variety of reasons. Individuals with greater education are more likely to be aware of the historic and institutional discrimination against women.
[quote will go here]
In addition, persons with higher education are likely to marry others with similar educational background, making the practice of non-traditional gender roles a likely possibility in their relationships. Educated individuals are more likely than uneducated persons to work in areas of employment where women have attained some degree of success in male-dominated environments. Observing these achievements could have the effect of changing a person's views from believing women do not "belong" in the workplace to encouraging their continued success.
The Study
Data for this paper comes from mail surveys sent to probability samples of residents in metropolitan Toronto and Detroit in 1988. The response rate was 69 percent, yielding a total sample size of 1805. The data and percentage distribution of the responses are shown in the table below, along with column and row totals used in the statistical analysis.
[Insert Data Table Here]
Findings
The table shows the results of a probability sample survey. The results support my hypothesis. Specifically, while less than 20 percent of those with a high school education reported having non-traditional views toward gender roles, 42 percent of those with some college and over half of those sampled with college degrees hold non-traditional views. In addition, the data show that almost half of those with high school only and less than 15 percent of those with a college degree hold traditional views. This demonstrates that with increased education, the likelyhood of having non-traditional views also increases.
If there were no correlation between educational level and nontraditional views, the survey responses would be expected to be distributed as shown in the following table.
[Expected response table goes here]
A Chi Square analysis shows the actual data and expected results differ significantly at the 0.01 level. For this reason I must reject the null hypothesis. I conclude that as a person receives more education, the likelyhood that his or her views toward gender roles will become non-traditional increases.

Figure 5.1

The research paper is currently formatted as Normal style using Word's default set of styles. If you click the Style box on the Formatting toolbar, you will find a small collection of predefined paragraph styles usually including Normal, for normal paragraphs, and three heading styles for different heading levels. Word's Normal template actually contains many more built-in styles, but to reduce formatting confusion, they don't appear in the Style box until you begin using them. You will be using and redefining the Normal style and adding several of your own styles as you format the research paper.

Standard research paper format calls for a typewriter font like Courier and double-spaced lines, with the first line in each paragraph indented about ½ inch. You will begin by redefining Normal style to conform to this standard.

To prepare the draft and redefine Normal style:

1 Type the draft as shown, or retrieve the *Sociology Paper* file if it is available.

2 Select a few words within the text of the document, and format that text as 12-point Courier New (or a similar typewriter-style face).

3 With the text still selected use the ruler to set the first-line indent to ½ inch, as shown in Figure 5.2.

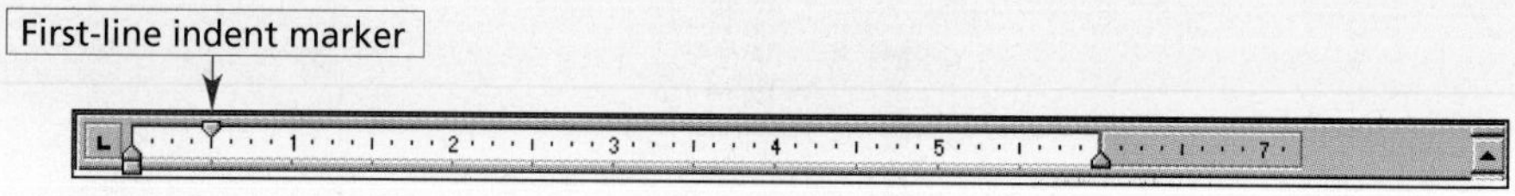

First-line indent marker

Figure 5.2

4 Press CTRL + **2** to double-space the text in the selected paragraph.

5 Select Normal in the Style box at the left end of the Formatting toolbar, and press ENTER
The Reapply Style dialog box will appear.

6 Select the top option: Redefine the style using the selection as an example?

7 Select OK to redefine the Normal style as 12-point Courier New, double-spaced and indented 1/2 inch.

All text in the research paper will change to the new style as soon as you redefine Normal style. Now you need to set up and apply different styles for the headings and titles. The section headings will be boldfaced and will not be indented.

To define and apply the Section Heading style:

1 Select the entire line for the first section heading: *The Study.* (Recall that the easiest way to select an entire line is to click in the selection bar to the left of the paragraph.)

2 Select the Bold button on the Formatting toolbar to boldface the heading.

3 Move the first-line indent marker on the ruler to the left margin to remove the first-line indent so that the heading is flush to the left margin.

4 Select Normal in the Style box at the left end of the Formatting toolbar.

5 Type in the name of the new style: **`Section Heading`**

6 Press ENTER to define the style.

7 Select the second heading: *Findings.*

8 Select Section Heading from the Style box to apply the style.
The title at the top of the research paper will be boldfaced, centered, and single spaced.

To define and apply the Paper Title style:

1 Select the entire first line of the title: *Impact of Educational Level on.*

2 Remove the first-line indent, as you did with the heading style.

3 Press CTRL + **1** to change the line spacing to single space.

4 Select the Center button on the Formatting toolbar to center the title line.

5 Select the Bold button on the Formatting toolbar to boldface the title.

6 Select the Style box on the Formatting toolbar.

7 Type in the name of the new style: **`Paper Title`**

8 Press ENTER to define the new style.

9 Select all three title lines as well as the blank lines above and below the title lines, and apply the new Paper Title style.
The top of the research paper should look like Figure 5.3.

```
        Sociology·415¶

        Professor·R.·Warner¶

        December·6,·1995¶

                              ¶
              Impact·of·Educational·Level·on¶
                   Views·of·Gender·Roles¶
                      by·B.J.·Mitchell¶
                              ¶
        I·am·interested·in·discovering·if·there·is·a·

relationship·between·educational·level·and·views·on·gender·

roles.·I·believe·I·will·find·that·as·one's·level·of·
```

Figure 5.3

To define and apply the Course Number style:

1 Select the entire first line of the document, which contains the course number.

2 Remove the paragraph indent, and press (CTRL) + **1** to single-space the line.

3 Select the Align Right button on the Formatting toolbar to move the line to the right margin.

4 Use the Style box on the Formatting toolbar to define a new style called Course Number.

5 Apply the Course Number style to the two lines below, containing the instructor's name and the date.

6 Save your document, changing the file name to *Revised Gender Roles Paper*.

EXIT If necessary, you can exit Word now and continue this project later.

WORKING WITH SECTIONS AND SECTION BREAKS

A ***section*** in Word is a portion of a document that can be formatted with specific margin settings, page orientation (vertical or horizontal), page-numbering sequence, or other features affecting page layout. When you begin a new document in Word, the entire document is a single section. If necessary, you can insert section breaks to divide the document into separate sections and vary the section formatting from one section to another. For instance, you could number the first few pages of a report with small roman numerals and then switch to another section to use conventional arabic numerals for the rest of the report. Or you could include a horizontal page in a separate section to accommodate a wide table within a series of conventional vertical pages. For most simple documents, however, the entire document will be a single section. That will be the case with this research paper.

Changing the Margins

Formatting sections in Word follows the same general rule as character and paragraph formatting: select, and then do. When formatting sections, you first select the section, and then you format it. A section is selected when any part of it is selected. If your whole document is a single section, that makes selecting it very straightforward: you just need to have the insertion point somewhere inside the document to format the whole document.

The standard margin settings for a research paper are at least 1 inch on all sides. You will set the top, bottom, left, and right margins for the paper to 1 inch exactly.

To set the margins:

1 Choose Page Setup from the File menu.
The Page Setup dialog box, shown in Figure 5.4, appears.

Figure 5.4

The margin settings on your screen may not exactly match those shown in Figure 5.4, but you are about to change them.

2 Select the Margins tab if it is not already on top.

3 Select the measurement within the Top box, shown in Figure 5.4, if not already selected.

4 Type **1** in the Top box.
The new measurement you type replaces the old measurement for the top margin. You can use the arrow keys, BACKSPACE, and DEL to edit the measurement in any of the boxes.

5 Select the measurement within the Bottom box, located just below the Top box.
As soon as you advance to the Bottom box, the Preview display within the dialog box is updated to indicate how the new setting for the top margin will affect general page appearance.

6 Type **1** in the Bottom box.

7 Change the measurement to **1** in the Left box.

8 Change the measurement to **1** in the Right box.

9 Select Whole Document in the Apply To box if it is not already selected.

10 Select OK.

To make the document easier to read on the screen, you can adjust the magnification of the display using the Zoom Control box at the right edge of the Standard toolbar. You can magnify your document as much as 200 percent to check intricate alignments, or as low as 10 percent to see a tiny facsimile of the page. For most of the figures in this project, the Zoom Control box is set to Page Width so that an entire line can be seen on the screen without scrolling from side to side. You will probably find it easiest to work at that magnification.

To set the screen magnification:

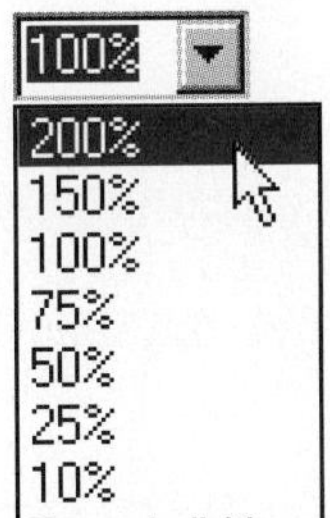

1 Select 200% from the Zoom Control box at the right end of the Standard toolbar.

2 Select 10% from the Zoom Control box.

3 Select Page Width from the Zoom Control box.

Creating a Bulleted List

To make clearer what you mean by nontraditional views of gender roles, you decide to list on separate lines each of the three example lifestyle choices mentioned in the first paragraph. To make it easier for the reader to compare these examples and understand the pattern of your thought, you will put the three examples in a bulleted list. A ***bullet*** is a typographical device, usually a large dot, that indicates separate items in a list, just as numbers do in a numbered list. Unlike numbered lists, however, bulleted lists don't suggest that items are in any particular sequence.

First you will edit the text so that each item in the list appears on a separate line and in a separate paragraph. Then you'll indent the list and add the bullets.

To create an indented list:

1 Place the insertion point just after the colon following *choices*.

2 Press (ENTER) to separate the list from the rest of the paragraph and establish a new paragraph.

3 Remove the first-line indentation using the top-left indent marker on the ruler.
The screen may scroll to the left when you move the marker. If necessary, you can adjust the display using the horizontal scroll bar at the bottom of the screen.

4 Edit the list so that it appears as shown in Figure 5.5. Be sure to eliminate all unneeded commas and spaces as well as the word *and* that connects the last item to the rest of the list and the period that ends the list.

```
likelyhood·of·having·non-traditional·views·toward·gender·roles·
increases.·Examples·of·non-traditional·views·include·regarding·
the·following·as·acceptable·lifestyle·choices:¶
women·working·in·male-dominated·fields¶
men·sharing·responsibility·for·work·in·the·home¶
women·able·to·hold·any·job·solely·on·the·basis·of·qualification.¶
     I·think·there·will·be·a·positive·connection·between·higher·
education·and·non-traditional·views·toward·gender·roles·for·a·
```

Figure 5.5

5 Select the three new paragraphs that compose the list.

6 Click the Increase Indent button on the Formatting toolbar to indent these lines.
The list should now look like Figure 5.6 although the way you selected the paragraphs might differ.

```
increases.·Examples·of·nontraditional·views·include·regarding·the·
following·as·acceptable·lifestyle·choices:¶
     women·working·in·male-dominated·fields¶
     men·sharing·responsibility·for·work·in·the·home¶
     women·able·to·hold·any·job·solely·on·the·basis·of·
     qualification¶
     I·think·there·will·be·a·positive·connection·between·higher·
education·and·nontraditional·views·toward·gender·roles·for·a·
```

Figure 5.6

Tip If necessary, you can increase the size of the indentation by selecting the Increase Indent button repeatedly or by pressing CTRL+**M** Each time you increase the indentation, the text moves to the next tab, ordinarily ½ inch. To decrease the size of an indentation, you can select the Decrease Indent button or press CTRL+SHIFT+**M** You can also adjust paragraph indentation using the indent markers on the ruler, as shown in Figure 5.7.

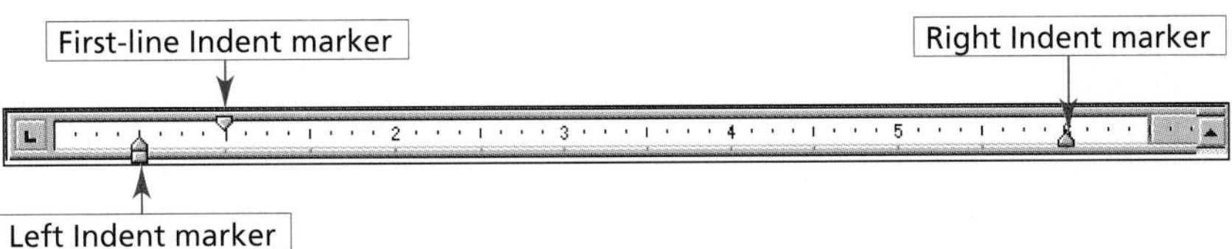

Figure 5.7

To format a series of lines as a bulleted list, you can call up the Bullets and Numbering dialog box, shown in Figure 5.8. You can use this dialog box to create both bulleted lists and numbered lists on a single level (like the one in the research paper) or on multiple levels (like an outline). You can change the character used for a bullet and customize the line spacing. For the list in the research paper, however, the default bullet style will work well. The default bullet style will have a blue border around it.

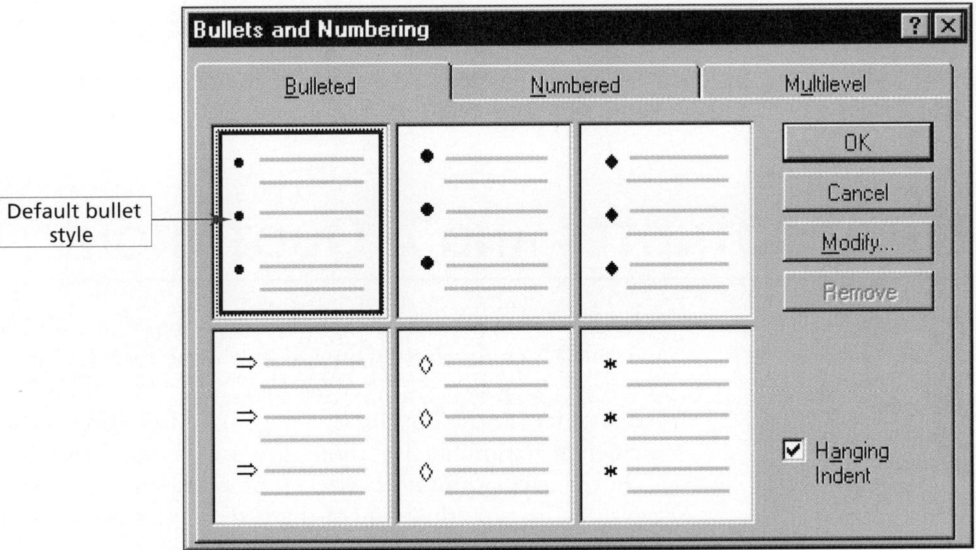

Figure 5.8

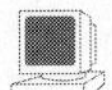

To create a bulleted list:

1 Select the three list items, as shown in Figure 5.6.

2 Choose Bullets and Numbering from the Format menu.

3 Select the Bulleted tab if it is not already on top.

4 Select OK to add bullets to the list.

The list should now look like Figure 5.9. Each item in the list stands out clearly, and the distinction between traditional and nontraditional views is made apparent.

```
increases.·Examples·of·nontraditional·views·include·regarding·the·
following·as·acceptable·lifestyle·choices:¶
    •  women·working·in·male-dominated·fields¶
    •  men·sharing·responsibility·for·work·in·the·home¶
    •  women·able·to·hold·any·job·solely·on·the·basis·of·
       qualification¶
    I·think·there·will·be·a·positive·connection·between·higher·
education·and·nontraditional·views·toward·gender·roles·for·a·
```

Figure 5.9

Tip If you want to use the bullet style already selected in the Bullets and Numbering dialog box, you can produce a bulleted list quickly by selecting the list items and then selecting the Bullets button on the Formatting toolbar. The button is a toggle, so selecting it a second time will eliminate the bullets.

If necessary, you can save your file as *Revised Gender Roles Paper,* exit Word now, and continue this project later.

Adding Footnotes and a Quotation

The data for the research paper came from a study published in an academic journal. To credit those who conducted the research, you need to add a footnote citing that study. A ***footnote,*** as you are probably aware, is a brief block of text at the bottom of a page used for citing authorities or making incidental comments. Footnotes are usually numbered in sequential order.

In the days of the typewriter, footnoting was a painful operation. The typist had to type the body of the text, being careful to stop short of the bottom of the page and leave exactly enough room for the footnote. Then the typist had to switch to single spacing and type whatever footnotes belonged on that page. Word, by contrast, makes the process of footnoting relatively painless. When you insert a footnote reference in the body of a paper, Word automatically numbers and formats the footnote reference as a superscript. Word then opens a footnote window where you can enter the text of the footnote as it should appear at the bottom of the page. If you insert or delete a footnote, Word automatically renumbers all other footnotes. When you print out the paper, Word puts footnotes at the bottom of the appropriate pages, or places them at the end of the section if you select the ***endnotes*** option. Unlike footnotes, which always appear at the bottom of the page, endnotes appear at the end of the section.

To add a footnote, you use the Footnote and Endnote dialog box, shown in Figure 5.10. This dialog box allows you to customize footnotes or endnotes to suit nearly any style guide. You can click the Help button if you want more information about available options. For the research paper, however, the default—numbered footnotes—is exactly what you want.

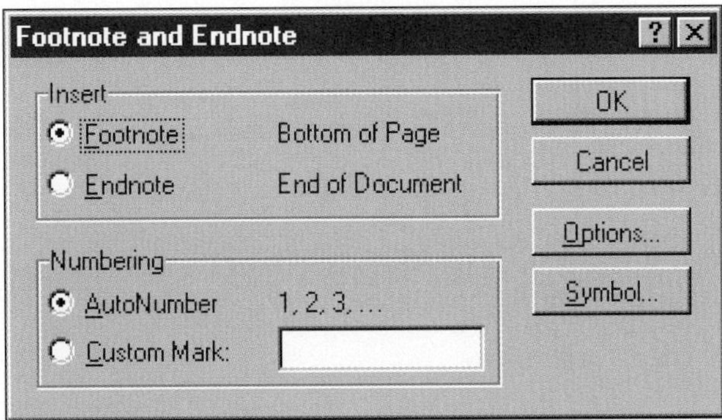

Figure 5.10

To add a footnote reference:

1 In the first paragraph after the heading *The Study,* position the insertion point immediately after the period following *Detroit in 1988,* at the end of the first sentence.

2 Choose Footnote from the Insert menu.

3 Select OK to add the footnote.

The footnote window opens at the bottom of the screen, as shown in Figure 5.11. This is a separate window, with its own vertical scroll bar, and you can switch from one window to the other by clicking inside the window or by pressing F6 Notice that Word has inserted a superscript footnote reference mark just after *1988* in the text window and at the beginning of the footnote text in the footnote window. Now you will type the reference.

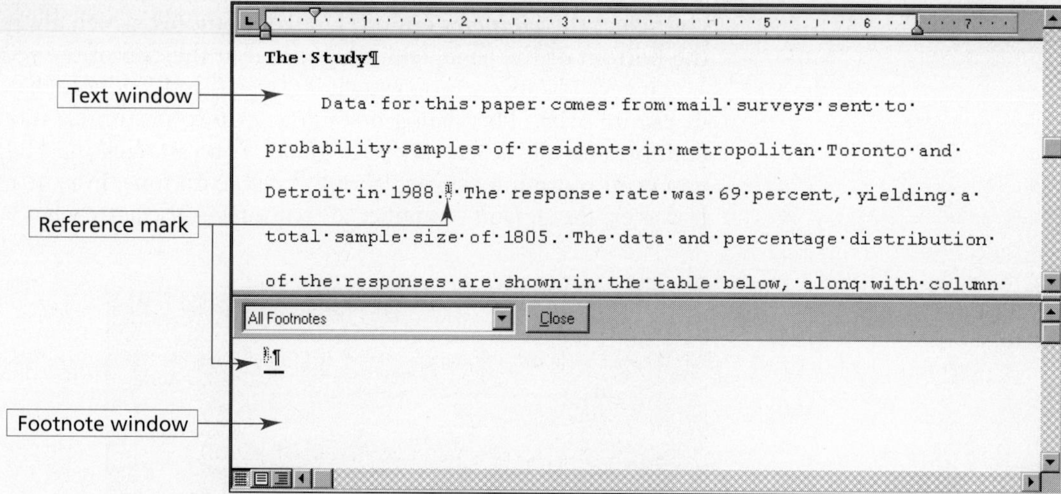

Figure 5.11

To add the footnote text and set the Footnote Text style:

1 Type the footnote text shown in Figure 5.12.

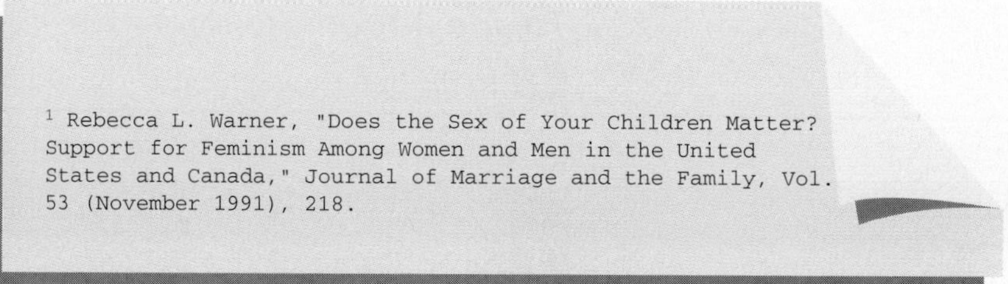

Figure 5.12

2 Press (CTRL) + 1 to single-space the footnote text.

3 Select Ruler from the View menu to open the ruler in the footnote window.

4 Move the first-line indent marker on the footnote window ruler to the left margin to remove the indent from the footnote.

5 Select Ruler from the View menu to close the ruler in the footnote window.

6 Select one or two words within the footnote text and change the size to 12 point.

7 Select Footnote Text in the Style box at the left end of the Formatting toolbar, and press (ENTER)
The Reapply Style dialog box will appear.

8 If not already selected, select the top option: Redefine the style using the selection as an example?

9 Select OK to redefine the Footnote Text style as 12-point Courier New.
Any future footnotes you enter will also appear in this new Footnote Text style.

Titles of books and journals should be underlined in standard research-paper style. Recall that underlining is a character format in Word, so you will need to select the words you want to underline and then format them as underlined. You can easily select a block of words by dragging the pointer from the first word to the last. As usual, the selection will be "rounded off" to include whole words only.

To underline the journal title:

1 Select the title of the journal, as shown in Figure 5.13.

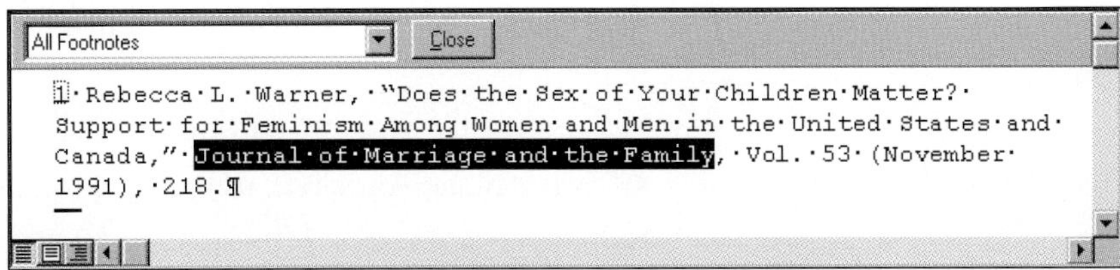

All Footnotes | Close

1·Rebecca·L.·Warner,·"Does·the·Sex·of·Your·Children·Matter?·Support·for·Feminism·Among·Women·and·Men·in·the·United·States·and·Canada,"·Journal·of·Marriage·and·the·Family,·Vol.·53·(November·1991),·218.¶

Figure 5.13

2 Click the Underline button on the Formatting toolbar to underline the title.

You will need to cancel the text selection to see the underlining.

3 Select the Close button to close the footnote window.

Next you need to add a supporting quotation and footnote it as well. Assume that in your notes for the research paper, you have a quotation that supports the argument that education influences attitudes about gender roles. The quotation will go just after the second paragraph in the body of the paper. The research paper format for longer quotations is to set them off as a separate block of single-spaced text, indented on the left side.

To add the quotation:

1 Select the line [*quote will go here*].

2 Type the quotation shown in Figure 5.14.

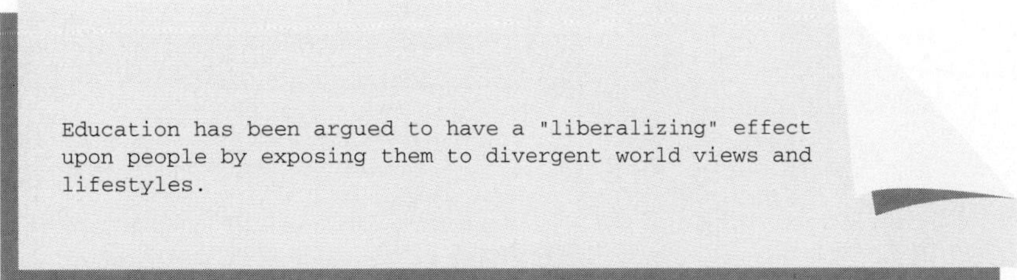

Education has been argued to have a "liberalizing" effect upon people by exposing them to divergent world views and lifestyles.

Figure 5.14

The material you type should replace the bracketed note, and it will be double spaced and indented like the other paragraphs in the body of the paper. You will need to single-space the block quotation and indent it on the left.

To single-space and indent the quotation:

1. Position the insertion point somewhere within the quotation you just added.
2. Press CTRL + 1 to single-space the quotation.
3. Remove the first-line indentation using the top-left indent marker on the ruler.
4. Select the Increase Indent button on the Formatting toolbar.
5. Use the *right* mouse button to click inside the new paragraph.
6. Select Paragraph from the pull-down menu to open the Paragraph dialog box.
7. Select the Indents and Spacing tab if it is not already on top.
8. Select the After box in the Spacing area.
9. Type `1 li` to set the spacing after the paragraph to one line.
10. Select OK to close the Paragraph dialog box.

If your paper were going to include more than one block quotation, you could use this paragraph to define a Block Quote style. As it is, you now need to add the footnote that gives the citation for the quotation.

To add a footnote reference for the quotation:

1. Position the insertion point just after the period at the end of the block quotation.
2. Choose Footnote from the Insert menu.
3. Select OK to add the footnote.

As before, Word inserts a footnote reference in the body of the paper and opens a footnote window for you to type the footnote text. Note that the previous footnote number 1 has already been renumbered and a new number 1 inserted for you where you can type the text for the new footnote.

To add the text for the new footnote:

1. Type the footnote text shown in Figure 5.15, underlining the name of the journal as shown.

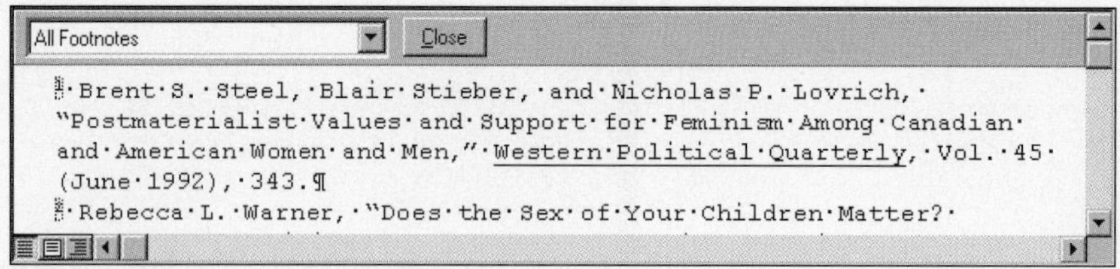

Figure 5.15

2. Position the insertion point somewhere within the second footnote.

Notice that when you move from one footnote to another in the footnote window, Word adjusts the text in the main window so that the footnote reference is displayed. This makes it easy to check the correspondence between a footnote reference and the footnote text itself.

3 Close the footnote window.

Tip To switch quickly between footnote references and text, double-click a footnote reference to open the footnote window and view the associated footnote text. Then double-click the footnote number in the footnote window to close the footnote window and return to the document window.

If necessary, you can save your file as *Revised Gender Roles Paper,* exit Word now, and continue this project later.

ADDING HEADERS AND FOOTERS

You are nearly done with the basic formatting of the research paper. All that remains is to add a ***header,*** a repeating section of text at the top of each page. Word also accommodates ***footers,*** which are like headers but appear at the bottom of the page. Headers and footers often list the title of a book, the name of the chapter, or the page number. The header for the research paper will include the name of the author and the page number, a common convention for research papers.

Because the name of the author already appears on the first page, however, and because it is obvious which page that is, you won't put the header on page 1. Thus you will need to make the first page of the paper an exception in the series of headers.

To make the header for the first page different from other pages:

1 Position the insertion point anywhere within the document, but be sure no text is selected.

2 Choose Page Setup from the File menu.

3 Select the Layout tab, as shown in Figure 5.16.

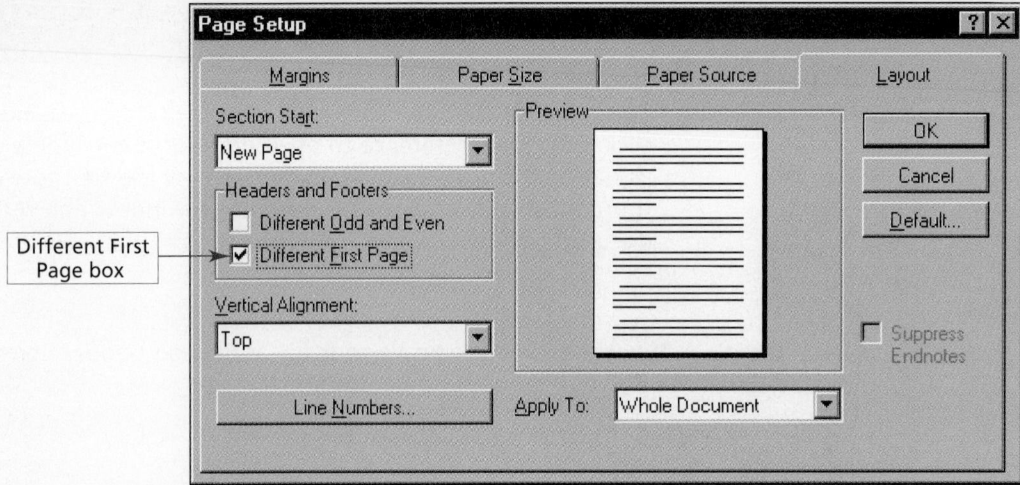

Figure 5.16

4 Select Different First Page so that a check mark appears in the box.

5 Select OK to complete the formatting choice.

You have just created two types of headers: one for the first page and one for all other pages. You will leave the first page header blank so that no header will appear on page 1, and you will use the other header to print the author name and page number on subsequent pages.

When you work with headers and footers, the display will change to Page Layout View, and a box for the header will appear at the top of the page, as shown in Figure 5.17. If the box is for page 1, it will be labeled First Page Header. Otherwise, it will simply be labeled Header. The Header and Footer toolbar will also appear, floating on the page. You can move the toolbar to other parts of the screen as needed to see what you are doing. If the magnification of the page is too small, you can change it using the Zoom Control box on the Standard toolbar near the right edge. The text of the paper itself appears dimmed because you can't edit the paper when you're working on headers and footers. You can move from page to page by selecting the Previous Page and Next Page buttons at the bottom of the vertical scroll bar. You can move between the header and footer on the page by selecting the leftmost button on the Header and Footer toolbar.

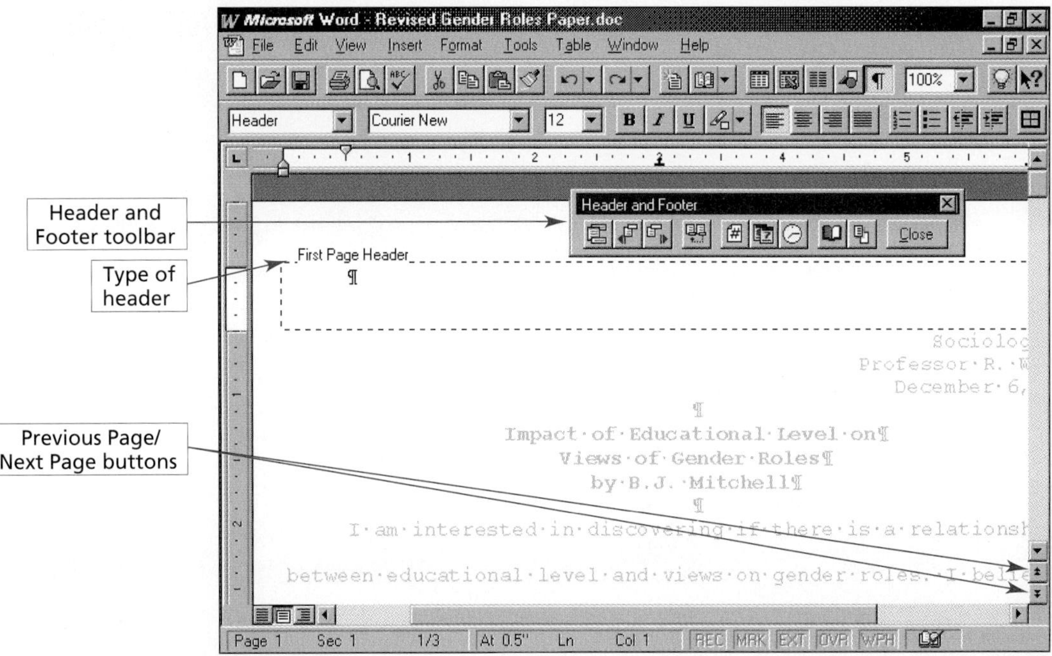

Figure 5.17

To create a header:

1 Choose Header and Footer from the View menu.

2 If you are in the first-page header, move to the next page by selecting the Next Page button on the vertical scroll bar.

3 Position the insertion point in the Header box.

4 Select Page Width in the Zoom Control box.

5 Type `Mitchell,` then a space, then a slash character (/), and then another space.

6 Click the Page Numbers button on the Header and Footer toolbar, as shown in Figure 5.18.

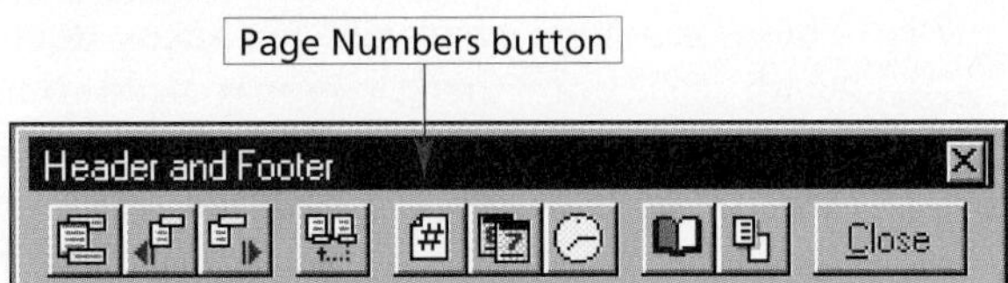

Figure 5.18

You have inserted a special code in the header that Word replaces with the appropriate page number. The code appears as a page number immediately after the header text.

To format the header:

1 Click the Align Right button on the Formatting toolbar to justify the header on the right.

The header should now look like Figure 5.19. Move from page to page to see that the page numbers do change and that the first page has a blank header.

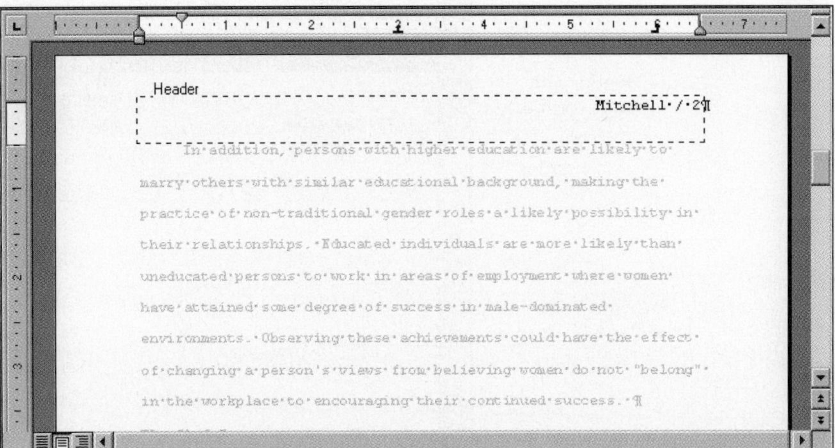

Figure 5.19

2 Select the Close button to close the Header and Footer window.

To save the paper and print a copy of it:

1 Save the paper.

2 Click the Print button on the Standard toolbar or choose Print from the File menu to print a copy of the paper.

3 Close the file.

The Next Step

When it comes to commonly used document features, Word makes many standard operations nearly automatic. You can produce standard headers, footers, footnotes, endnotes, bulleted lists, or numbered lists with a few clicks or a few keystrokes. For many documents, Word's standard formats work well. For others, you may need to modify the format. You may want to return to the Paragraph dialog box to see how you can control line spacing both within and between paragraphs on the Indents and Spacing tab. You can also switch to the Text Flow tab and format a paragraph so that it will not be split at a page break or so that a heading will be kept with the text that follows it. You may want to experiment more with the Bullets and Numbering dialog box to try other typographical devices, indentations, or even multilevel lists. You also could experiment with changing the position of headers and footers by changing the From Edge settings on the Margins tab in the Page Setup dialog box. Word can be as flexible as you need it to be, but you'll need to invest some time in learning how to accomplish what you want.

The standard research paper format used here will work for many papers you are asked to write. If you want more detail, a common authority for style and format questions is *The Chicago Manual of Style*, available in nearly any library. An adaptation of *The Chicago Manual of Style* that is especially for students is *A Manual for Writers of Term Papers, Theses, and Dissertations*, by Kate L. Turabian, also published by The University of Chicago Press. In addition, each academic field tends to have its own particular style and format. Many fields in the humanities use Modern Language Association style, many social sciences use the style of the American Psychological Association, and many life sciences use the style of the Council of Biology Editors. Your field may have its own set of conventions, and you should be relatively familiar with what those conventions are.

This concludes Project 5. You can either exit Word or go on to work the Study Questions, Review Exercises, and Assignments.

SUMMARY AND EXERCISES

Summary

- Page layout—such as margins, page orientation, page numbering, positions of headers and footers—is referred to as section formatting in Word.
- Although most simple documents are a single section, Word allows you to divide a document into many sections and change the page layout choices from section to section.
- You can set page margins in the Page Setup dialog box (choose Page Setup in the File menu).
- You can set paragraph indentation, including the first-line indentation, in the Paragraph dialog box from the Format menu or by moving the indent markers on the ruler.
- You can create a bulleted or numbered list with the Bullets and Numbering dialog box in the Format menu or by selecting either the Bullets or the Numbering button on the Formatting toolbar.
- To create a footnote, open the Footnote and Endnote dialog box from the Insert menu. Word will open a footnote window where you can type the text of the footnote.
- You can add headers or footers by choosing Header and Footer from the View menu.
- You can have a header and footer for the first page different from those on the other pages in a section if you specify Different First Page on the Layout tab of the Page Setup dialog box.
- Headers and footers can contain a special code that automatically inserts page numbers.

Key Terms and Operations

Key Terms
bullet
endnote
footer
footnote
header
section

Operations
Change margins
Indent paragraphs
Create bulleted lists
Add footnotes
Set up headers and footers

Study Questions

Multiple Choice

1. Which of the following is *not* controlled by section formatting in Word?
   a. page numbering
   b. margins
   c. line spacing
   d. page orientation
2. Which of the following is not a paragraph format in Word?
   a. bulleted lists
   b. line spacing
   c. numbered lists
   d. line width
3. The Center button aligns:
   a. a single line of text.
   b. an entire paragraph.
   c. the characters selected.
   d. to the next tab.
4. A typographic device used to set off items in a list is called a:
   a. dingbat.
   b. logo.
   c. typo.
   d. bullet.
5. The Increase Indent button moves text to:
   a. the right ¼ inch.
   b. the next tab.
   c. align with the text above.
   d. the right margin.
6. You can double-space text by pressing:
   a. CTRL+S
   b. CTRL+2
   c. SHIFT+S
   d. CTRL+D
7. The footnote number that goes in the text of the document is called:
   a. the reference mark.
   b. the footnote text.
   c. the subscript.
   d. an asterisk.
8. Document headers or footers often contain:
   a. page numbers.
   b. copyright disclaimers.
   c. charts and graphs.
   d. footnotes.
9. You can indent the first line of a paragraph by using:
   a. the Indent dialog box.
   b. CTRL+I
   c. the Increase Indent button.
   d. the indent markers on the ruler.
10. To select a section:
    a. Triple-click in the selection bar.
    b. Select the entire document.
    c. Position the insertion point inside the section.
    d. Select all text in the section.

Short Answer

1. To change page orientation within a docum
   zontal, you must establish a new ___________
2. You can change line spacing in the ___________
3. Endnotes appear at the end of a ___________
4. To indent a paragraph from the right, you
   the ruler.
5. Footnotes are usually used for ___________ or ___________.
6. Word's footnote window contains the footnote ___________.
7. Most section formatting is done in the ___________ dialog box.
8. The buttons for paragraph alignment (center, right, left) are on the ___________ toolbar.
9. If you insert or delete a footnote, Word will ___________ other footnotes.
10. If you want each chapter in a book to start numbering from page 1, you should make each chapter a separate ___________.

For Discussion

1. What is a section in Word? What are sections used for?
2. Explain the general procedure for adding a footnote to a document.
3. How can you suppress a header on the first page of a section or document?

Review Exercises

Changing the Research Paper Format

Reformat the research paper you worked on in this project according to a new set of style guidelines.

1. Change the margin settings to 1 inch for the top and bottom and 1.25 inches for the sides.
2. Reorganize the header and add a footer as follows: for the header, use tabs or a table to center the date and place the course number at the right edge; for the footer, place the word *Page,* followed by the page number, at the right edge.
3. Turn the bulleted list into a numbered list beginning with number 1.
4. Add a new footnote to the research paper. Place the footnote reference at the end of the first sentence in the last paragraph, which ends *at the 0.01 level.* Add the following footnote text:

   That is, there is only a 1% chance that education and gender role attitudes are not significantly related.

5. Save the file as *Third Gender Roles Paper,* and print it out.

Formatting the Paper in Publication Style

Reformat the research paper from the preceding exercise in a style suitable for publication as a report or journal article.

1. Set margins to 1.25 inches all around (top, bottom, and sides).
2. Delete the course number, instructor's name, and date.
3. Change the font for the entire document to 12-point Times New Roman (or a similar serif face).
4. Change the title to 18-point Times New Roman bold.
5. Change all other headings to 14-point Helvetica or Arial bold (or a similar sans serif face).
6. Single-space the entire document.
7. On the Indents and Spacing tab in the Paragraph dialog box, set extra spacing before or after paragraphs as needed to separate headings from the text above them.
8. Remove the header.
9. Format the footnotes in 10-point Times New Roman (or equivalent).
10. Insert blank lines if needed to keep the table on one page.
11. Save the file as *Publication Style Paper,* and print the result.

Assignments

Numbering with Multiple Levels

Use the Multilevel Numbering option in the Bullets and Numbering dialog box to number the agenda created at the end of Projects 2, 3, and 4. (The agenda should be in a file named *Meeting Agenda.*)

Formatting Your Own Paper

Take a term paper you've already written and saved to disk, and format that paper according to the conventions used for the research paper in this project. Word can read word processing files from many other word processors, so try this even if you didn't use Word to write your paper in the first place. You can almost always transfer text from one word processor to another if you first save the file as an ASCII, or plain text, file. The drawback is that you will lose most of your formatting information this way.

Formatting a Draft as a Finished Publication

Retrieve the file *Pasteur on Germ Theory* from the Word 7 web site (http://www.aw.com/is/word7), or ask your instructor where to get the file. This document is the presentation Louis Pasteur gave to the French Academy of Science in 1878 announcing his discoveries in germ theory. The document is formatted as a draft for publication. Your job is to turn it into a finished publication, as shown in Figure 5.20.

Germ Theory and its Applications to Medicine and Surgery[1]

by Louis Pasteur

The Sciences gain by mutual support. When, as the result of my first communications on the fermentations in 1857-1858, it appeared that the ferments, properly so-called, are living beings, that the germs of microscopic organisms abound in the surface of all objects, in the air and in the water; that the theory of spontaneous generation is chimerical; that wines, beer, vinegar, the blood, urine and all the fluids of the body undergo none of their usual changes in pure air, both Medicine and Surgery received fresh stimulation. A French physician, Dr. Davaine, was fortunate in making the first application of these principles to Medicine, in 1863.

Our researches of last year, left the etiology of the putrid disease, or septicemia, in a much less advanced condition than that of anthrax. We had demonstrated the probability that septicemia depends upon the presence and growth of a microscopic body, but the absolute proof of this important conclusion was not reached. To demonstrate experimentally that a microscopic organism actually is the cause of a disease and the agent of contagion, I know no other way, in the present state of Science, than to subject the microbe (the new and happy term introduced by M. Sedillot) to the method of cultivation out of the body. It may be noted that in twelve successive cultures, each one of only ten cubic centimeters volume, the original drop will be diluted as if placed in a volume of fluid equal to the total volume of the earth. It is just this form of test to which M. Joubert and I subjected the anthrax bacteridium.[2] Having cultivated it a great number of times in a sterile fluid, each culture being started with a minute drop from the preceding, we then demonstrated that the product of the last culture was capable of further development and of acting in the animal tissues by producing anthrax with all its symptoms. Such is—as we believe—the indisputable proof that anthrax is a bacterial disease.

Our researches concerning the septic vibrio had not so far been convincing, and it was to fill up this gap that we resumed our experiments. To this end, we attempted the cultivation of the septic vibrio from an animal dead of septicemia. It is worth noting that all of our first experiments failed, despite the variety of culture media we employed—urine, beer yeast water, meat water, etc. Our culture media were not sterile, but we found—most commonly—a microscopic organism showing no relationship to the septic vibrio, and presenting the form, common enough elsewhere, of chains of extremely minute spherical granules possessed of no virulence whatever.[3] This was an impurity, introduced, unknown to us, at the same time as the septic vibrio; and the germ undoubtedly passed from the intestines—always inflamed and distended in septicemic animals—into the abdominal fluids from which we took our original cultures of the septic vibrio. If this explanation of the contamination of our cultures was correct, we ought to find a pure culture of the septic vibrio in the heart's blood of the animal recently dead of septicemia. This was what happened, but a new difficulty presented itself; all our cultures remained

---

[1] Read before the French Academy of Sciences, April 29th 1878. Published in *Comptes rendus de l'Academie des Sciences*, lxxxvi., pp. 1037-43. Translation by H.C. Ernst, M.D.

[2] In making the translation, it seems wiser to adhere to Pasteur's nomenclature. *Bacillus anthracis* would be the term employed today.—Translator.

[3] It is quite possible that Pasteur was here dealing with certain septicemic streptococci that are now known to lose their virulence with extreme rapidity under artificial cultivation.—Translator.

Figure 5.20

Here are the specifications:

- Page margins will be 1 inch top and bottom, 1½ inches at the sides.
- The main text is to be 11-point Times New Roman, single spaced, with a first-line indentation of ¼ inch.
- Underlining in the draft should be changed to italic in the final publication.
- The title of the paper should be 18-point Arial bold.
- Footnote references in the draft are given as ^ 1 for the first footnote, ^ 2 for the second, and so on. Footnote text is given in brackets with a heading such as *Footnote 1 text:* in front of the text. Change the references and text to conventional forms, like those used in the research paper in this project. All footnote text should be formatted as 10-point Times New Roman.

- All pages, including the first page, should have a footer containing the page number only. The page number should be on the right side on odd pages and on the left side on even pages. The first page should not have a header. Even pages should have headers that say *Germ Theory* on the left side of the page. Odd pages should have headers that say *by Louis Pasteur* on the right side of the page. All headers and footers should be formatted as 12-point Times New Roman bold italic.
- Save the revised document as *Revised Germ Theory,* and print it out.

PROJECT 6: WRITING AND EDITING TOOLS

Objectives

After completing this project, you should be able to:

- Find words and phrases automatically
- Replace one word or phrase with another
- Check spelling
- Use the thesaurus
- Get a quick word count

In this project, you will continue with the research paper you formatted in Project 5. You'll use some of Word's writing and editing tools to make corrections and revisions in the paper. You'll see how to find words and phrases using the Find tool, and how to replace those words and phrases with new text using the Replace tool. You'll check the spelling of every word in the paper with Word's spelling checker. And you'll use the built-in thesaurus to look at alternative word choices. At the end of this project, the paper should be relatively polished and free of errors. You'll also see how to get a quick word count of the length of the paper.

CASE STUDY: MAKING REVISIONS AND CORRECTIONS

Writing projects almost always involve writing, revising, rethinking, revising some more, adding and subtracting, tinkering, polishing, correcting, re-thinking again—all that and more, and in no particular order. As mentioned before, a word processor makes this circular, sometimes circuitous, process much less complicated because it makes it easy to change what you don't like and still retain what you're satisfied with. In short, it saves retyping as you revise and reconsider.

In addition, as they have evolved, word processors have added tools that assist the writing and editing process in other ways. The ***find and replace*** feature allows you to find all instances of a certain word or phrase in a document and, if you want, to replace each instance with another word or phrase. For example, if you misspelled someone's name consistently and frequently throughout a document, Word will track down every instance of the incorrect spelling and substitute the correct spelling, in seconds. Spelling checkers look up every word in a document in a dictionary-on-disk to make sure each one is a legitimate word. Word's online thesaurus will give you alternative word choices in a flash. You can use the built-in word counter to get a quick statistical profile of a document. None of these tools replaces thinking and writing skill, but they can take some of the labor out of writing well.

Designing the Solution

Assume that as you reviewed the paper you started in Project 5, you made some notes about revisions you wanted to make. Those notes are shown in Figure 6.1. In addition to those changes, assume that you had Word's automatic spelling feature turned off so that you didn't have to attend to misspelled words while drafting. Now, even though you've already read through the research paper for spelling errors, you want to check through it once again with Word's built-in spelling checker. This sort of revision and polishing is made much easier with Word's writing and editing tools.

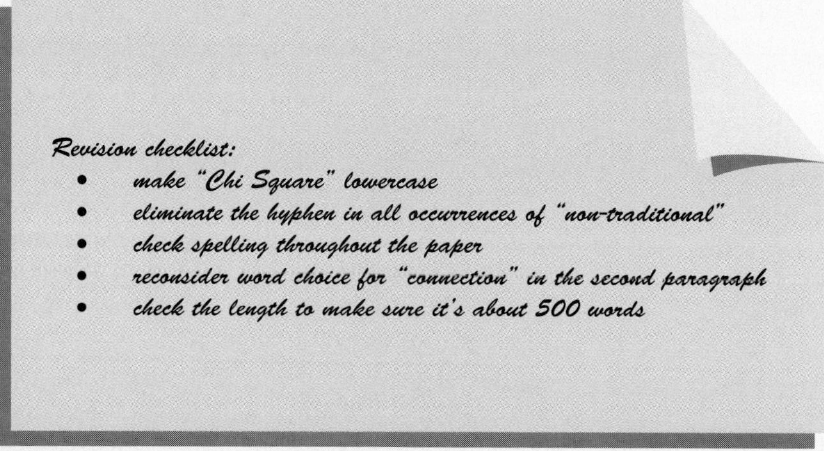

Revision checklist:
make "Chi Square" lowercase
eliminate the hyphen in all occurrences of "non-traditional"
check spelling throughout the paper
reconsider word choice for "connection" in the second paragraph
check the length to make sure it's about 500 words

Figure 6.1

FINDING TEXT

In checking a style guide, you found that the term *chi square*, the name of a common statistical test, is always lowercased. So, the first item on the revision list involves finding all mentions of *Chi Square* in the research paper and changing them to *chi square*. You recall that you used the term only once or twice, and you know that if you read through the paper, you would find the term in a few minutes. But Word can find it faster. In a ***find*** operation, the word processor searches through every character pattern in the document looking for the characters or words you specify.

You initiate a search operation using the Find dialog box, shown in Figure 6.2. You can type the search characters in lowercase, all capital letters, or in caps and lowercase. If the Match Case box is not checked, Word will ignore differences in capitalization when searching. In word processing parlance, this would not be a ***case-sensitive*** search.

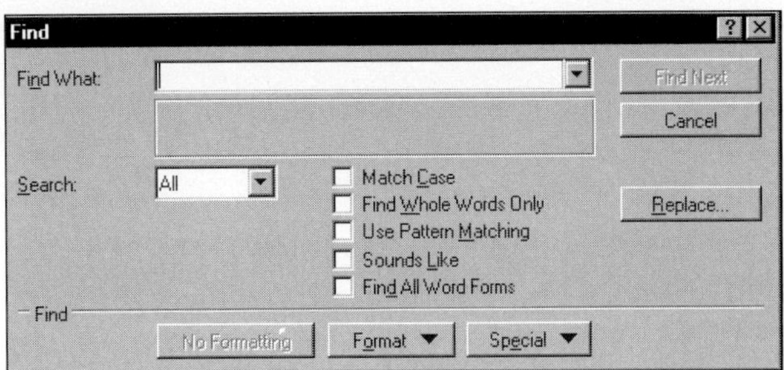

Figure 6.2

To find a word or phrase:

1 Load Word and open the paper as you left it at the end of Project 5. (The document should be in a file named *Revised Gender Roles Paper*.)

2 Choose Find from the Edit menu.

3 Type the search characters `Chi Square` in the Find What box.

4 Make sure All is selected in the Search box, as shown in Figure 6.2, so that the whole document will be searched.

5 Select Find Next to find the next occurrence of the term.
Word takes you immediately to the first occurrence of the search characters and highlights them, as shown in Figure 6.3. The Find dialog box stays on the screen in case you want to search for another occurrence of the characters or modify the search. Even though the dialog box is on the screen, you can still edit the document. For now, however, you will close the dialog box.

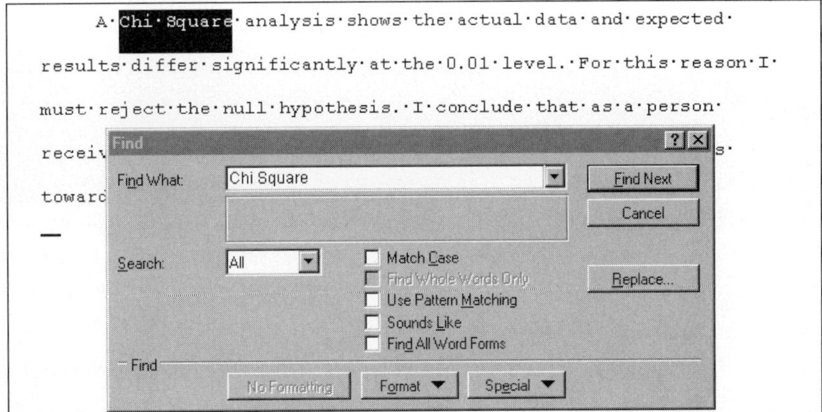

Figure 6.3

6 Select Cancel to remove the dialog box and leave the text highlighted.

One way to correct this capitalization error would be to retype all the characters, or replace the capital letters with lowercase. But Word provides an easier way.

You can use the Change Case dialog box, shown in Figure 6.4, to change the uppercase/lowercase format of selected text in any of the five ways shown in the dialog box.

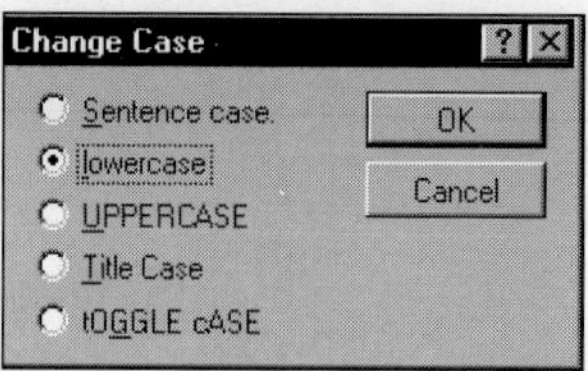

Figure 6.4

To change the case of selected text:

1. Choose Change Case from the Format menu.
2. Select lowercase in the dialog box.
3. Select OK to make the change.

> ***Tip*** You can toggle selected text from all UPPERCASE, to all lowercase, to Title Case by pressing SHIFT+F3 repeatedly.

Just to make sure you caught all instances of the *Chi Square* search characters, you will perform the search again.

To search for the same characters again:

1. Choose Find from the Edit menu to open the Find dialog box again.
The dialog box already contains the search characters you used before, so you only need to start the search process again.
2. Select Find Next to find the next occurrence of the term.
This time, Word cannot find the search characters and gives you the information box shown in Figure 6.5.

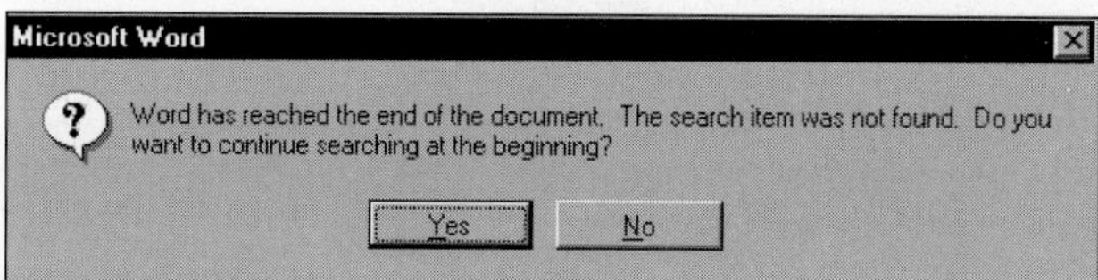

Figure 6.5

3. Select No to close the box.
4. Select Cancel to close the Find dialog box.

> ***Tip*** When you are working on a document that is several pages long, it can become a real chore to find your way around. This is especially true when you have a set of printed pages marked with revisions and you're trying to find the right place to make each needed correction. You can use Word's Find feature instead of hunting through screen after screen of text. Pick out an unusual word or phrase on the printed page, type that word or phrase in the Find dialog box, and press ENTER to go to that spot instantly. You can also use Word's Go To feature to move to a certain page. Use the Answer Wizard to look up *go to a page* to find out more about Go To.

Replacing Text

Now turn to the second item on the revision checklist: eliminating the hyphen in all occurrences of *non-traditional*. You are making the change because accepted style discourages the use of hyphens in compound words beginning with prefixes like *pre-*, *post-*, *semi-*, or *non-*. The word appears in the research paper many times, and finding each one and editing it would be time consuming. Instead, you will find and replace the word automatically. Word will first search out the word and then allow you to replace each occurrence with a click of the mouse.

To find and replace one word with another:

1 Choose Replace from the Edit menu.
The Replace dialog box, similar to the Find dialog box, appears. The search characters you used before are still there, and there is a new box for a set of replacement characters.

2 Type **`non-traditional`** in the Find What box.

3 Type **`nontraditional`** in the Replace With box.

4 Make sure All is selected in the Search box so that the whole document will be searched.
The dialog box should look like Figure 6.6. Now you will execute the find and replace operation a step at a time to see how it works.

Figure 6.6

5 Select Find Next to find the next occurrence of the term.
Word finds the first instance of the search characters following the insertion point and highlights them, just as with a find operation (they may be hidden behind the dialog box). But now you can replace the search characters with those in the Replace With box.

6 Select Replace to replace *non-traditional* with *nontraditional*.
The first occurrence is replaced, and the second occurrence is highlighted, ready to be replaced as well.

You could continue in this fashion, replacing each instance one by one, but there's a faster way. Word can replace every occurrence of the search characters with the replacement characters in one step.

To find and replace all occurrences:

1 Select Replace All to replace all occurrences of one term with another. When the procedure is finished, Word reports how many replacements were made.

2 Select OK to close the report box.

3 Select Close to close the Replace dialog box.

Find and replace can be a powerful tool. But you need to be aware that it also can be hazardous. The following experiment will show you why.

Assume for a moment that you frequently use the first person singular (*I*) in your writing, but that because of a lazy Shift key finger the word often comes out lowercased, as *i.* That might work for e.e. cummings, but it doesn't for you. You decide to use Word's find and replace feature to correct all errant *i*'s. Try the following procedure on the research paper to see what happens.

To change **i** to **I** in the entire file:

1 Save the file first as a precaution.

2 Choose Replace from the Edit menu.

3 Type **i** in the Find What box.

4 Type **I** in the Replace With box.

5 Make sure that All is selected in the Search box and that all the check boxes are cleared.

6 Select Replace All to replace all occurrences of *i* with *I.*
Word reports what should seem like a large number of replacements. You probably don't recall using the first person singular that much.

7 Select OK to close the report box.

8 Select Close to close the dialog box.
Now inspect the text. You may have intended to replace the word *i* with the word *I,* but instead you replaced every lowercase *i* with a capital *I,* and made a mess of the document in the process. Thanks to Word's Undo feature, that's easily remedied.

9 Click the Undo button on the Standard toolbar to return the document to the way it was before the find and replace operation.

Notice that the Replace All command is capable of doing a lot of damage in a hurry. In this particular instance, the solution would have been to check the Find Whole Words Only box in the Replace dialog box. Then only whole words, not single characters, would have been replaced. If Find Whole Words Only is selected, and if you're looking for *cat,* Word will find only *cat.* But if Find Whole Words Only is not selected, Word will find not only *cat,* but also *cat*alog, con*cat*enate, and predi*cat*e.

The real lesson here is to treat the find and replace feature with respect, especially until you have some experience with it. Do one or two substitutions a step at a time before you select Replace All.

Word's find and replace feature will do much more than substitute characters and words for other characters and words. You can also look for characters that are formatted in a specific way or substitute one kind of formatting for another. For example, you could have Word change all underlined words to italicized words. You can also search for special characters such as tabs, paragraph marks, and page breaks. That can be handy if you have to reformat a file. To find out more, use the Answer Wizard to look up *replace text.*

Tip Now for the truth about lowercase *i*'s (the word). They're not likely to occur in your documents if you have Word's AutoCorrect feature turned on. AutoCorrect watches as you type and automatically corrects common typing errors that appear on its list. It turns *i*'s into *I*'s, *teh*'s into *the*'s, and *adn*'s into *and*'s. To find out more about this feature, use the Answer Wizard to look up *autocorrect.* You also can customize the correction list to suit your own typing imperfections.

EXIT If necessary, you can save your file, exit Word now, and continue this project later.

CHECKING SPELLING

Next on your list of revisions is checking the spelling in the research paper. Word's ***spelling checker*** compares every word in a document with an online dictionary, the same dictionary used by Word's autospelling feature. If a word is not in the dictionary, Word reports that fact to you.

You need to be aware of what a spelling checker can and cannot do. Spelling checkers can be a great help in uncovering words you misspelled or mistyped. But they have two significant limitations. First, the spelling checker may look in the dictionary for a word and simply not find it there even though the word is spelled correctly. This error commonly happens with proper names, such as names of cities, or with technical terms not likely to be found in a small general dictionary. For proper names or technical terms that you use frequently, you can simply add them to your personal dictionary, and the spelling checker will ignore them in the future. The second problem, however, is more troublesome: the spelling checker may find a word in the dictionary, but it's not the word you intended. If you misspell *cat* as *cut,* the spelling checker won't report it as a problem because both are legitimate words. The latter problem is the reason you need to keep proofreading documents and depend on the spelling checker only to double-check yourself.

Assume that you have already checked through your research paper and corrected all the errors you saw. Now you will be using Word's spelling checker to check yourself. Begin by setting options for the spelling checker that will make the spelling checker work in parallel with the following numbered steps.

To set spell-check options:

1. Choose Options from the Tools menu.
2. Select the Spelling tab if it is not already on top.
3. Make sure that Automatic Spell Checking is off (check box cleared) and that all options under Suggest and under Ignore are selected (have check marks). When you finish, the dialog box should look like Figure 6.7.

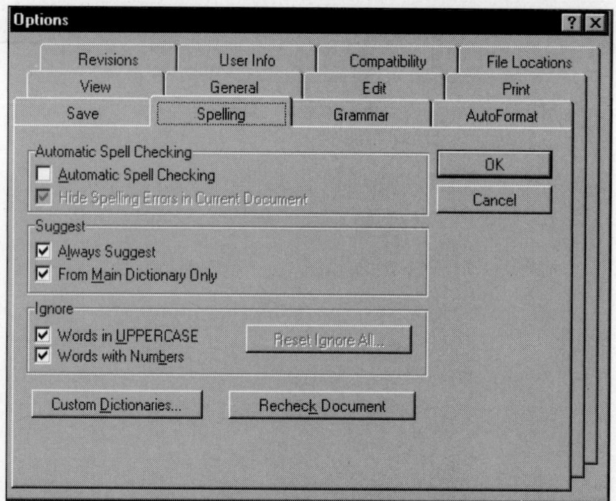

Figure 6.7

4 Select OK to put the settings into effect.

These settings, by the way, are not the "right" settings. They will just ensure that when you check spelling, Word will work in the same way as the numbered steps that follow. Now you are almost ready to check spelling.

Before you start, however, you should be aware that if you typed the research paper into the computer yourself, you may have accidentally introduced typographical errors in addition to those deliberately put in the file for this series of numbered steps. If you encounter a misspelling and aren't sure what to do, just select the Ignore button. You'll be able to go back and correct those errors later, after you are more familiar with the spelling checker.

To start the spelling checker:

1 Press (CTRL)+(HOME) to position the insertion point at the beginning of the research paper.

2 Select the Spelling button on the Standard toolbar.

Word will start checking spelling immediately, and the Spelling dialog box will appear, as shown in Figure 6.8, in this case reporting a word that did not match the dictionary: *likelyhood.* At the same time, Word scrolls down the document and highlights the misspelled word in context to make it easier to determine whether the word is really a misspelling you need to correct. Word also suggests a possible correction in the Suggestions box. This time the spelling checker is right: the correct spelling is *likelihood.* Word can correct the error automatically.

Figure 6.8

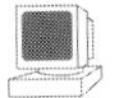

To correct misspellings:

1 Select Change to substitute a correct spelling for a misspelling. Notice that the correct spelling replaces the incorrect one in the document and that the spelling checker moves on to another instance of the misspelled *likelyhood.* Rather than reconsider this same change each time it occurs, you can correct all occurrences of this misspelled word in the entire document in one step.

2 Select Change All to correct the misspelled word throughout the document.
Now the spelling checker will move on to the footnotes and won't be able to find one of the author's names, a proper noun, in the dictionary. You will tell the checker to ignore this word.

To ignore correctly spelled proper nouns:

1 Select Ignore to accept this word as is.

2 Continue to ignore proper names reported by the spelling checker, until you come to *Postmaterialist,* another word not in the dictionary.

Postmaterialist is a specialized term used by social scientists. If this were a word that came up frequently in your field of study, you could add it to your custom dictionary by selecting Add. Once the word was added to your custom dictionary, Word would no longer report it as an error. For now, however, you will simply ignore this word like the others.

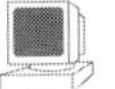

To ignore a technical term:

1 Select Ignore to accept this word as is.
An information box appears, telling you that the spelling check is complete.

2 Select OK to close the information box.

If you ran into other errors in the document and skipped past them, go back now and correct these errors with the spelling checker. You may want to change the Spelling options back to the settings they had when you began this series of numbered steps. And you may want to turn the Automatic Spell Checking feature back on.

Tip If you want to confine a search or want to spell-check only a portion of a document, select that portion first. On the other hand, if you want to search or spell-check an entire document, remember that you should not have text selected.

EXIT If necessary, you can save your file, exit Word now, and continue this project later.

USING THE THESAURUS

The next item on the revision list is to reconsider the choice of *connection* in the second paragraph of the research paper. That particular word seems imprecise. Word's built-in ***thesaurus*** makes it easy to look at alternatives. Like a printed thesaurus, it contains lists of words with similar but distinct meanings. It's up to you, the author, to decide the precise shade of meaning you want.

You look up alternative words using the Thesaurus dialog box, shown in Figure 6.9. The dialog box displays the word you are looking up in the box at the upper left. (Word will also highlight the word you are looking up in the text so that you can see the word in context.) At the bottom left of the dialog box is a list of different meanings for the word you are looking up. To the right is a list of synonyms (words with similar meanings). If you press ↑ or ↓ you can scroll through the list of meanings.

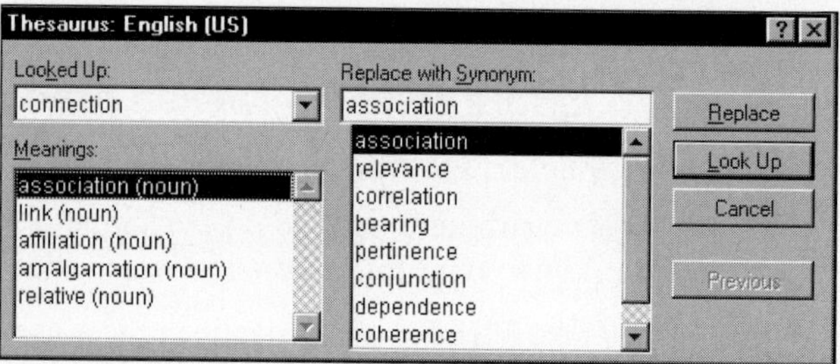

Figure 6.9

To check for synonyms with the thesaurus:

1 Position the insertion point somewhere within the word *connection* in the second paragraph of the body of the research paper.

2 Choose Thesaurus from the Tools menu.

3 Press ↓ several times to scroll through the list of meanings.
Note that each time you select a new meaning, the list of synonyms changes to give you new options to consider.

4 Press ↑ several times to select *association.*
As you look through the synonyms that are listed when *association* is selected, you notice that *correlation* would be a better word choice for the research paper because it is a more precise term in this statistical context.

5 Select *correlation* in the synonym list.
Now *correlation* appears in the Replace with Synonym box above.

6 Select Replace to replace *connection* with *correlation.*

7 Save the file, and print a copy of the revised research paper.

Tip The thesaurus can be very handy when you are revising, as here, or when you are writing and get stuck for the right word. Just type in a trial word, select it, and start the thesaurus. You can even browse in the thesaurus by selecting a word in the Replace with Synonym list and selecting the Look Up button to find another list of words related to that one.

CHECKING DOCUMENT LENGTH

Many writing projects involve writing to a specific length. You may be asked to produce at least *x* words but no more than *y* words. In this instance, the instructor asked that the research paper be about 500 words. You could count the words one by one or estimate the number of words by counting the words on a typical line and then counting the number of lines. But there's an easier way. Word has a built-in word counter that will give you a quick statistical profile of the research paper.

To check the number of words in a document:

1 Choose Word Count from the Tools menu.
The Word Count report box appears, as shown in Figure 6.10. (The numbers on your screen may vary slightly from those in the figure.) To include footnotes and endnotes, check that box and count again.

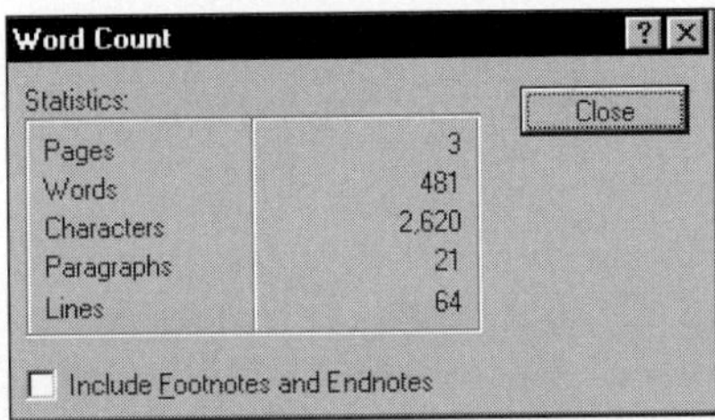

Figure 6.10

2 Select Close to close the report box.

THE NEXT STEP

Word's writing and editing tools are an invaluable resource. A spelling checker, especially, is helpful to those of us who didn't do so well in grade-school spelling bees. And there's even more that you didn't explore in this project. Word also has a grammar checker that can inspect documents for possible style and usage problems, report these problems, and give you hints about what you might do to revise if needed. The grammar checker is much more complex than the spelling checker and consumes so much disk space that many people don't install it. But if it is installed on the system you are using, you should try it to see what it does. (If available, the grammar checker is in the Tools menu.)

None of these online tools, however, will replace a sharp proofreading eye and a set of essential reference books. You'll still need a dictionary to check word meanings, if not spellings. You'll probably still want a basic thesaurus for occasions when the online thesaurus doesn't come up with the right word. And you'll need a basic style and grammar guide even if you use the grammar checker. One popular style guide is Strunk and White's *The Elements of Style*. Keep in mind that carefully crafted writing requires thought, not a computer. Much of the world's great literature was written with a quill pen and an ink pot. Nonetheless, tools such as find and replace or a spelling checker are very handy. Shakespeare probably would have loved the modern word processor.

This concludes Project 6. You can either exit Word or go on to work the Study Questions, Review Exercises, and Assignments.

SUMMARY AND EXERCISES

Summary

- You can find text quickly by choosing Find from the Edit menu.
- Find operations can be case sensitive, for which capitalization and lowercase characters must match, or can be set so that capitalization is ignored.
- Find operations may involve whole words only or may be set to find character sequences within words.
- You can find and replace text by choosing Replace from the Edit menu.
- A spelling checker compares words in a document with words stored in an on-line dictionary.
- If you frequently use proper names, technical terms, or other words that are not already in the dictionary, you can add these to a custom dictionary.
- A spelling checker will not report a word as misspelled if the misspelling is itself a word, such as *two* when you meant *too*.
- Word's thesaurus can give you a list of alternative word choices similar in meaning to a word you've selected.
- For a quick count of words in a document, choose Word Count from the Tools menu.

Key Terms and Operations

Key Terms
case-sensitive
find
find and replace
spelling checker
thesaurus

Operations
Find and replace text
Check spelling
Use the thesaurus
Check document length

Study Questions

Multiple Choice

1. Which of the following is *not* one of the writing or editing tools in Word?
   a. spelling checker
   b. word counter
   c. thesaurus
   d. reference dictionary

2. You can use a thesaurus to look up:
   a. synonyms.
   b. word meanings.
   c. derivations.
   d. spellings.

3. A spelling checker does not check:
   a. footnotes.
   b. grammar.
   c. headers.
   d. proper names.

4. To substitute a correction in a misspelled name throughout a document, you should use:
   a. AutoCorrect.
   b. a thesaurus.
   c. find and replace.
   d. the built-in dictionary.

5. When the spelling checker reports a word not found in the dictionary, which of these is *not* an option?
   a. Replace the word.
   b. Add the word to the dictionary.
   c. Ignore the word.
   d. Look for alternative words.

6. Word's spelling checker will correctly report a problem when your document contains:
   a. *5* instead of *five*.
   b. *fbi* instead of *FBI*.
   c. *there* instead of *they're*.
   d. *more better* instead of *better*.

7. You can set the spelling checker to routinely ignore which of these:
   a. words in all caps
   b. proper nouns
   c. names of cities
   d. hyphenated words

8. If the thesaurus cannot find a workable synonym, you can:
   a. add new ones to the dictionary.
   b. look in an alternative dictionary.
   c. look up alternative words.
   d. use find and replace instead.

9. If you are using Find, Match Case is on, and Find Whole Words Only is off, which of these will result in a match for *ate*?
   a. Atenbrugh
   b. predicate
   c. POTENTATE
   d. sixty-eight

10. The Word Count tool does *not* report the number of:
    a. characters.
    b. words.
    c. sentences.
    d. paragraphs.

Short Answer

1. If you find *one* and replace with *two* in the sentence, "One of the tones hit the high range," what is the result: ________.
2. A find operation in which *Dog* does not match *dog* is ________.
3. You can get a quick tabulation of the number of pages, words, characters, paragraphs, and lines in your document by using Word's ________ feature.
4. A thesaurus will find words that are ________ for the selected word.
5. The thesaurus can sometimes also find antonyms, which are word ________.
6. If a proper noun appears repeatedly in a document and you don't want the spelling checker to report every occurrence, you can select the ________ button or the ________ button.
7. To spell-check only a portion of a document, ________ that portion first.
8. Word processors save time in writing primarily because they eliminate ________.
9. If a find-and-replace operation results in disaster, you should ________.
10. The Word feature that fixes typing errors like *teh* "on the fly" is called ________.

For Discussion

1. What two types of errors can a spelling checker miss? What can you do about these errors?
2. Suppose the thesaurus doesn't immediately suggest a usable synonym. Explain how to use the thesaurus to browse for other choices.
3. Suppose you have a file in which paragraphs are indented by five spaces (someone typed five spaces at the beginning of the first line of each paragraph). Now you want to eliminate those spaces so that you can use the First-Line Indent in the Paragraph dialog box to reformat the paragraphs. Explain how you could use find and replace to eliminate the spaces.

Review Exercises

Adding to the Dictionary

1. Spell-check the research paper again, but this time add the proper names and technical terms to the dictionary.
2. Spell-check the paper again to see what happens after the words have been added.
3. Go to the Spelling tab in the Options dialog box and edit the dictionary to remove the proper names, but not the technical terms.
4. Spell-check the paper again.
5. Remove the technical terms from the dictionary.

Polishing Your Own Paper

Take the term paper you had written earlier and then formatted at the end of Project 5 and spell-check it. Use the thesaurus to reconsider word choices as appropriate. Compute the average number of characters in the words in your paper.

Assignments

Personalizing AutoCorrect

AutoCorrect can be used to correct common typing errors, but you can also set it up to do automated shorthand transcription. Choose AutoCorrect from the Tools menu. Modify AutoCorrect so that it will translate the following personal abbreviations:

Abbreviation	Spelled Out
asap	as soon as possible
fubar	fouled up beyond all recognition
imho	in my humble opinion

Add others if you wish. Try AutoCorrect with these additions.

Reformatting with Find and Replace

Retrieve the file *Two Cities*. Once the file is loaded in the word processor, make paragraph marks visible, and inspect the structure of the file. Note that each line ends with a paragraph mark and that the file is double spaced using blank lines. Note also that paragraphs are indented five spaces. Using find-and-replace operations, reformat the file as follows:

- Remove all paragraph marks except at the end of paragraphs.
- Single space the text.
- Change two spaces to one space between sentences.
- Convert the five-space paragraph indentations to ½-inch first-line indentations.
- Convert two hyphens to a one-em dash, one of the special characters in the Replace dialog box.

The beginning of the file is shown in Figure 6.11.

```
                    A•Tale•of•Two•Cities¶
                    by•Charles•Dickens¶
                             ¶
              Book•the•First--Recalled•to•Life¶
                        The•Period¶
                             ¶
•••••It•was•the•best•of•times,•it•was•the•worst•of•times,¶
¶
it•was•the•age•of•wisdom,•it•was•the•age•of•foolishness,¶
¶
it•was•the•epoch•of•belief,•it•was•the•epoch•of•incredulity,¶
¶
it•was•the•season•of•Light,•it•was•the•season•of•Darkness,¶
¶
it•was•the•spring•of•hope,•it•was•the•winter•of•despair,¶
¶
we•had•everything•before•us,•we•had•nothing•before•us,¶
¶
we•were•all•going•direct•to•Heaven,•we•were•all•going•direct¶
¶
the•other•way--in•short,•the•period•was•so•far•like•the•present¶
¶
period,•that•some•of•its•noisiest•authorities•insisted•on•its¶
¶
being•received,•for•good•or•for•evil,•in•the•superlative•degree¶
¶
of•comparison•only.¶
¶
•••••There•were•a•king•with•a•large•jaw•and•a•queen•with•a•plain•face,¶
¶
on•the•throne•of•England;•there•were•a•king•with•a•large•jaw•and¶
¶
a•queen•with•a•fair•face,•on•the•throne•of•France.••In•both¶
¶
countries•it•was•clearer•than•crystal•to•the•lords•of•the•State¶
¶
preserves•of•loaves•and•fishes,•that•things•in•general•were¶
¶
settled•for•ever.¶
¶
•••••It•was•the•year•of•Our•Lord•one•thousand•seven•hundred•and¶
¶
seventy-five.••Spiritual•revelations•were•conceded•to•England•at¶
¶
that•favoured•period,•as•at•this.••Mrs.•Southcott•had•recently¶
¶
attained•her•five-and-twentieth•blessed•birthday,•of•whom•a¶
¶
prophetic•private•in•the•Life•Guards•had•heralded•the•sublime¶
¶
appearance•by•announcing•that•arrangements•were•made•for•the¶
¶
swallowing•up•of•London•and•Westminster.••Even•the•Cock-lane¶
¶
ghost•had•been•laid•only•a•round•dozen•of•years,•after•rapping¶
¶
out•its•messages,•as•the•spirits•of•this•very•year•last•past¶
¶
(supernaturally•deficient•in•originality)•rapped•out•theirs.¶
¶
```

Figure 6.11

Checking Spelling

Retrieve the file *Pasteur on Germ Theory*. This is Pasteur's presentation to the French Academy in 1878 that you reformatted at the end of Project 5. Check the spelling of the document. Change words that are incorrectly spelled, and add technical terms to your own custom dictionary. Count the number of words in the document. Save the file as corrected, and print a copy of it.

PROJECT 7: BUILDING TABLES

Objectives

After completing this project, you should be able to:

- Create a table
- Modify a table
- Adjust table and column widths
- Format a table
- Create a table from text

In this project, you will complete the research paper you began in Project 5 by adding two tables. Word has powerful tools you can use to create, modify, and format tables. You can add blank tables and fill them in, or you can take existing text and turn it into a table. You can add text to or subtract text from the table. You can also use font and paragraph formatting to make the table attractive and readable.

CASE STUDY: ADDING TABLES TO THE RESEARCH PAPER

Tables are an excellent way to organize information in a way that visually exhibits relationships. From the grid listings in *TV Guide* to the stock exchange results in *The Wall Street Journal,* a single table can lay out complex information in a way that is clearly seen and easily understood.

The problem with tables, at least in the days before word processors, was that they took an immense amount of trouble to produce. If you were working at a typewriter, you usually had to retype a table several times to get the spacing of the columns adjusted correctly. Even with a simple word processor, you had to fuss with tabs and alignment to make the table look right.

With Word, tables are nearly automatic. If you specify the number of rows and columns you need, Word will give you a blank table to fill in. You also can take existing text and turn it into a table. You can add or subtract rows or columns. You can adjust column widths or have Word do the adjusting for you automatically. You can reformat the text within a table just as you do other text in a document.

Designing the Solution

The research paper, as planned from the outset, will contain two tables: one to present the results of the survey and one to support the analysis of the data. Markers for the locations of the two tables are already included in the research paper. Now you need to design the tables and replace the markers with the tables themselves.

Tables are made up of a series of cells organized into columns and rows, as shown in Figure 7.1. An individual ***cell,*** where a column and row intersect, can contain numbers or text. A horizontal series of cells is a ***row.*** A vertical series of cells is a ***column.***

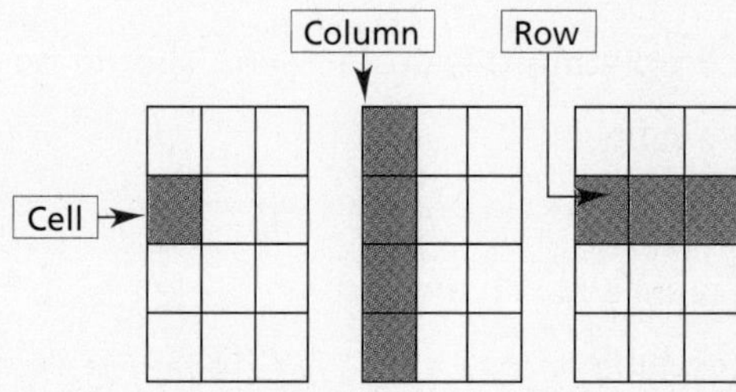

Figure 7.1

The first table will present the data from the survey. The people who responded to the survey were divided into three groups: those with a high school education, those with some college, and those who completed college. Their responses to the gender roles questionnaire were divided into three categories: traditional, mixed, and nontraditional. The result is a three-by-three (3×3) data set that looks like Figure 7.2 when headings are added.

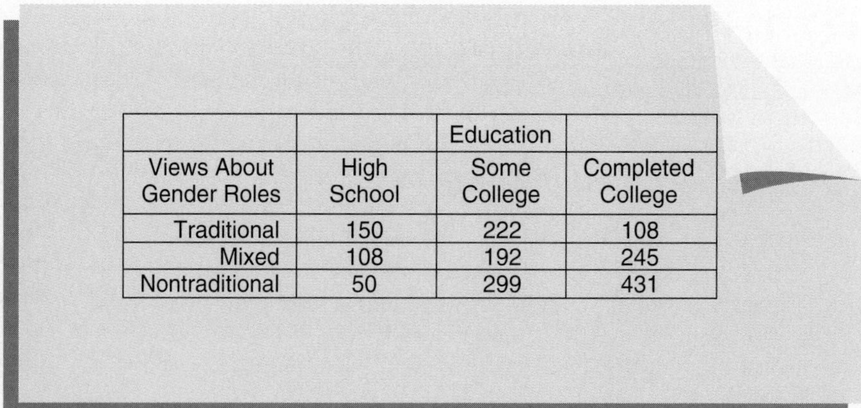

		Education	
Views About Gender Roles	High School	Some College	Completed College
Traditional	150	222	108
Mixed	108	192	245
Nontraditional	50	299	431

Figure 7.2

The second table will follow the same pattern and layout, but the data cells will contain an analysis of the data rather than the raw data itself.

DEFINING A TABLE

You will begin by inserting a blank table, and then you will fill it with data and headings.

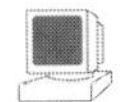

To insert a table:

1 Load Word and open the research paper file—*Revised Gender Roles Paper*—that you saved at the end of Project 6.

2 Position the insertion point at the beginning of the line that reads [*Insert Data Table Here*] on the second page of the research paper.

3 Click the Insert Table button on the Standard toolbar.
A grid of table cells drops down. You want to insert a table that is five rows deep by four columns wide (a 5 x 4 table).

4 On the table grid, drag to select five cells deep by four cells wide, as shown in Figure 7.3, and then release the mouse button.

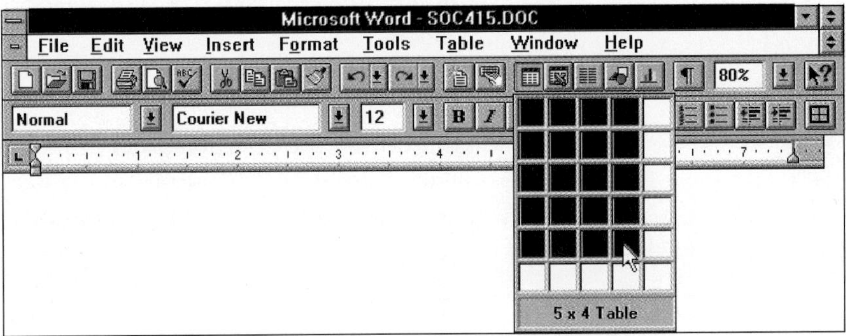

Figure 7.3

The table grid expands as needed when you drag the mouse. The label at the bottom of the grid shows the table size to be inserted. If you move the pointer to the left off the grid or above the grid, *Cancel* appears as the label, and no table is inserted.

5 Select the line [*Insert Data Table Here*] and delete it.

You will now have a blank table in the research paper, ready for you to enter data. The table should appear as shown in Figure 7.4. The dotted ***gridlines*** will help you visualize the structure of the table on the screen while you work, but they will not print. Each cell will contain an ***end-of-cell mark,*** and each row will end with an ***end-of-row mark.***

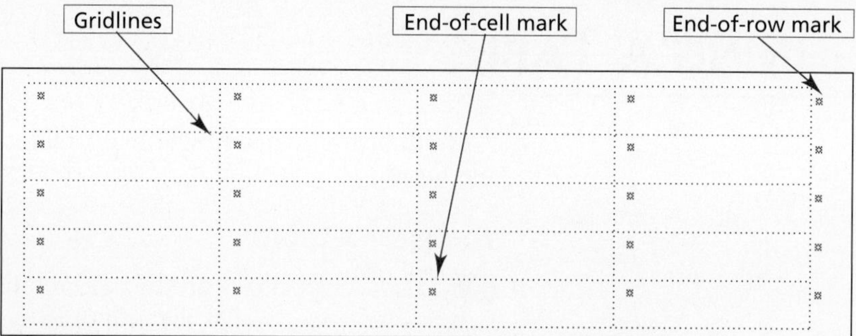

Figure 7.4

Do the following steps if either the gridlines or the end marks do not show on the screen.

To make gridlines and end marks visible:

1 If gridlines are not visible, choose Gridlines from the Table menu.

2 If end marks are not visible, select the Show/Hide ¶ button on the Standard toolbar.

To fill in the table with headings and data:

1 Position the insertion point inside the top left cell of the table, immediately in front of the end-of-cell mark.

2 Press TAB twice to skip to the third column in the top row.

3 Type **`Education`**

4 Press TAB twice to skip to the first column in the second row.

5 Type **`Views About Gender Roles`**
The text you type word wraps within the cell automatically.

6 Press TAB to advance to the next cell, and continue filling in the table with the rest of the headings and data. When you are finished, the table should look like Figure 7.5.

¤	¤	Education¤	¤	¤
Views·About· Gender·Roles¤	High·School¤	Some·College¤	Completed· College¤	¤
Traditional¤	150¤	222¤	108¤	¤
Mixed¤	108¤	192¤	245¤	¤
Nontraditional¤	50¤	299¤	431¤	¤

Figure 7.5

Quick Fix If you press TAB after inserting the last data item, you will add an extra row at the bottom of the table. If you catch the error right away, just click the Undo button on the Standard toolbar. You can also eliminate a row at any time by selecting that row and then deleting it. Select a row by clicking in the selection bar to the left of the row. Then choose Delete Rows from the Table menu.

Some of the columns will be too narrow for the headings, so text will wrap awkwardly. Other columns will be wider than they need to be. Later in this project, you will adjust column widths to make the table more readable.

MODIFYING A TABLE

The basic data table is in place. You now review the assignment for the research paper and discover that the table was also to include column and row totals as part of the statistical analysis required. Accomplishing this will require a 6 x 5 table. You will need to add a new column on the right side of the table and a new row at the bottom.

To add a new row:

1. Position the insertion point at the end of the cell at the bottom right of the table (just after *431*).
2. Press TAB to insert a new row at the bottom of the table.
3. Fill in the new row with the heading and data shown in Figure 7.6.

Mixed¤	108¤	192¤	245¤	¤
Nontraditional¤	50¤	299¤	431¤	¤
Column·Totals¤	308¤	713¤	784¤	¤

Figure 7.6

Tip The Insert Table button has multiple personalities. If you are working inside normal text, click this button to insert a new table. If you already have a table, you can click the same button to modify the table. For instance, you can use the button to add a new row as follows. Select a row by positioning the pointer somewhere within the row. Insert a new row above the selected row by clicking the Insert Rows button (otherwise known as the Insert Table button) on the Standard toolbar. You can also add a row by choosing Insert Rows from the Table menu.

To add a new column:

1 Position the pointer above the end-of-row marks at the right edge of the table.

2 When the pointer turns into a down arrow, as shown in Figure 7.7, click to select all the end-of-row marks.

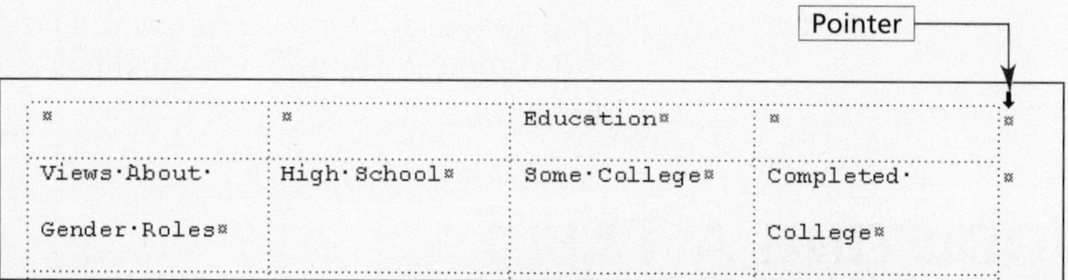

¤	¤	Education¤	¤	¤
Views·About· Gender·Roles¤	High·School¤	Some·College¤	Completed· College¤	¤

Figure 7.7

3 Choose Insert Columns from the Table menu, or click the Insert Columns button (the Insert Table button) on the Standard toolbar. The new column makes the table too wide to fit on the screen, a problem you will fix in the next section. First, you need to add the new heading and data.

4 Scroll to the right so that the new column is visible.

5 Select the second cell from the top in the new column, and type in the heading: **`Row Totals`**

6 Fill in the other cells in the new column with the data shown in Figure 7.8.

	Education¤	¤	¤	¤
School¤	Some·College¤	Completed· College¤	Row·Totals¤	¤
	222¤	108¤	480¤	¤
	192¤	245¤	545¤	¤
	299¤	431¤	780¤	¤
	713¤	784¤	1805¤	¤

Figure 7.8

EXIT

If necessary, you can save your file, exit Word now, and continue this project later.

ADJUSTING TABLE AND COLUMN WIDTHS

The new column has made the table too wide to fit inside the page margins, and the column widths still need to be adjusted to accommodate the headings and make better use of white space. You will adjust the table in two steps. First you will reduce the overall width of the table, and then you will resize the columns within the table.

To adjust table size and column widths with AutoFit:

1. Position the insertion point somewhere within the table.
2. Choose Select Table from the Table menu to select the entire table.
3. Choose Cell Height and Width from the Table menu.
4. Select the Column tab to view the dialog box shown in Figure 7.9.

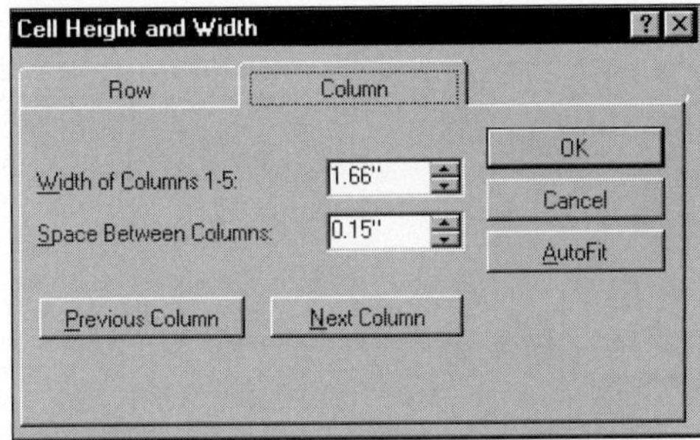

Figure 7.9

5. Select the AutoFit button.

   Word will resize the table to fit within the document margins and, at the same time, will change the column widths so that headings and data are displayed more clearly. This is a distinct improvement, but the table is not yet really finished. The data columns and row totals will look better if they are the same width because they contain equivalent kinds of data.

To adjust column widths in the table:

1. If the ruler is not visible, choose Ruler from the View menu.
2. Position the insertion point anywhere inside the table.
3. Press CTRL and hold it down.
4. Position the pointer on the gridline at the right edge of the first column.
   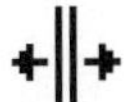
   When the pointer is directly on the gridline, it changes shape to a grabber handle.
5. While you continue to hold down CTRL press the mouse button.
   You can use the mouse to move the gridline from side to side.
6. Continue to hold down CTRL and the mouse button, and now also press ALT
   The ruler displays the column widths when you hold down ALT as shown in Figure 7.10.

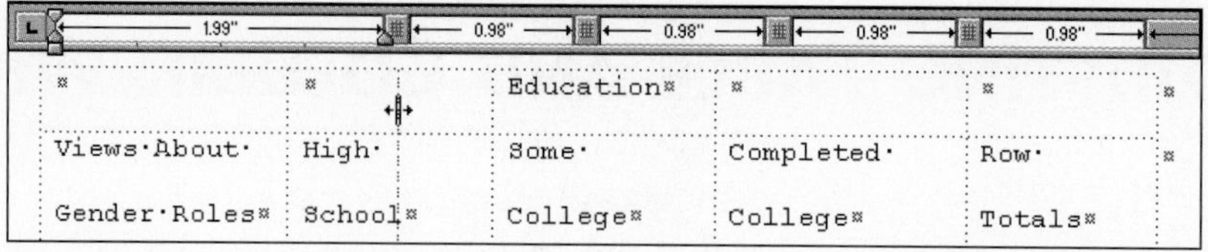

Figure 7.10

7 Drag the gridline to the right until the width of the first column is 1.99″ then release all keys.

As you drag the column boundary gridline while holding down the CTRL key, Word will automatically equalize the width of all the columns to the right. You can use the mouse together with different key combinations to drag column boundaries and reshape a table in various ways, as described next.

- Drag the column boundary without holding down any key to adjust the width of the current column and resize all columns to the right in proportion to their original width. Overall table width does not change.
- Drag the column boundary while holding down CTRL to adjust the current column and make all columns to the right equal width. Overall table width does not change.
- Drag the column boundary while holding down SHIFT to adjust the current column and the width of the column to the right. Overall table width does not change.
- Drag the column boundary while holding down SHIFT+CTRL to adjust the current column and change the overall table width.

Formatting a Table

The table is now complete except for formatting. The text within the table is all double spaced, like the rest of the text in the research paper. The double spacing results in a clumsy distribution of space within the table. In addition, the headings do not stand apart from the data. Paragraph and font formatting can be applied to the contents of a table just as to any other text in a document.

To single-space the table:

1 Position the insertion point somewhere within the table.

2 Choose Select Table from the Table menu to select the entire table.

3 Choose Paragraph from the Format menu.

4 Select the Indents and Spacing tab if it is not on top.

5 Set the Line Spacing box to Single.

6 Select OK.

Each individual cell in the table has a selection bar along its left edge that will allow you to select the entire contents of the cell with a single click. When the pointer is in the selection bar, its shape changes to an arrow pointing upward and to the right. To select several adjacent cells, you can click and drag.

To boldface major headings:

1 Position the pointer to the left of *Education* at the top of the third column.
The pointer changes to an arrow pointing up and to the right, as shown in Figure 7.11.

		Education			
Views About Gender Roles	High School	Some College	Completed College	Row Totals	
Traditional	150	222	108	480	
Mixed	108	192	245	545	
Nontraditional	50	299	431	780	
Column Totals	308	713	784	1805	

Figure 7.11

2 Click to select the cell.

3 Click the Bold button on the Formatting toolbar to boldface the heading.

4 Select the cell containing *Views About Gender Roles,* near the top of the first column.

5 Click the Bold button.

To center the column headings:

1 Select the four column headings as shown in Figure 7.12.

		Education			
Views About Gender Roles	High School	Some College	Completed College	Row Totals	
Traditional	150	222	108	480	
Mixed	108	192	245	545	
Nontraditional	50	299	431	780	
Column Totals	308	713	784	1805	

Figure 7.12

2 Click the Center button on the Formatting toolbar to center all four headings.

Tip The Center button on the Formatting toolbar centers text within cells. It does not center the table itself. To center a table between page margins, choose Cell Height and Width from the Table menu. Select the Row tab, and then select Center in the Alignment box.

To position the numbers in the data cells:

1 Select the data cells as shown in Figure 7.13.

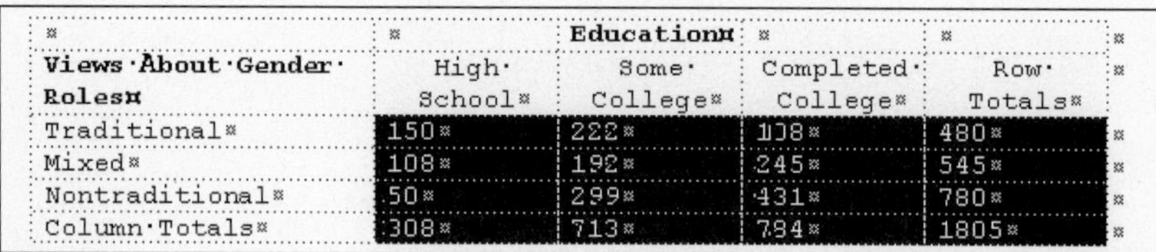

		Education		
Views About Gender Roles	High School	Some College	Completed College	Row Totals
Traditional	150	222	108	480
Mixed	108	192	245	545
Nontraditional	50	299	431	780
Column Totals	308	713	784	1805

Figure 7.13

2 Click the Align Right button on the Formatting toolbar.
The numbers are now all aligned to the right edge of the cells, but they are jammed too tightly against the cell edges. If you indent the cells from the right edge, the cell contents will be easier to read.

3 With all the data cells still selected, grab the right indentation marker on the ruler, above and to the right of the second column, and drag the marker to the 2¾-inch mark, as shown in Figure 7.14.

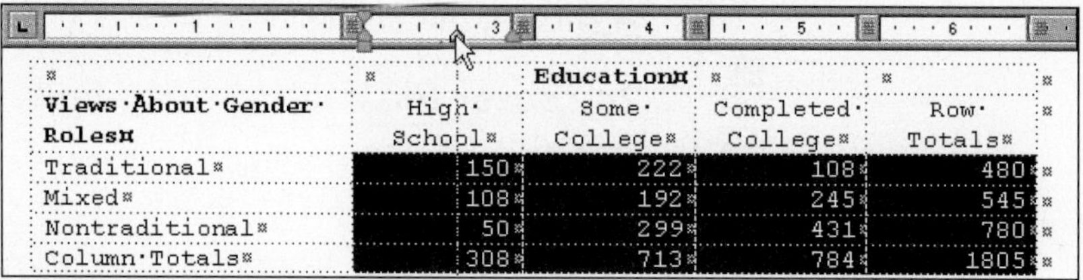

		Education		
Views About Gender Roles	High School	Some College	Completed College	Row Totals
Traditional	150	222	108	480
Mixed	108	192	245	545
Nontraditional	50	299	431	780
Column Totals	308	713	784	1805

Figure 7.14

Adjusting the indentation marker above the second column simultaneously adjusts the indentation in all the selected cells.

To make the table clearer and easier to read, you will next add borders to the cells.

To add borders to the table cells:

1 Choose Select Table from the Table menu.

2 Click the Borders button on the far right end of the Formatting toolbar.
The Borders toolbar appears, as shown in Figure 7.15.

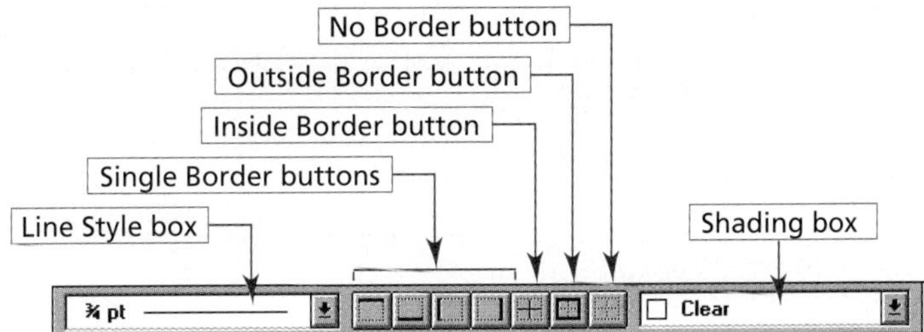

Figure 7.15

3 Click the Inside Border button and the Outside Border button.

To differentiate the raw data from the column and row totals, you will now add light shading to the column and row total cells.

To add shading to cells:

1 Position the pointer above the rightmost column, and when the pointer becomes a down arrow, click to select the column.

2 Click the down arrow beside the Shading box on the Borders toolbar.

3 Select 12.5% shading, as shown in Figure 7.16.

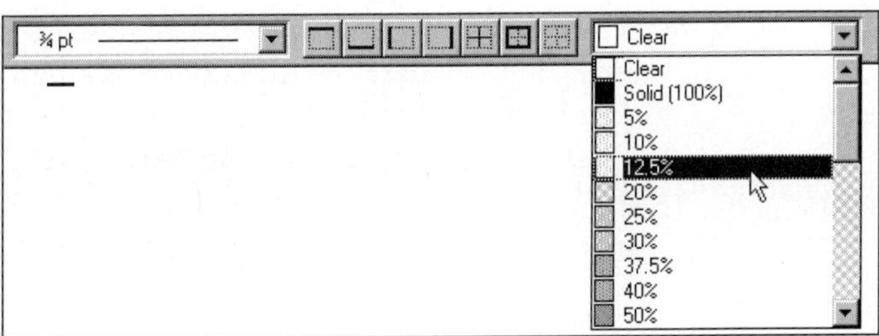

Figure 7.16

4 Click the Borders button on the Formatting toolbar to close the Borders toolbar.

5 Position the pointer in the selection bar to the left of the bottom row of the table, and click to select the bottom row.

6 Select Repeat Shading Pattern from the Edit menu (or press CTRL + Y).

7 Click outside the row to deselect it.

The first table is now complete and should look like Figure 7.17.

		Education		
Views About Gender Roles	High School	Some College	Completed College	Row Totals
Traditional	150	222	108	480
Mixed	108	192	245	545
Nontraditional	50	299	431	780
Column Totals	308	713	784	1805

Figure 7.17

Tip Borders and shading are paragraph formats and can be used on text outside tables also. Just select the paragraphs you want to format, and click the Borders button to open the Borders toolbar.

If necessary, you can save your file, exit Word now, and continue this project later.

TURNING TEXT INTO A TABLE

Assume that one of your lab partners in Soc 415 who worked with you in analyzing the data has already entered a table of expected responses. The data for the table is in a file called *Table Two Data.* If you already have that file, skip the next series of steps, labeled "To create the *Table Two Data* file" and go to the "To insert the data from the file Table Two Data" section. If you don't have the file, follow these steps to create it.

To create the Table Two Data *file:*

1 Click the New button at the far left of the Standard toolbar to open a new document.
You don't need to quit the document you are working on to open another document. In Word, you can have several documents open simultaneously.

2 Type the information shown in Figure 7.18.

```
  →  High·School  →  Some·College  → Completed·College¶
Traditional  →  81.9→189.6  →  208.5¶
Mixed  →  93.0→215.3  →  236.7¶
Nontraditional→133.1  →  308.1  →  338.8¶
```

Figure 7.18

Recall that the → symbol on the screen represents a TAB character.

3 Format the text as 12-point Courier New.

4 Save the file as *Table Two Data.*

5 Choose Close from the File menu.
You should be back in the research paper document window.

Tip In Word, you can have several documents open at the same time. To switch from one open document to another, select the document you want from the list at the bottom of the Window menu.

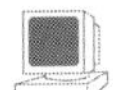

To insert the data from the file Table Two Data*:*

1 Select the line [*Expected response table goes here*].

2 Choose File from the Insert menu.
The Insert File dialog box appears. You may need to adjust the drive and directory to locate *Table Two Data.*

3 Select the *Table Two Data* file.

4 Select OK to open the file.

The contents of the file will be inserted into the research paper document. The text is now ready to be turned into a table.

To convert the text to a table:

1 Press (ENTER) to insert a blank line between the bottom of the data and the beginning of the next paragraph if a blank line is not already there.

2 Select the four lines of data, as shown in Figure 7.19.

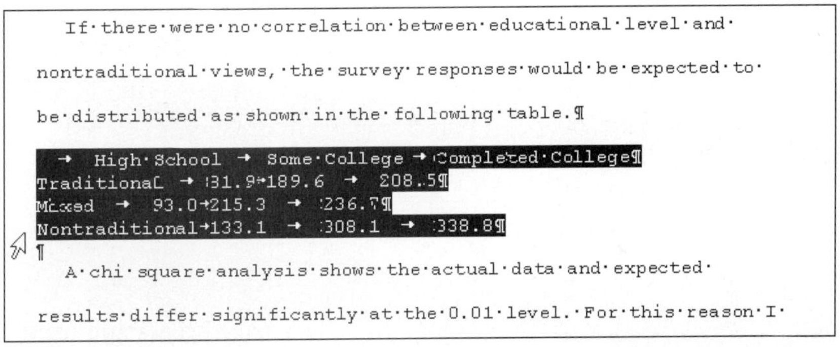

```
    If·there·were·no·correlation·between·educational·level·and·

nontraditional·views,·the·survey·responses·would·be·expected·to·

be·distributed·as·shown·in·the·following·table.¶

→   High·School  →  Some·College →  Completed·College¶
Traditional  → 131.9→189.6  →  208.5¶
Mixed  →  93.0→215.3  →  236.7¶
Nontraditional→133.1  →  308.1  →  338.8¶
¶
    A·chi·square·analysis·shows·the·actual·data·and·expected·

results·differ·significantly·at·the·0.01·level.·For·this·reason·I·
```

Figure 7.19

3 Choose Convert Text to Table from the Table menu.
The Convert Text to Table dialog box appears, as shown in Figure 7.20.

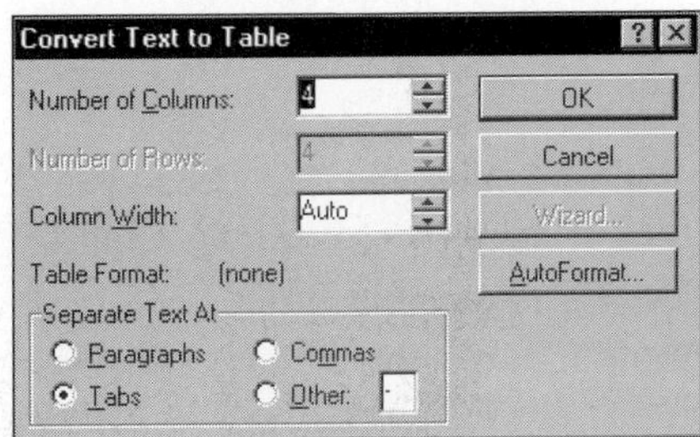

Figure 7.20

4 Select OK to convert the text.

The new table now needs to be formatted so that it resembles the first table.

To format the table:

1 Click in the selection bar at the left of the table to select the top row.

2 Click the Center button on the Formatting toolbar to center the headings.

3 Press CTRL and ALT while you drag the boundary for the first column to 1.99″.

4 Select the nine data cells containing numbers.

5 Click the Align Right button on the Formatting toolbar.

6 On the ruler, grab the right indentation marker above and to the right of the second column, and slide the marker to the 3-inch mark.

7 Choose Select Table from the Table menu.

8 Click the Borders button at the far right of the Formatting toolbar.

9 On the Borders toolbar, click the Inside Border and Outside Border buttons.

10 Close the Borders toolbar.

11 Click anywhere in the table to deselect it.

The second table is formatted. It should look like Figure 7.21.

¤	High·School¤	Some·College¤	Completed· College¤	¤
Traditional¤	81.9¤	189.6¤	208.5¤	¤
Mixed¤	93.0¤	215.3¤	236.7¤	¤
Nontraditional¤	133.1¤	308.1¤	338.8¤	¤

Figure 7.21

Once you check page breaks and print the research paper, it will be complete. You don't want a page break in the middle of a table or between a heading and the text that follows it, so check your document in Page Layout View before printing it. Where necessary, you can insert a page break in front of a table or heading to force it onto the next page.

To check page breaks and print the research paper:

1 Choose Page Layout from the View menu (or select the Page Layout View button at the left side of the horizontal scroll bar at the bottom of the screen).

2 Check the document for any tables that are split at a page break, and check for any headings separated from the text that follows them.

3 If you need to insert a page break, position the insertion point in front of the table or heading, choose Break from the Insert menu, select Page Break, and then select OK to insert the page break.

4 When you have resolved the page breaks, save the file, and print a copy of the finished research paper.

THE NEXT STEP

The table feature in Word is a powerful and flexible tool. Tables are often the best way to organize and present data. Keep your eye out for tabular data you think is presented well and clearly. You can use Word's AutoFormat feature to add punch to your own tables. If you put the insertion point in a table and choose Table AutoFormat from the Table menu, you can quickly review a variety of format options.

The table structure can be useful in Word even when you're not presenting tabular data. If you want to use side heads—headings to the left of the text, like the ones in this module—a table format is often the easiest way to do that. You can put the side heads in one column and the text in the second column, and the two will word wrap independently of one another and always stay aligned at the top edge.

You also can put formulas in a table, like a spreadsheet. You can turn table data into a chart. You can add graphics or use tables to position graphics and text side-by-side. To find out about these and other uses for tables, look up *Table* using the Answer Wizard.

This concludes Project 7. You can either exit Word or go on to work the Study Questions, Review Exercises, and Assignments.

SUMMARY AND EXERCISES

Summary

- You can insert a blank table using the Insert Table button on the Standard toolbar.
- To move from cell to cell in a table, use the arrow keys or TAB
- To add a new row at the bottom of a table, position the insertion point at the end of the lower-right cell and then press TAB
- To add a new row above an existing row, position the pointer inside the existing row, then click the Insert Rows button on the Standard toolbar.
- To add a new column to the left of the selected column, click the Insert Columns button on the Standard toolbar.
- You can use AutoFit in the Column tab of the Cell Height and Width dialog box to automatically adjust overall table width and individual column widths.
- You can manipulate column widths by grabbing the column gridlines with the mouse and moving the gridlines left or right. Holding down ALT while you are moving gridlines displays column widths on the ruler.
- You can add shading or borders to tables by using the Borders toolbar.
- You can change text to a table by choosing Convert Text to Table from the Table menu.

Key Terms and Operations

Key Terms
cell
column
end-of-cell mark
end-of-row mark
gridline
row

Operations
Add a border or shading
Add a column or row
Adjust column and table width
Convert text to a table
Insert a table

Study Questions

Multiple Choice

1. A table column:
   a. is a horizontal series of cells.
   b. ends with an end-of-column mark.
   c. cannot be changed in width.
   d. is a vertical stack of cells.
2. To add a column to the left of the selected column:
   a. press INS
   b. double-click above the column.
   c. click the Insert Columns button.
   d. double-click the left gridline.
3. To select a row:
   a. double-click within the row.
   b. press ALT+→.
   c. click the end-of-row mark.
   d. click in the selection bar to the left of that row.
4. To select an entire table:
   a. triple-click the table.
   b. choose Select Table from the Table menu.
   c. select the end-of-row marks.
   d. double-click to the right of the table.
5. To adjust table and column width automatically:
   a. select AutoFit in the Column tab of the Cell Height and Width dialog box.
   b. click the AutoFit button on the Table toolbar.
   c. double-click the gridline at the top of the table.
   d. double-click the end-of-table mark.
6. To display column widths on the ruler when you resize a column with the mouse:
   a. hold down the ALT key.
   b. hold down the SHIFT key.
   c. hold down the CTRL key.
   d. click the Table button first.
7. To select a single cell:
   a. click the end-of-cell mark.
   b. click the right-edge gridline.
   c. click in the cell selection bar at the left of the cell.
   d. click the top-edge gridline.

8. To add borders and shading to a table, you can:
   a. press CTRL + B
   b. use the Borders toolbar.
   c. click the Formatting toolbar.
   d. choose Gridline from the Table menu.

9. To convert text into a table, select the text and then:
   a. choose Convert Text to Table from the Table menu.
   b. click the Borders button on the Standard toolbar.
   c. click the Convert button on the Tables toolbar.
   d. press CTRL + T

10. To insert one file into another:
    a. click the Paste button on the Standard toolbar.
    b. choose File from the Insert menu.
    c. choose Add File from the File menu.
    d. click the Open button on the Standard toolbar.

Short Answer

1. The smallest component of a table is a __________.
2. The boundaries and divisions of a table are shown on the screen by nonprinting __________.
3. To select a column, position the pointer at the top of the column so that the pointer changes to a __________, and then click.
4. To move from one cell to the cell to its right, press __________.
5. To insert a row above the selected row in a table, click the __________ button on the Standard toolbar.
6. To change the width of a column, grab the vertical __________ and drag sideways.
7. To add borders and shading to a table, use the __________ toolbar.
8. To automatically resize the width of all columns and the overall table, select the table and then select AutoFit in the __________ tab of the Cell Height and Width dialog box.
9. To insert the contents of a file into a document, choose File from the __________ menu.
10. If end-of-row and end-of-cell marks are not showing in a table, you can click the __________ button.

For Discussion

1. How would you apply shading only to the headings of a table?
2. How can you control overall table width?
3. How would you construct a table to present the win–loss records of eight different teams in each of three categories: conference, nonconference, and overall?

Review Exercises

Making a Calendar

Make a calendar for your birthday month this year.

1. Choose Page Setup from the File menu. Change the page orientation to landscape in the Paper Size tab, and change all margins to 1 inch in the Margins tab.
2. Type the name of your birthday month (for example, March) and the current year, and press (ENTER)
3. Insert a six-row-by-seven-column table.
4. In the top row, enter the days of the week in each cell beginning with Sunday.
5. Fill out the other cells with the dates for each day (1, 2, 3, and so on).
6. If needed, add another row to the bottom of the table to accommodate all the dates for your month.
7. Select the month and year at the top of the table. Format them as 36-point Arial bold. Add a blank 12-point line below the month–year heading.
8. Select the top row of the calendar. Format the headings as 12-point Arial bold, and center them.
9. Select the remaining cells in the table (those with dates in them). Format them as 24-point Times New Roman bold.
10. Open the Paragraph dialog box, and select the Indents and Spacing tab. In the Spacing After box, set the spacing after each paragraph to 48 points.
11. Select the cell for your birthday, and add 10% shading to the cell.
12. Add inside and outside borders to the table.
13. Save the document as *My Calendar,* and print a copy.

Making a TV Listing

Make your own TV program listing guide. Feel free to substitute your own programs for those listed in Figure 7.22.

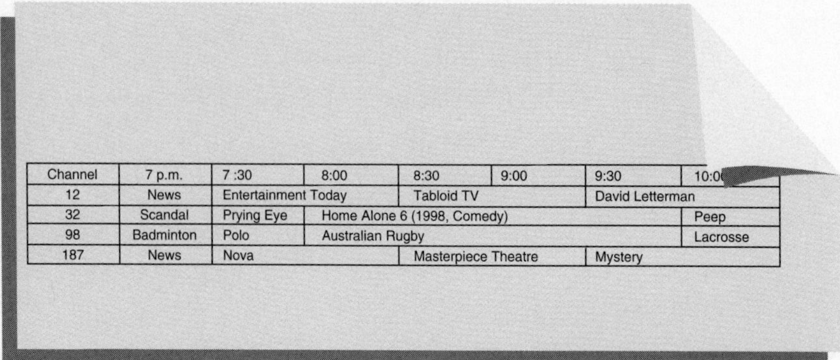

Channel	7 p.m.	7 :30	8:00	8:30	9:00	9:30	10:0
12	News	Entertainment Today		Tabloid TV		David Letterman	
32	Scandal	Prying Eye	Home Alone 6 (1998, Comedy)				Peep
98	Badminton	Polo	Australian Rugby				Lacrosse
187	News	Nova		Masterpiece Theatre		Mystery	

Figure 7.22

1. Create a five-row-by-eight-column table.
2. Format the entire table as 9-point Arial.
3. Place the column headings in the top row as shown.
4. Place the channel numbers in the first column as shown.
5. Enter **News** in the 7 p.m. time slot for channel 12, and press TAB
6. Enter **Entertainment Today** in the 7:30 p.m. time slot for channel 12. The program name will word wrap inside the cell. To combine the 7:30 cell with the 8:00 cell, select both cells, and then choose Merge Cells from the Table menu. Delete the extra paragraph mark.
7. Continue to fill out the rest of the table, merging cells as needed.
8. Add inside and outside borders to the table.
9. Choose Table AutoFormat from the Table menu. When the Table AutoFormat dialog box appears, click AutoFit off (no *x* in the box). Try different table formats. Print samples of two formats you like.
10. Save the document as *TV Listing*.

Assignments

Sorting the Telephone List

Retrieve the telephone list you saved as *Telephone List* at the end of Project 4. Select all the name and telephone number lines. Choose Sort Text from the Table menu. When the Sort Text dialog box appears, select OK. The list will be sorted into alphabetical order.

Convert the telephone list into a table. What advantages will that format have?

Creating a Resume as a Table

Use Figure 7.23 as a guide to create your personal resume using a side-heading format. (Do not use borders in the table, however. They are shown in Figure 7.23 only to indicate the structure of the table.) Use different side headings if appropriate, and adjust the width of the left column to accommodate the headings you use. Format the side headings in bold, and right align them. Fill in the right column with your own resume information, leaving a blank line between each item.

Your Name
Address
City, State Zip
Telephone Number

Career Objective	State your career objective in one succinct sentence.
Education	List the schools you have attended in this cell. List the most recent first.
Experience	List experience relevant to your career path here, including on-campus experience as well as internships and employment. List the most recent first.
Employment	List the jobs you have had in this cell regardless of their relevance to your career goals. List the most recent first.

Figure 7.23

PROJECT 8: USING DESKTOP PUBLISHING

Objectives

After completing this project, you should be able to:

- Use WordArt to create typographical special effects
- Format text in multiple columns
- Use tables to place text and graphics side-by-side
- Insert graphics into a document and resize the graphics to fit
- Use frames to position elements anywhere on a page

In this project, you will get a glimpse of what Word can accomplish in the area of desktop publishing. You will produce a sample newsletter that uses multiple columns, special typographical effects, and graphics. Graphics and text will be positioned side-by-side using a table. You also will see how to use frames to position text or graphics anywhere on the page.

CASE STUDY: CREATING A NEWSLETTER

Just a few years ago, columns, typographical effects, and graphics were available only in expensive desktop publishing software. Now those same capabilities are integrated into the word processor you use every day. For many types of publications, Word is the only desktop publishing system you will ever need.

Designing the Solution

Assume that you are working for a sporting goods store in a mountain area where skiing and other winter sports are popular. The store has been keeping a list of customers and addresses for the past year, and now has a mailing list of several hundred names. Many of these are repeat customers who come in every season to rent ski equipment or to update the equipment they own. The store owner wants to publish a small newsletter for customers that would be informative and identify the store with what's current in skiing and other winter sports.

Before committing to publishing the newsletter, the owner wants to see some ideas for design and format. She wants the newsletter to look "newsy" and credible, not like an advertising flyer. She wants it to contain information that would be of genuine interest to recreational skiers. She asks you to design a sample front page as a starting point in the planning process.

The sample will give the two of you something concrete to look at when you discuss the newsletter in more detail.

You don't have a lot of time to put the sample front page together, so you won't be able to write actual copy for the newsletter. Instead, you'll use a technique that graphic designers have used for years to prepare sample layouts, called ***greeking***. Greeking is simply dummy text formatted in the type size and style that you intend to use. Greeked text usually doesn't make sense if you try to read it, but it does give an accurate impression of the appearance of the final publication. You decide to use realistic headlines, however, to give a better sense of newsletter content, and you will also prepare a custom logo (identification symbol) for the newsletter nameplate.

To give the newsletter the "newsy" look the owner wants, you'll design it to resemble a miniature newspaper. The newsletter will have a logo like a newspaper nameplate and multiple columns with headlines above the stories. The newsletter will use what newspaper designers call modular layout, in which items on the page are arranged in simple rectangular blocks.

In Word, the number of columns and column widths are part of the section format. Because part of the newsletter page will have a single column and part of it will have three columns, you will need to divide the page into separate sections. The general page design will be like the preliminary sketch shown in Figure 8.1.

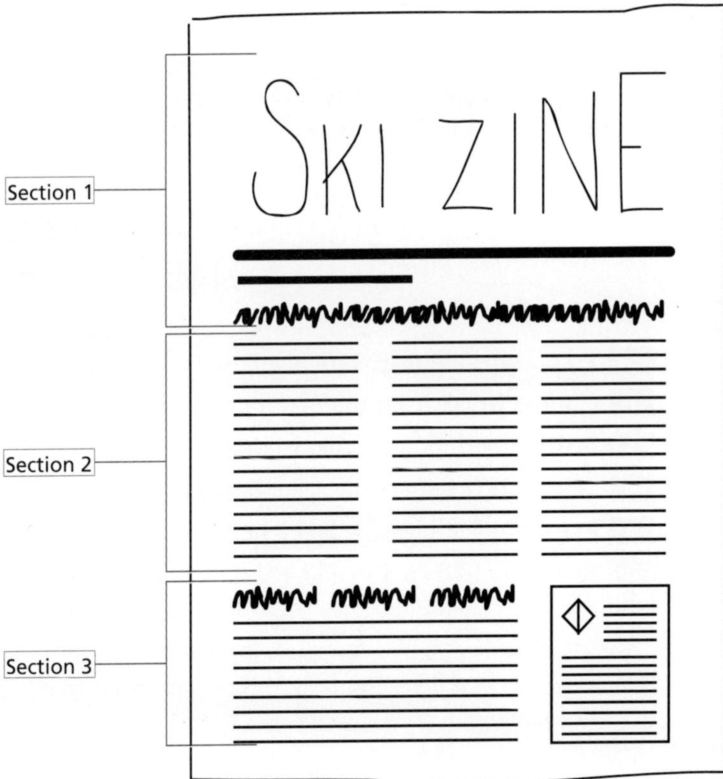

Figure 8.1

The top section will be one column wide and will include the logo, the store identification, the dateline heading, and the headline for the first story. The middle section will be divided into three columns and will include the text of the first story. The bottom section will be one column wide and will include the headline and text for the second story, as well as a boxed announcement on the right side.

You will begin the sample newsletter by establishing the basic page layout and dividing the page into three sections. Then you will design the logo and add the headings for the first section. Next, you will insert the text for the top story. Last, you will add the headline for the bottom story, insert the text for that story, and create the boxed announcement.

Organizing the Layout

The general page design calls for 1-inch margins and a page that is divided into three sections.

To set the page margins:

1. Open a new document if one is not already on the screen.
2. Choose Page Setup from the File menu.
3. Select the Margins tab if it is not already on top.
4. Set the top, bottom, left, and right margins to 1 inch.
5. Select OK to complete the margin settings.

When you set a section break, Word inserts a double line and the label *End of Section,* marking the boundary between two sections of a document. Because you will use a ***continuous section break,*** Word will not start a new page at the section break. (Section breaks are also often used to divide a document into chapters, in which case you could set the section break to begin a new page, and even stipulate whether the new page were to be a right- or left-hand page.)

To create the sections:

1. Press (ENTER) to leave one blank line.
2. Choose Break from the Insert menu.
3. Select Continuous in the Section Breaks box.
4. Select OK to insert the section break.
5. Press (ENTER) to leave a blank line.
6. Repeat steps 2 to 4 to add a second continuous section break, which will divide the document into three separate sections.

At this point, you have created the structural outline for the newsletter, which should look like Figure 8.2. Now you need to add the textual and graphic elements.

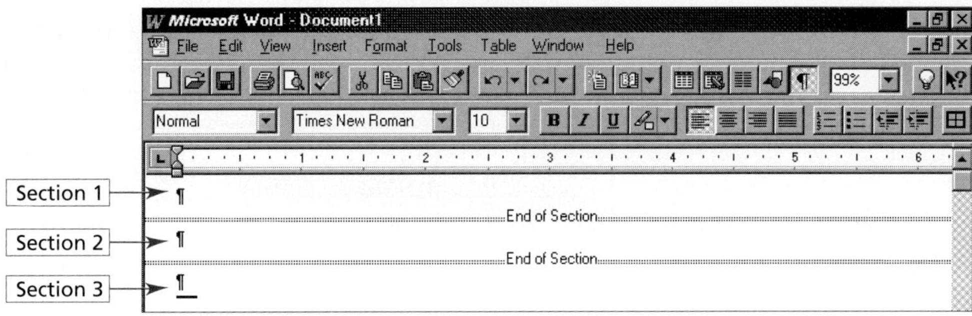

Figure 8.2

Setting up the Headings for the First Section

The newsletter will be identified by a logo at the very top, with a reverse (white on black) line below the logo that gives the name of the sporting goods store. Below the reverse line is a line that gives the date of publication and, below that, the headline for the main story. You'll create the top part of the newsletter in two stages. First you'll create the logo using Word's built-in typographical special effects program, WordArt. Then you'll add the heading information, including the reverse type.

Creating a Logo Using WordArt

WordArt is a miniprogram built into Word that allows you to create typographical special effects. You will be using it here to create the logo for the newsletter masthead at the top of the page. When you are finished, the document will contain a WordArt object. An ***object*** in Word is a graphic, a chart, an equation, or some similar nontext item that originates outside the word processor itself, but that is included as part of a document.

To insert a WordArt object:

1. Position the insertion point at the beginning of the document.
2. Choose Object from the Insert menu.
3. Select the Create New tab if it is not already on top.
4. Select Microsoft WordArt 2.0 in the Object Type box.
5. Select OK.

The WordArt toolbar and a rectangular WordArt object will appear, as shown in Figure 8.3. You will type the title of the newsletter and then manipulate the letter forms to create the logo.

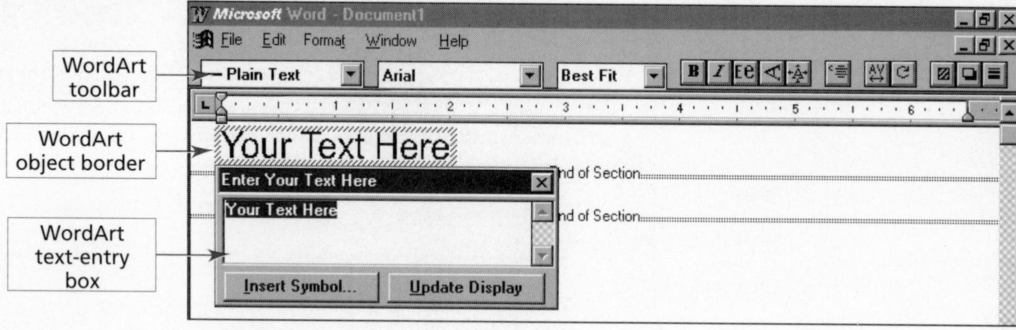

Figure 8.3

Quick Fix Word is a very complex application program, requiring a large amount of storage space. To save space, some systems omit some of Word's auxiliary programs, such as WordArt. If you do not have access to WordArt and cannot create the logo yourself, you may have access to the *SkiZine Logo* file, which has the logo in it, ready to copy to another document. If you do not have that file, you can make a simple nameplate as follows: type the name of the newsletter, format it as boldface Arial, and set the font size to 100 points. Center the line, choose Paragraph from the Format menu, and set the Line Spacing at Exactly 144 points. That will create a substitute logo that is nearly page-width and exactly 2 inches high. If you have to use the substitute logo, you should skip the next set of numbered steps, which deal with creating the logo, and the two sets of numbered steps that follows, which deal with sizing the logo.

To create the logo:

1 Type **SKI ZINE**

Your text replaces *Your Text Here* in the WordArt text-entry box.

2 Choose Arial (or a similar sans serif typeface) from the font box on the WordArt toolbar.

3 Select Update Display if necessary so that the new text appears in the WordArt object border.

4 Select Deflate Top in the Shape box, located at the far left of the toolbar, as shown in Figure 8.4.

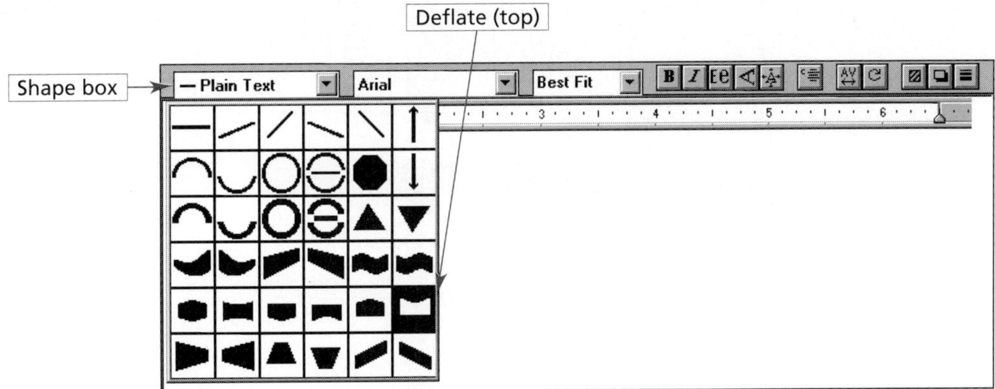

Figure 8.4

The text is reshaped in the WordArt object border so that the text curves downward at the top.

5 Choose the Straight-Back Shadow option in the Shadow box, as shown in Figure 8.5.

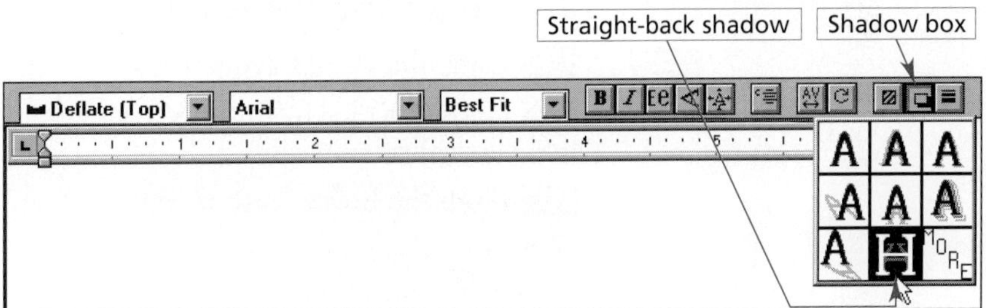

Figure 8.5

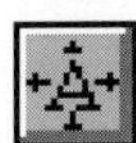

6 Click the Stretch to Frame button.

7 Click outside the WordArt object border and text-entry box to return to Word.

The Stretch to Frame option will force the logo to fill the object border no matter how you later size or stretch the border. If you compress the object border, the logo will compress with it. If you elongate the object border, the logo will also elongate. If you want to edit the object, you can double-click it to open WordArt again.

The logo is complete and needs only to be resized so that it is larger and unmistakably identifies the newsletter. This WordArt object is really a graphic—a picture—in Word. It has a nonprinting rectangular border around it with handles at the edges and corners, as shown in Figure 8.6.

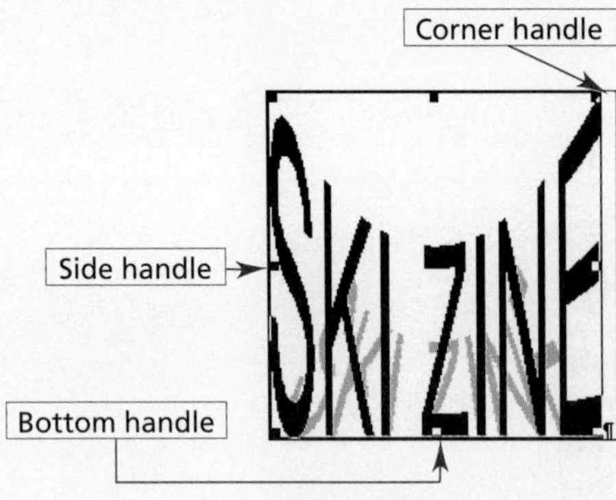

Figure 8.6

You can use the mouse to grab the handles and stretch, compress, or resize the object. You can also control the shape and size of the graphic using a dialog box. You will first stretch the logo into a shape that is close to the final size and then use the dialog box to make the logo the precise shape needed. You will begin by changing to Page Layout view so that you have both a horizontal and a vertical ruler available.

To manipulate the logo using the mouse:

1. Click the Page Layout View button.
2. Choose Ruler from the View menu if needed to make the horizontal and vertical rulers visible.
3. Grab the lower-right handle of the picture rectangle.
4. Drag the corner around to see how the change affects the size of the rectangle, but not its proportions. The rectangle's shape stays the same when you drag the corners.
5. Grab the right-edge handle and drag it to see how both the shape and size of the rectangle change. As you change the shape, the logo is distorted in different ways.
6. Drag the right edge of the rectangle to the right margin of the document, the 6 1/2-inch mark.
7. Grab the bottom-edge handle and drag the bottom edge of the rectangle to the 2-inch mark on the vertical ruler.

The logo should be close to the right size, 6 1/2 inches wide by 2 inches deep, but it is difficult to be precise with the mouse. To make the logo the precise size, you will refine its dimensions with a dialog box.

To set the size of a graphic using the Picture dialog box:

1. Select the logo so that the graphic rectangle and handles are displayed.
2. Choose Picture from the Format menu.
3. Set Width in the Size box to 6.5″.
4. Set Height in the Size box to 2″.
5. Select OK to set the size of the object.

Using the dialog box is obviously faster and more precise if you know the exact final dimensions of a graphic. But using the mouse makes it easier to try different options to see how the shape and size will look in a layout.

Creating the Headings and Headline

Now you will add a reverse heading, a dateline heading, and the main headline below the logo.

To enter the heading information:

1. Click the Normal View button, or select Normal from the View menu.
2. Position the insertion point just to the right of the WordArt object.
3. Press (ENTER) to begin a new line.
4. Type the three lines shown in Figure 8.7.

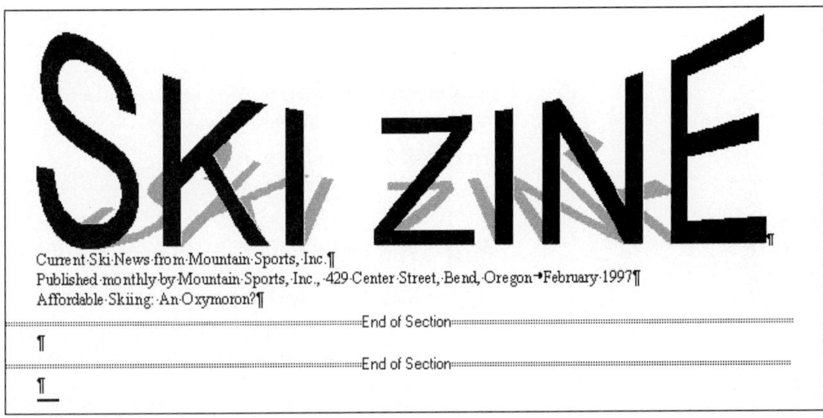

Figure 8.7

5. Select all three lines and set the type font to Arial, or a similar sans serif font.

Now you will reverse the top heading so that it has white letters against a black background. To create a reverse in Word, you will set the paragraph shading to solid black. Word will automatically change the font color to white. In the newsletter layout, the heading line that identifies the store is reversed to give the store's name extra visibility and to separate the logo from the body of the newsletter.

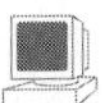

To create the reverse heading:

1. Select the top line, *Current Ski News from Mountain Sports, Inc.*
2. Boldface the line, and set the font size to 20 point.
3. Center the line.
4. Choose Borders and Shading from the Format menu.
5. Click the Shading tab if it is not already on top.
6. Select Solid (100%) in the Shading box.
7. Select OK to make the changes.
8. Move the insertion point or click outside the selected line to unselect it.

The heading should appear as shown in Figure 8.8.

Current·Ski·News·from·Mountain·Sports,·Inc.¶
Published·monthly·by·Mountain·Sports,·Inc.,·429·Center·Street,·Bend,·Oregon → February·1999¶
Affordable·Skiing:·An·Oxymoron?¶

Figure 8.8

To format the dateline heading:

1 Click in the selection bar to select the second heading line, which begins *Published monthly by* . . . .

2 Set the font size to 8 point.

3 Click the Tab Alignment button at the far left of the ruler until you see a right-tab marker (see Figure 8.9).

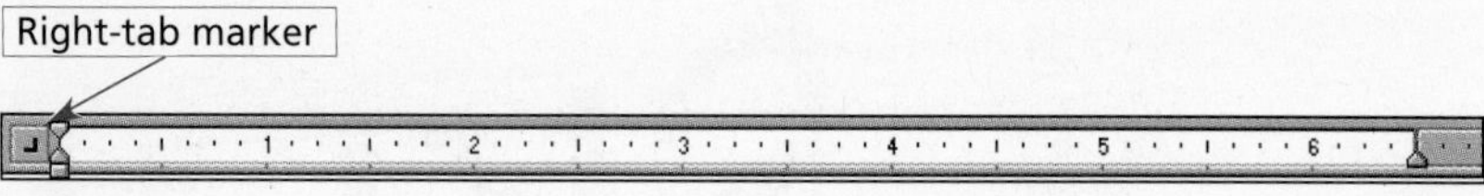

Figure 8.9

4 Set a right tab at the 6-inch mark on the ruler.

5 Drag the right-tab marker to the 6 1/2-inch mark on the ruler. Word will not accept a tab setting directly on top of one of the margin settings. But you can set a tab nearby and then drag the tab marker over to the margin.

6 Click outside the dateline to remove the selection. The dateline heading should now look like Figure 8.10.

Published·monthly·by·Mountain·Sports,·Inc.·429·Center·Street,·Bend,·Oregon → February·1999¶

Figure 8.10

To format the headline:

1 Select the headline *Affordable Skiing: An Oxymoron?*

2 Set the font size to 28 point.

3 Boldface the line.

4 Choose Paragraph from the Format menu.

5 Select the Indents and Spacing tab if it is not already on top.

6 Set the Before value in the Spacing box to 12 points to separate the headline from the nameplate information.

7 Select OK to add the space before the headline.

8 Click outside the headline to remove the selection.

That completes work on the top section of the page. The newsletter design should now look like Figure 8.11.

Figure 8.11

If necessary, you can save your file as *SkiZine Newsletter*, exit Word now, and continue this project later.

CREATING MULTIPLE COLUMNS

The middle section of the newsletter will consist of greeked text formatted in three columns. The greeked text is already prepared in the file *Greeking Text*. If this file isn't available, you can easily prepare your own greeked text by following the next series of numbered steps. The content of the text doesn't matter, but most people create greeked text in a foreign language so that people viewing the sample design don't begin reading the text and get distracted from the design. Despite the name, most greeked text is usually Latin, not Greek.

The format of the greeked text is really what counts. For the newsletter, text will be formatted as 11-point Times New Roman. Paragraphs will be single spaced with the first line indented. Typographers commonly indent paragraphs between one and two ems. An ***em*** is a measure of width that is as wide as the type is high. Thus an em in 10-point type is 10 points wide, and an em in 36-point type is 36 points wide. By indenting one em, the typographer ensures that the paragraph indentation is proportional to the size of the type. You will set the first-line indentation at 11 points, or one em. If you already have the *Greeking Text* file available, it has been formatted this way. If you have *Greeking Text,* skip the next set of numbered steps and pick up again with the set of numbered steps labeled "To insert the greeked text."

To prepare the greeked text:

1. Open a new file, and type a paragraph of about three or four sentences.
2. Copy and paste the text several times so that it is repeated six to eight times to get adequate length.

If your greeked text is in a foreign language (or just nonsense words), the automatic spell checker will flag nearly every word as misspelled. You will fix that shortly.

3 Select all the text.

4 Format the text as 11-point Times New Roman (or a similar serif typeface).

5 Format the paragraphs so that they are flush left (aligned to the left).

6 Select Language from the Tools menu.

7 Select *(no proofing)* in the Language dialog box, then select OK so that Word does not spell-check the selected text.

8 Open the Paragraph dialog box, and select the Indents and Spacing tab if it is not already on top.

9 In the Indentation section, set Special to First Line, and type **11pt** in the By box.

10 Select OK to apply the first-line indentation.

11 Save the file as *Greeking Text*.

12 Close the document window.

Now that you have the dummy text, you will place it into the layout.

To insert the greeked text:

1 Position the insertion point at the beginning of the middle section, immediately after the end-of-section marker for the top section.

2 Choose File from the Insert menu.

3 Select *Greeking Text* in the file list. (It may be necessary to adjust the Look in box for the drive and directory settings.)

4 Select OK to insert the file.

The text will be inserted into the document in the middle section. The text will be one column wide and longer than needed. You will next format the text in three columns and later prune it back to the needed length. If you are in Normal view, the screen will show only one column. To see the columns side by side, you will begin by switching to Page Layout view.

To format the section into three columns:

1 Click the Page Layout View button, or choose Page Layout from the View menu.

2 Position the insertion point somewhere inside the greeked text you just inserted.

3 Choose Columns from the Format menu.
The Columns dialog box appears, as shown in Figure 8.12.

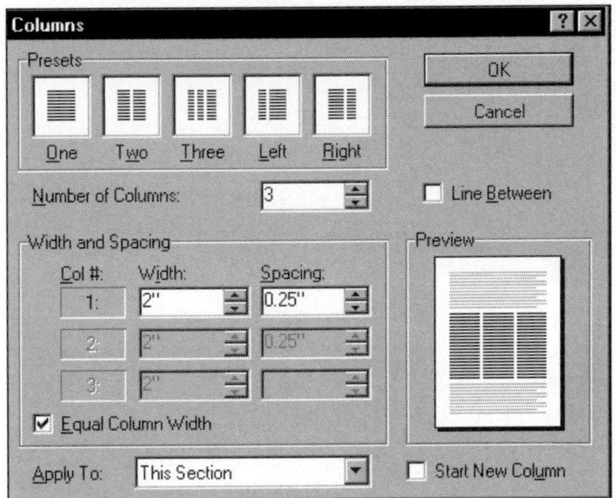

Figure 8.12

4 Set the Number of Columns box to 3.

5 For Col #1 in the Width and Spacing box, set the width to 2″ and the spacing to 0.25″, as shown in Figure 8.12.

6 Select OK to complete the settings.

The text will now appear in three columns, each 2 inches wide, with a ¼-inch gap between columns. The greeked text will probably be much longer than needed. The layout will require a column depth of 18 lines per column, or 54 total lines of text. You will switch back to Normal view to make it easier to count the lines.

To cut the text to length:

1 Click the Normal View button, or choose Normal from the View menu.

2 Position the insertion point in the first line of greeked text.

3 Note the current line number in the status bar at the bottom of the screen, as shown in Figure 8.13. (Your line numbers may be different from those shown in Figure 8.13.)

Line number

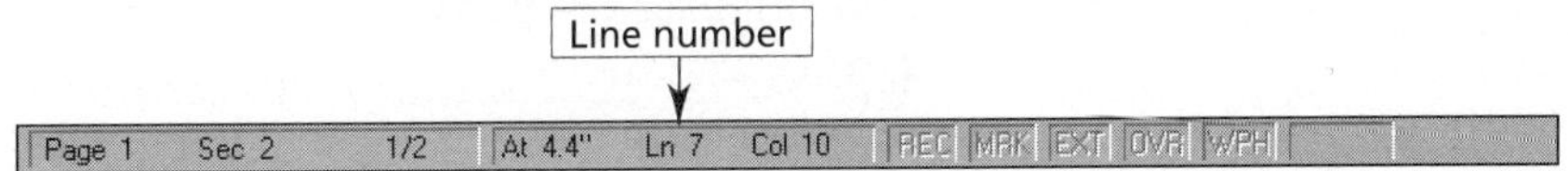

Figure 8.13

The insertion point is in the first line of greeked text, and you need 53 more lines.

4 Add 53 to the current line number to find the line number of the last line of greeked text required.
For example, if the first line of greeked text is line 7, the last line will be 53 + 7, or line 60.

5 Move the insertion point down the column of greeked text until the insertion point is on the line number you just calculated.

6 Delete the lines following that line, but be careful *not* to delete the end-of-section marker.

7 If necessary, cut a word or two off the end of the last line, and add a period to make the line look more like the last line in a typical paragraph.

8 Click the Page Layout View button, or choose Page Layout from the View menu.
The screen should display three columns of equal length, each 18 lines deep. If needed, you can adjust the greeked text to get the correct length.

EXIT If necessary, you can save your file, exit Word now, and continue this project later.

Inserting the Second Story

The bottom section of the newsletter will consist of two elements: the second story and a boxed announcement. The text of the story will be one column, but this column will be about two-thirds of a page wide after the boxed announcement is in place.

To insert the headline for the second story:

1 If necessary, open the Ski Zine Newsletter file and change to Normal view.

2 Position the insertion point at the beginning of the third section, immediately following the section break at the end of the middle section.

3 Type the headline for the second story: **`Snowboarding New at the Olympics`**

4 Press ENTER to begin a new line.

5 If Automatic spell checking is on, click *Snowboarding* with the right-hand mouse button, and select Ignore All to clear the red underline marking the word as a misspelling.

6 Select the entire headline you just typed.

7 Format the headline as 18-point Arial (or a similar sans serif font).

8 Boldface the headline.

9 Choose Paragraph from the Format menu.

10 Select the Indents and Spacing tab if it is not already on top.

11 Set Before in the Spacing box to 12 points.

12 Select OK to set the format.

To insert the greeked text for the second story:

1 Position the insertion point on the blank line immediately following the headline for the bottom story.

2 Choose File from the Insert menu.

3 Select *Greeking Text*. (Adjust the drive and directory if necessary.)

4 Select OK to insert the file.

The greeked text will be too long, but until the boxed announcement is in place, it will not be clear how much of the text should be cut.

Creating the Boxed Announcement

The boxed announcement is really a table. Using a table allows you to place graphics side-by-side with text and arrange the column widths as needed. After the table is complete, you will place the table inside a frame. ***Frames,*** which can contain text or graphics, allow you to position text or graphic objects anywhere on a page. When you position a frame, Word will automatically move text aside to make space for the frame contents.

To create the boxed announcement table and insert the graphic:

1 Choose Normal from the View menu if Word is not already in Normal view.

2 Position the insertion point at the beginning of the greeked text for the second story.

3 Insert a table that is two columns by two rows.

4 Position the insertion point in the top left cell of the table.

5 Choose Picture from the Insert menu.

6 If needed, adjust the Look in box so that the clipart graphics files that come with Word are displayed in the Name box, as shown in Figure 8.14.

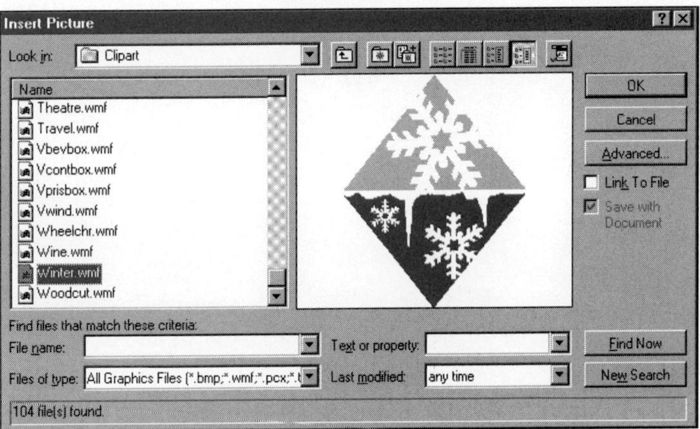

Figure 8.14

7 Select the *Winter.wmf* file.

8 Select OK to insert the graphic into the table.

Quick Fix If the *Winter.wmf* file is not available, but you have other graphics files, select one of those files to substitute. If you have no graphics files, you may be able to create your own: choose Object from the Insert menu, and select Paintbrush Picture. If this Word option is installed on the system, you will be transferred to a simple paint program that will allow you to create your own picture. If neither of these options is available to you, insert a boldface, 72-point *X* (for cross-country) into the cell.

The height of the table cell will expand to make room for the graphic, which is too large for the final boxed announcement. You will need to resize the graphic to 50 percent of its original size. The graphic you just inserted is the same kind of object as the WordArt logo. Just as you did with the WordArt object, you can resize this graphic by using the scaling handles on the graphic or by using a dialog box. Because the methods are sufficiently different, we will give them in two separate series of numbered steps. You should try both approaches to fully understand each.

First, you will resize the graphic using the scaling handles. This method is preferable if you need to experiment to visualize how the graphic will appear alongside other elements on the page.

To resize a graphic using scaling handles:

1 Select the graphic.

2 Grab the lower-right corner handle, as shown in Figure 8.15. The pointer changes shape to a diagonal double-headed arrow.

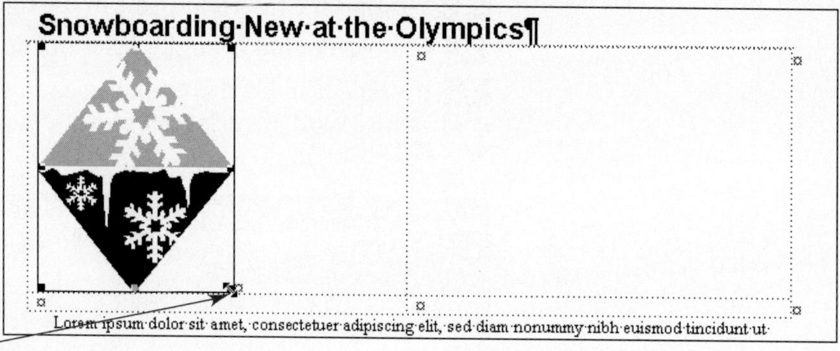

Figure 8.15

3 Drag the handle toward the upper-left corner until the scaling factors reported in the status bar at the bottom of the screen are as close to 50% as you can make them.

4 Release the mouse button.

Now you will repeat resizing the graphic using a dialog box. This method is usually faster if you know ahead of time exactly how much you will need to scale the graphic.

To resize a graphic using a dialog box:

1 Select the graphic.

2 Choose Picture from the Format menu.

3 In the Scaling box, set Width to 50%, and set Height to 50%.

4 Select OK to set the size of the graphic.

The graphic will be in place and correctly sized. Now you need to insert the text.

To insert the text into the boxed announcement table:

1 Position the insertion point in the top-right cell.

2 Type **`Mountain Sports Cross-Country Ski Program`**

3 Select the new text. Format the text as 10-point Arial and boldface it.

4 Select the bottom two cells of the table.

5 Choose Merge Cells from the Table menu to combine the bottom cells into a single cell.

6 Position the insertion point in the bottom cell.

7 Type the remaining information, as shown in Figure 8.16.

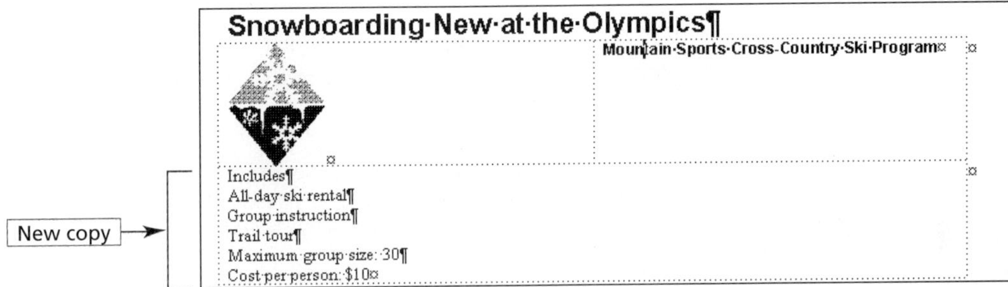

Figure 8.16

8 Format the bottom-cell text as 10-point Arial.

To create the numbered list within the table:

1 Select the three lines just below *Includes* in the bottom cell.

2 Choose Bullets and Numbering from the Format menu.

3 Select the Numbered tab if it is not already on top.

4 Select Modify so that you can adjust the numbered list settings.

5 Set the Distance from Indent to Text to 0.125″, as shown in Figure 8.17.

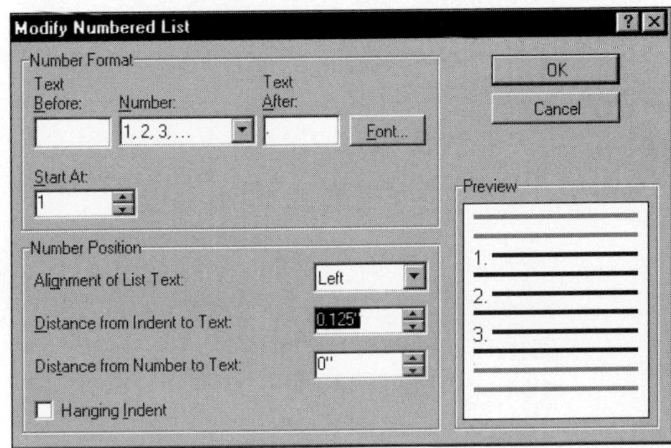

Figure 8.17

6 Select OK to complete the setting.

The elements of the table are now in place, but you will need to rework the overall proportions so that the table will fit into the layout. The table should be as wide as one of the columns: 2 inches.

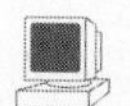

To resize the table:

1 Select the bottom cell.

2 Choose Cell Height and Width from the Table menu.

3 Select the Column tab if it is not already on top.

4 Set the Width of Column 1 box to 2″.

5 Select OK to complete the setting.

6 Select the top two cells in the table.

7 Choose Cell Height and Width from the Table menu.

8 Select the Column tab if it is not already on top.

9 Set the Width of Columns 1-2 box to 1″.

10 Select OK to complete the setting.

To put a border around the table:

1 Choose Select Table from the Table menu.

2 Choose Borders and Shading from the Format menu.

3 Select the Borders tab if it is not already on top.

4 Select Box.

5 Select OK to put a box around the table.

6 Insert a blank line at the top of the top-right cell to align the bottom of the text near the bottom of the graphic.

The format of the table is complete. Now you need to place the table in a frame. Once you place a text block or graphic inside a frame, you can position the frame (with the text block or graphic) anywhere on the page just by dragging the frame. To see what you are doing when moving frames, you need to be in Page Layout view.

To place the table into a frame:

1 Click the Page Layout View button, or choose Page Layout from the View menu.

2 Choose Select Table from the Table menu to select the entire table.

3 Choose Frame from the Insert menu.

The table will be enclosed in a frame, as shown in Figure 8.18. When the frame is selected, there will also be a small anchor visible to the left of one of the paragraphs in the document. The anchor icon indicates which paragraph anchors the frame. If the ***anchor paragraph*** moves to another page, the frame and its contents move with the paragraph. If the anchor paragraph is deleted, so are the frame and its contents. On the other hand, if you move a frame, Word will anchor the frame to another paragraph that is nearer the new location of the frame.

Figure 8.18

The frame and enclosed table are on the left side of the page. Eventually, they will need to be moved to the right side. Before doing the final positioning, however, you will have a chance to "drop" the framed table somewhere else on the page to see how Word shifts text around to accommodate a frame. To see the effects on page layout better, you will first zoom out so that an entire page is visible on the screen.

To reposition the frame:

1 Select Whole Page in the Zoom Control box at the right edge of the Standard toolbar, or choose Zoom from the View menu and then select Whole Page.

2 Position the pointer near one of the edges of the frame.

3 When the pointer changes shape to an arrow with a four-headed set of arrows attached to it, press and hold down the mouse button to grab the frame and contents.

4 Drag the frame to somewhere near the center of the page and drop the frame (see Figure 8.19 as an example).
If necessary, you can drag the frame from one page to another.

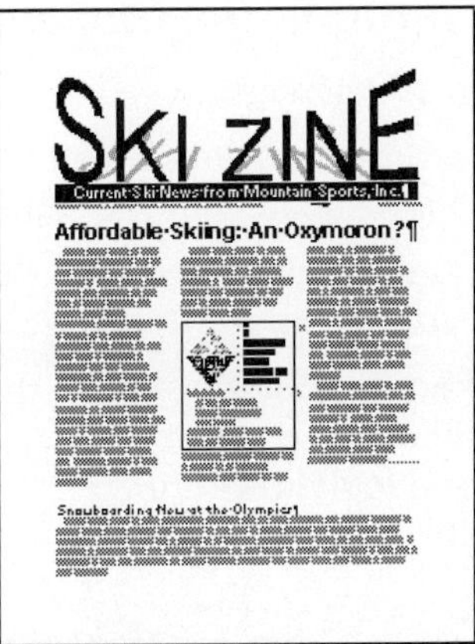

Figure 8.19

Notice how Word runs text around the frame.

5 Now drag the frame to the lower-right corner of the page so that the page looks similar to Figure 8.20.

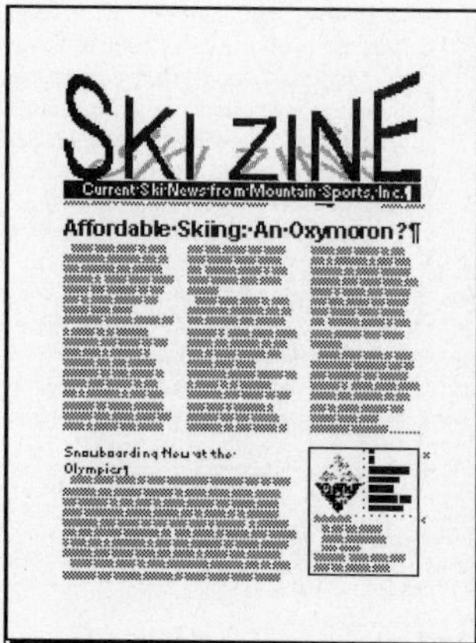

Figure 8.20

The headline for the bottom section may be slightly too long for one line. You can force it into a tighter space by condensing the character spacing.

To force the headline onto one line:

1 Select the headline for the bottom section: *Snowboarding New at the Olympics.*

2 Choose Font from the Format menu.

3 Select the Character Spacing tab if it is not already on top.

4 Select Condensed in the Spacing pull-down list box.

5 Select OK to condense the headline into a single, shorter line.

The frame will probably need to be positioned more precisely so that it lines up with text columns and headings. That is more easily done by zooming in tightly on the page.

To precisely position the frame:

1 Zoom in to 200 percent.

2 Scroll the screen horizontally and vertically so that the top-left corner of the frame is approximately in the center of the screen.

3 Grab the frame and position it so that the left edge aligns with the left edge of the column above the frame.

4 Grab the frame and position it so that the top edge aligns near the top of the headline to the left of the frame.
The screen should look like Figure 8.21.

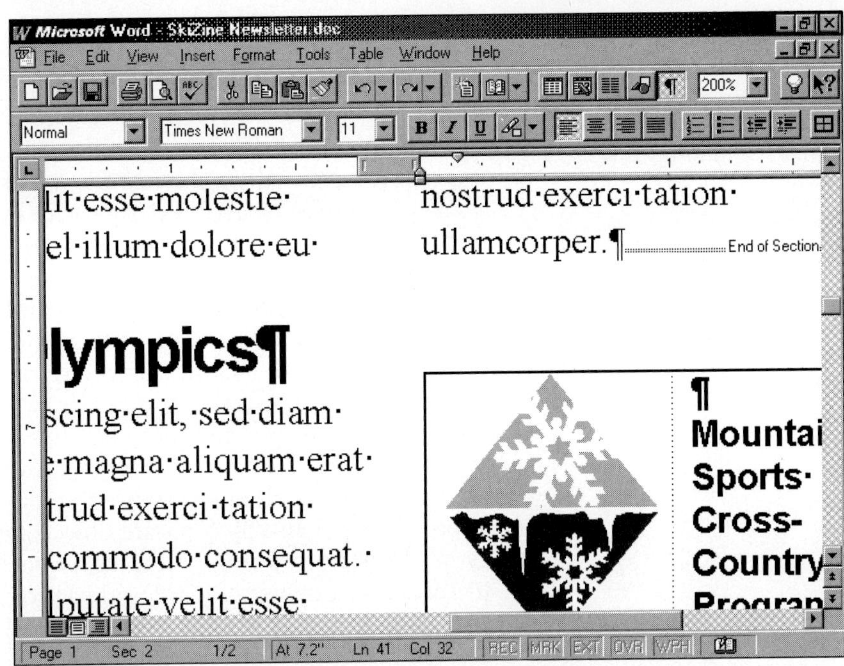

Figure 8.21

5 Zoom out to Page Width.

COMPLETING THE NEWSLETTER

The sample newsletter is nearly done. You still need to trim the excess lines in the second story and then save and print the newsletter.

To trim the second story to length:

1 Scroll down to the second page, which contains the unneeded greeked lines.

2 Select the excess lines.

3 Press (DEL) to delete the selected text.

4 Scroll back to the bottom of the first page.

5 If necessary, adjust the end of the text for the second story to make it appear as a normal paragraph.

To save and print the newsletter:

1 Save the newsletter as *SkiZine Newsletter*.

2 Print a copy of the sample newsletter.

The Next Step

We have introduced you to a number of desktop publishing techniques in this project. All of them deserve more exploration.

You can use WordArt to design with text. WordArt allows you to wrap text in circles, run text sideways, add shading and shadows, and distort text almost endlessly. Although well-designed typefaces deserve to be treated with respect, it is still fascinating to see what can be done with WordArt.

WordArt creates just one of the many types of objects you can add to a document. You can include charts fashioned in Word's built-in charting feature, Microsoft Graph. You can draw your own pictures using Word's Drawing toolbar or sketch out ideas in Paintbrush, Word's built-in paint program. You can even add mathematical equations using the equation editor. Those are all objects you can create using programs that come with Word. You can also incorporate objects created in other applications, such as spreadsheets, drawing programs, or database programs. You can add pictures and graphics drawn in other programs or scanned into a computer as a graphics file. If you have the right equipment, you can even add sound and video objects that will replay digitized sound and movies when you click them. Obviously, word processing is not just about words anymore.

Engineering a reverse is just the beginning of what you can do with color and type. Color printing is one of the fastest growing areas in desktop publishing. If you don't have access to a color printer now, you probably will within a few years. Word makes it easy to use color and see the results on the screen.

One of the most powerful of Word's desktop publishing features is the ability to use a frame to locate a graphic or piece of text anywhere on the page. You can use frames to position pictures, text blocks, headings, or graphics exactly where you want them. You can format frames so that text runs around the frame at a certain distance or so that text has to "leap over" the frame altogether.

Word's capabilities as a word processor, coupled with its desktop publishing features, make it an ideal tool for many types of publications—from simple brochures to complex technical reports and books. The time you spend learning its many features will be repaid in the control you will achieve in the preparation, formatting, and publication of many types of documents.

This concludes Project 8. You can either exit Word or go on to work the Study Questions, Review Exercises, and Assignments.

Summary and Exercises

Summary

- You can divide a document into sections by inserting section breaks.
- WordArt can be used to create a variety of typographical special effects.
- You can insert objects—including products of other computer applications such as charts, pictures, or spreadsheets—into a Word document.

- You can change the size and shape of objects by manipulating object handles with the mouse or by using the Picture dialog box.
- You can format the text within a section in multiple columns.
- Tables can be used to arrange text and graphics side-by-side.
- Text, graphics, and other objects can be encapsulated in a frame and then positioned anywhere on a page.

Key Terms and Operations

Key Terms	**Operations**
anchor paragraph	Format multiple columns
continuous section break	Insert a file
em	Insert a graphic
frame	Position a frame
greeking	Resize a graphic
object	
WordArt	

Study Questions

Multiple Choice

1. Which of the following is not an option for a section break?
   a. Begin New Page
   b. Begin Odd Page
   c. Continuous
   d. Begin New Column

2. Within a Word document, a WordArt object is like:
   a. text.
   b. a picture.
   c. a header or footer.
   d. a separate document.

3. If you want to change the size of a picture without changing its shape, you should use the mouse to manipulate:
   a. the right handle only.
   b. any corner handle.
   c. the top or bottom handle.
   d. either of the edge handles.

4. In typography and graphic arts, a reverse is when type:
   a. is a mirror image.
   b. runs from right to left.
   c. is white on black.
   d. runs over a picture.

5. If you want to indent paragraphs set in 12-point type by two ems, how much should you indent the first line?
   a. 3 points
   b. 6 points
   c. 12 points
   d. 24 points

6. The line number of the line containing the insertion point is displayed:
   a. in the status bar.
   b. in the Page dialog box.
   c. on the Standard toolbar.
   d. on the right edge of the ruler.

7. If you want to see multiple-column text displayed side-by-side, you must be in:
   a. Column view.
   b. Normal view.
   c. Page Layout view.
   d. Outline view.
8. To place an object in a frame:
   a. choose Frame from the Format menu.
   b. choose Frame from the Insert menu.
   c. click the Frame button on the Standard toolbar.
   d. choose Frame in the Object dialog box.
9. One of the main advantages of a frame is that it:
   a. produces an automatic border when printed.
   b. can manipulate the shape of any object.
   c. can run type vertically on a page.
   d. can position an object nearly anywhere on a page.
10. You can choose the type of tab you are inserting by:
   a. clicking the proper alignment button on the Formatting toolbar.
   b. dragging the appropriate tab marker from the Formatting toolbar to the ruler.
   c. clicking the tab marker on the ruler as many times as needed.
   d. clicking the Tab Alignment button on the ruler.

Short Answer

1. Products of other computer applications brought into Word—such as charts or pictures—are called __________.
2. By putting a picture in a __________, you can position the picture anywhere on a page.
3. If you wanted to create a typographical effect so that a heading “ran around” in a circle, you could use __________.
4. If you want some text in one column and other text in three columns, you will need to divide the text into two __________.
5. Designers call dummy text used in sample layouts __________.
6. To bring text into a document from another file, choose File from the __________ menu.
7. To put a text block or graphic beside another text block or graphic, it is usually easiest to use a __________.
8. Once a picture is inserted into a Word document, you can select the picture and use the handles to change both the picture’s __________ and its __________.
9. To magnify the view of a document, you can use the __________ command.
10. A frame is always associated with a paragraph, and the paragraph is marked by the __________ icon.

For Discussion

1. When is a section selected?
2. How would you create a yellow stripe with blue lettering on it?
3. Explain how to make a picture 75 percent of its original size without distorting the picture.

Review Exercises

Designing a Letterhead

You have been asked by a local business to set up an electronic letterhead, one that will be printed by the computer along with the body of the letter. It is to look like Figure 8.22.

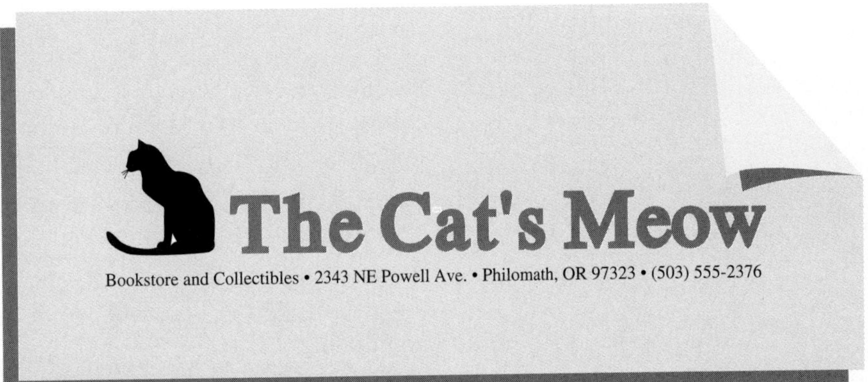

Figure 8.22

1. Begin by opening a new document and setting the left and right margins to 1¼ inches and the top and bottom margins to 1 inch. (The margins may already be at these settings because they are the usual default settings for Word.)
2. Insert a table that is two columns wide by one row deep.
3. Insert the picture *Cat.wmf* into the left cell of the table. (If you do not have access to this file, find another picture file you like. If you have access to a scanner, you can use almost any printed material as a picture source.) Scale the picture to 60 percent (1-inch square), without changing the proportions.
4. Insert a WordArt object into the right cell. Type the title of the business. Make the type Times New Roman, and boldface it. Do not distort the type, but use WordArt to "screen back" the name, which means to turn it into a fine dot pattern so that it is gray rather than black. Choose Shading from the WordArt Format menu. Use the Shading dialog box, shown in Figure 8.23, to set the shade of gray. You may need to experiment to get a shade that works well with your printer.

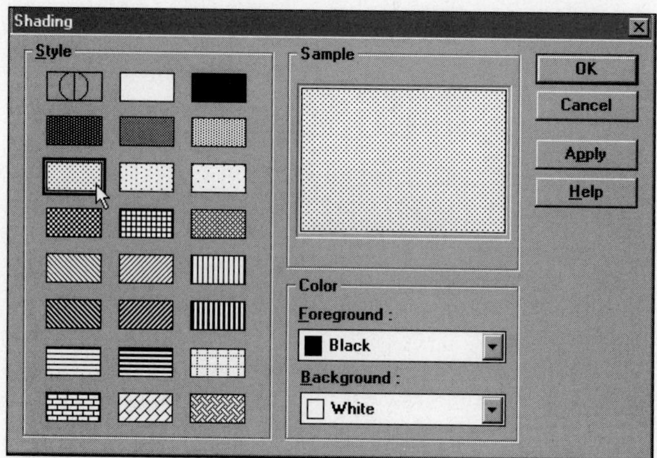

Figure 8.23

5. Set the column widths in the table to 1.2 inches for the left column (with the cat in it) and 4.8 inches for the right column (with the name in it).
6. Drag one of the corner handles on the WordArt object to expand the object horizontally to fill the right cell.
7. Insert one blank line above the WordArt object. Select the paragraph mark for the blank line, and set the paragraph to a point size (about 36 points) that makes the bottom of the WordArt object align with the bottom of the picture.
8. Type the address line. Separate items with two spaces, a bullet, and then two more spaces. Recall that you can add a bullet by choosing Symbol from the Insert menu. Format the address line as 11-point Times New Roman.
9. Save the letterhead, and print a copy of it.

Preparing a Book Chapter

You are preparing a sample chapter for a book of Sherlock Holmes mystery tales. The book will be 8 1/2 x 11 with the text in two columns.

1. Open a new document. In the Page Setup dialog box, set page margins at 1 inch all around. Set the layout so that there will be a different set of headers and footers both for the first page and for odd and even pages.
2. Insert the text from the file *Sherlock Holmes*. The text was in manuscript form, so you will need to select the text, single-space it, format it as 10-point Times New Roman, and set the first-line indentations at one-and-a-half ems.
3. Insert a continuous section break after the chapter title.
4. Format the title line as follows: 24-point Times New Roman, boldface, centered, and the first-line indentation removed. Use the Borders toolbar to put a line under the title.
5. Insert a blank line above the title line. On that blank line, insert the

picture *Scales.wmf,* to represent the scales of justice. Scale the graphic to 50 percent of the original size.

6. Select the second section of the chapter. Format the section for two columns.
7. Select all the text in the second section. Format the text as justified alignment. Choose Hyphenation from the Tools menu, select Automatically Hyphenate Document, and then select OK. Hyphenation will improve the between-word spacing of justified text.
8. Switch to view headers and footers. Insert page numbers in 10-point Times New Roman in the footers so that the page numbers will be at the outside edges of the page (at the right on odd pages and at the left on even pages). Insert an even page header that says *The Return of Sherlock Holmes* in italic 12-point Times New Roman. The even page header should be aligned to the left and have a rule beneath it, as the chapter title does. Insert an odd page header that gives the chapter title in the same font as the even header. Make the odd page header aligned to the right. Also put a rule under the odd page header.
9. You need to arrange things so that you don't have a header on the first page, which is the first odd header. Go to the page 3 header, and click the Same as Previous button to unlink the first and third page headers. Then erase the first page header. Check through the headers and footers to be sure they are formatted correctly.
10. The last page should contain two even columns. To have Word arrange this automatically, insert a continuous section break after the last paragraph in the document.
11. Save the chapter as *Student Mystery,* and print a copy of it.

Assignments

Producing a Menu

Prepare a sample menu based on the design shown in Figure 8.24. The basic layout is a horizontal (landscape) page with margins of 1/2 inch on all sides. Divide the page into three columns with a 1-inch gap between columns.

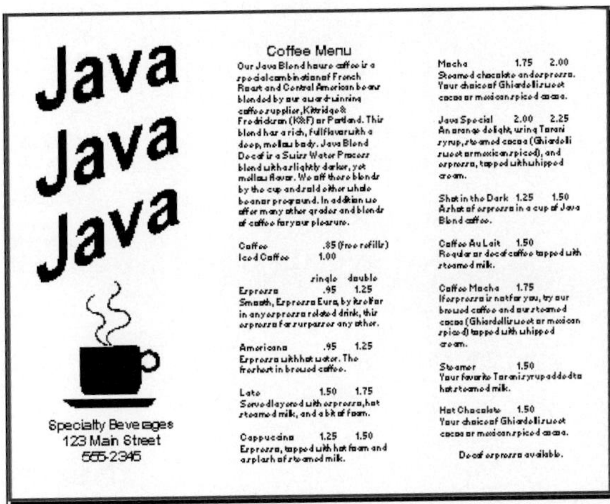

Figure 8.24

The logo is created in WordArt, and the graphic is in the file *Coffee.wmf*. The graphic file is included with Word, but may not be installed on the system you are using. If the file is not available, you can create your own graphic using Word's built-in paint program. You can use dummy text for the menu items or make up your own menu.

This basic three-panel format can also be used for brochures and programs.

Designing Your Own Newsletter

Create a sample newsletter for a club or organization you belong to, following the sample in Figure 8.25. Unlike the newspaper style used for the ski newsletter, this is essentially a bulletin board design, where all news items have equal typographic treatment. Headings are all the same size and style and are side heads rather than newspaper-style headlines.

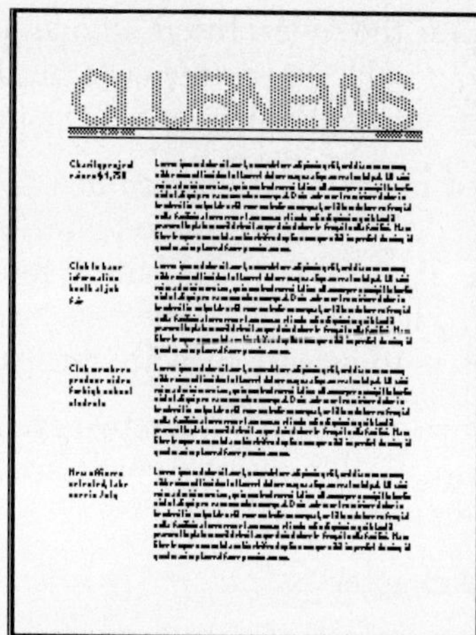

Figure 8.25

Use WordArt to create the logo. Use a two-column table to organize the body of the newsletter. Side heads go in the left column, and the news items go in the right column. If you don't have actual text for news items, use the greeked text you used for the ski newsletter.

Operations Reference

FILE

Button	Operation	Keystrokes	Description
	New	CTRL + N	Create a new document.
	Open	CTRL + O	Open an existing document.
	Close		Close a document.
	Save	CTRL + S	Save the current document.
	Save As		Save the current document under a new name.
	Page Setup		Set page layout: margins, orientation, paper size, treatment of headers and footers, and so on.
	Print Preview		Preview printer output on-screen.
	Print	CTRL + P	Print the current document.
	Exit		Exit to Windows.

EDIT

Button	Operation	Keystrokes	Description
	Undo	CTRL + Z	Undo the last operation.
	Repeat	CTRL + Y	Repeat the last operation.

Button	Operation	Keystrokes	Description
	Cut	CTRL + X	Cut selected text to clipboard.
	Copy	CTRL + C	Copy selected text to clipboard.
	Paste	CTRL + V	Paste clipboard text segment into document.
	Select All	CTRL + A	Select entire document.
	Find	CTRL + F	Find specified text.
	Replace	CTRL + H	Replace one text string with another.
	Go To	CTRL + G	Go to certain page (or other marker).

VIEW

Button	Operation	Keystrokes	Description
	Normal		Display in normal editing view.
	Outline		Display in Outline view.
	Page Layout		Display in Page Layout view.
	Full Screen		Display text only (no menus, toolbars, etc.).
	Toolbars		Display or hide toolbars.
	Ruler		Display or hide ruler.
	Header and Footer		Show headers and footers.
	Footnotes		Open footnote window.
100%	Zoom		Increase/decrease document magnification.

INSERT

Button	Operation	Keystrokes	Description
	Break		Insert page, column or section break.
	Symbol		Insert special symbol.

	Operation	Keystrokes	Description
	Footnote		Insert footnote reference.
	File		Insert another file into document.
	Frame		Insert selected text or object into frame.
	Object		Insert object, such as a WordArt object, equation, graph, and so on.

FORMAT

Button	Operation	Keystrokes	Description
	Font		Set character formats.
	Paragraph		Set paragraph formats.
	Tabs		Set, change, and clear tabs.
	Borders and Shading		Format paragraphs and tables with borders and shading.
	Columns		Set width and number of columns.
	Change Case	SHIFT + F3	Switch from capital to lowercase letters or vice versa.
	Bullets and Numbering		Establish bulleted or numbered lists.
Normal	Style		Define, edit, and apply styles.
	Frame		Adjust size and position of frame.

TOOLS

Button	Operation	Keystrokes	Description
	Spelling	F7	Check spelling.
	Thesaurus	SHIFT + F7	Suggest alternative word choices.
	Word Count		Count words, characters, paragraphs, lines, or pages.
	AutoCorrect		List errors to be corrected as you type.
	Options		Change various options for Word.

Table

Button	Operation	Keystrokes	Description
	Insert		**Insert table, row, or column.**
	Delete		Delete row or column.
	Merge		Merge several cells into one.
	Select Table	ALT + 5	Select an entire table.
	Table AutoFormat		Suggest format options for a table.
	Cell Height and Width		Change height or width of rows or columns.
	Convert Text to Table		Change text into a table or a table into text.
	Sort		Sort text or rows in a table.
	Gridlines		Turn table gridlines on or off.

Window

Button	Operation	Keystrokes	Description
	New Window		Open new window into active document.

Help

Button	Operation	Keystrokes	Description
	Microsoft Word Help Topics		Access Help via Contents, Index, Find, or Answer Wizard.
	Answer Wizard		Get help by typing questions.

Formatting Reference

CHARACTER

Button	Operation	Keystrokes	Description
B	Bold	CTRL + B	Boldface selected text.
I	Italic	CTRL + I	Italicize selected text.
U	Continuous Underline	CTRL + U	Underline selected text and spaces between words.
	Word Underline	CTRL + W	Underline words only in selected text.
	Double Underline	CTRL + D	Double underline selected text.
	Subscript	CTRL + =	Make selected text into a subscript.
	Superscript	CTRL + SHIFT + =	Make selected text into a superscript.
Times New Roman	Font	CTRL + D	Bring up Font dialog box.
11	Point Size	CTRL + SHIFT + P	Activate font-size selection box.
	Reset Character	CTRL + SPACE	Change selected text to underlying style.

Paragraph

Button	Operation	Keystrokes	Description
	Left Align	CTRL + L	Align text to the left.
	Center	CTRL + E	Center text between margins.
	Right Align	CTRL + R	Align text to the right.
	Justify	CTRL + J	Justify text along both edges.
	Increase Indentation	CTRL + M	Indent left edge to next tab.
	Decrease Indentation	CTRL + SHIFT + M	Move left indent to previous tab.
	Hanging Indent	CTRL + T	Indent lines following the first line.
	Remove Hanging Indent	CTRL + SHIFT + T	Remove indentation from lines following the first line.
	Single-Space	CTRL + 1	Single-space lines.
	Double Space	CTRL + 2	Double-space lines.

Glossary

aligned left Paragraph format in which lines are aligned along the left edge. Used for most text. To align text to the left, select the paragraph and then select the Align Left button on the Formatting toolbar, or press (CTRL) + **L**.

aligned right Paragraph format in which lines are aligned along the right edge. Difficult to read, but can be used for small amounts of text such as a figure caption or a short heading. To align text to the right, select the paragraph and then select the Align Right button on the Formatting toolbar, or press (CTRL) + **R**.

Aligns text on the right side under the tab. You can choose from various tab options by selecting the Tab Alignment button at the left edge of the ruler.

anchor paragraph The paragraph to which a frame is attached, indicated on the screen by a small anchor icon next to the paragraph.

body text The main text of a report, letter, or other document, as contrasted with headings or headlines.

bullet A small typographical device, usually a large dot, that indicates separate items in a list. Used to create bulleted lists.

case sensitive A Find or Replace operation in which *Cat* matches *Cat* but not *cat* is case sensitive. If *Cat* matches *cat* or *cAt*, the Find or Replace operation is not case sensitive.

cell Where a row and column intersect in a table. A table is made up of a collection of cells.

center tab Centers text under a tab. You can choose from various tab options by selecting the Tab Alignment button at the left edge of the ruler.

centered alignment Paragraph format in which lines are centered between margins or column edges. Often used with headings or small amounts of text that require a formal presentation. To center text, select the paragraph and then select the Center button on the Formatting toolbar, or press (CTRL) + **E**.

clipboard A temporary storage location for text or graphics. You can copy or delete a text selection or graphic to the clipboard and later paste that item into a Word document or another application.

column A vertical series of cells in a table. You can select a column by positioning the pointer above the column so the pointer turns into a down arrow and then clicking.

context-sensitive Help Takes you directly to Help information about a feature you have selected or are using without having to search through a list of Help topics.

continuous section break Breaks a document into two sections, but without creating a page break at the same time. Could be used to combine a one-column section (for a heading) and a multicolumn section (for text) on the same page.

decimal tab Aligns text—or, more commonly, numbers—on the decimal point under the tab. You can choose from various tab options by selecting the Tab Alignment button at the left edge of the ruler.

em A measure of width for type that is as wide as the type is high. An em in 12-point type is 12 points wide, and an em in 24-point type is 24 points wide. The first line of a paragraph is commonly indented either one to two ems.

endnote Like a footnote, a brief block of text used for citing authorities or making incidental comments. An endnote appears at the end of a section rather than at the bottom of a page.

end-of-cell mark Indicates the end of the contents of a cell in a table.

end-of-document mark (end mark) A short horizontal line that marks the end of a document. You cannot insert characters after the end-of-document mark.

end-of-row mark Indents the rightmost edge of a row of cells in a table.

file A block of storage on disk that contains the text and formatting information for a document.

find operation Searches through a document for a certain word or phrase. To start a find operation, choose Find from the Edit menu.

find-and-replace operation Allows you to find all instances of a certain word or phrase and replace each instance with a different word or phrase. To initiate a find-and-replace operation, choose Replace from the Edit menu.

fixed-space font A type style, such as Courier New, in which all characters are allotted the same width regardless of the letterform.

font A particular style of type, such as Arial or Times New Roman.

footer A repeating block of text at the bottom of each page in a section. Might contain a chapter heading, page number, or similar information. Word allows different footers for even and odd pages.

footnote A brief block of text at the bottom of a page that is used for citing authorities or making incidental comments.

Formatting toolbar Contains information, menus, and buttons related to formatting a document.

frame Text or graphics inserted into a frame can be positioned anywhere on the page by dragging them to the new location. Working with frames is easiest in Page Layout view.

greeked text Dummy text used to prepare sample layouts. Greeked text is correctly formatted in type size and style, but often does not make sense.

gridlines Dotted lines that show the basic structure of a table. Can be turned on and off by choosing Gridlines from the Table menu.

hanging indentation Paragraph format in which the first line is not indented but subsequent lines are indented. The fastest way to create a hanging indentation is to press CTRL + T.

header A repeating block of text at the top of each page in a section. Might contain a chapter heading, page number, or similar information. Word allows different headers for even and odd pages.

indentation marker Triangular markers on the ruler. The marker at the top left controls the first-line indentation. The marker at the bottom left controls the left edge indentation. The marker at the right side of the ruler controls the right indentation.

insert mode In insert mode, characters that you type on the keyboard are inserted into whatever text already exists in the document. Sclcct the Overtype indicator (OVR) in the status bar to switch between insert mode and overtype mode.

insertion point A blinking vertical bar that marks the position where text will be inserted or deleted when you type on the keyboard.

jump In a Help screen, a reference to related definitions or Help topics. A jump is displayed in a contrasting color. Select a jump to see that definition or related topic.

justified alignment Paragraph format in which lines are aligned along both left and right edges. Often used with text that appears in multiple columns on a page. To justify text, select the paragraph and then select the Justify button on the Formatting toolbar, or press CTRL + J.

left tab Aligns text on the left side under the tab. You can choose from various tab options by selecting the Tab Alignment button at the left edge of the ruler.

menu bar Gives access to word processing commands via drop-down menus. Located near the top of the screen.

nonprinting characters Characters that can be displayed on the screen but will not be printed. Include spaces, paragraph marks, and tabs. You can toggle screen display of nonprinting characters on and off by selecting the Show/Hide ¶ button on the Standard toolbar.

object A graphic, chart, equation, or similar nontext item originating outside the word processor itself, but that is included as part of a document.

overtype mode In overtype mode, characters you type replace existing characters. Select the Overtype indicator (OVR) on the status bar to switch between overtype mode and insert mode.

paragraph mark Marks the end of a paragraph in Word. Inserted with the ENTER key. Shows on-screen as a ¶ symbol.

points The measurement system used to describe type sizes. A point is 1/72 of an inch, thus 72-point type is 1 inch high. Text matter is usually from 8 to 12 points. Headings are usually 14 points or larger.

proportionally spaced font A type style, such as Arial or Times New Roman, in which the width of a letter depends on the letterform. For example, the letter *i* is thinner than the letter *M*.

Redo command Restores editing or typing that has been reversed with the Undo feature.

reverse White letters on a black background. To create a reverse in Word, set the paragraph shading to black and set the color of the font to white.

row A horizontal series of cells in a table. You can select a row by clicking in the selection bar to the left of the table.

ruler Displays and allows you to control margins, indentation, tab settings, and column widths. Page Layout view shows a vertical as well as a horizontal ruler.

sans serif font Typefaces that lack serifs, or small crosslines at the end of the main letter strokes. Arial is a sans serif font.

scroll bar Used to move around in a document. The horizontal scroll bar also includes buttons to display documents in different ways.

section A portion of a document that can be formatted with specific margin settings, page orientation (portrait or landscape), page numbering sequence, multiple columns, or other features affecting page layout.

selection bar Allows you to select part of a document using a mouse.

serif font Typefaces that have small crosslines, called serifs, at the end of the main letter strokes. Times New Roman is a serif font.

spelling checker Word's spelling checker will compare every word in a document with an online dictionary. If a word is not in the dictionary, Word reports the word as a possible misspelling.

Standard toolbar Contains buttons that allow you to perform many word processing tasks with a click of a mouse.

status bar Gives basic information about a document or about word processing modes.

style A collection of formatting characteristics that is given a name and is accessible from the Style box in the Formatting toolbar.

subscript Characters that appear below the normal baseline for text, such as the *2* in H_2O. You can format text as subscripted using the Font dialog box or the keyboard shortcut CTRL + +.

superscript Characters that appear above the normal baseline for text, such as the *2* in $E=mc^2$. You can format text as subscripted using the Font dialog box or the keyboard shortcut CTRL + SHIFT + +.

template Preformatted skeleton document that can be everything from a memo to a newsletter. A template is like a blank, formatted document you can fill in with your own text.

thesaurus Word's built-in thesaurus can look up a word and provide a list of synonyms, or words with similar meanings.

title bar Contains the title of the application (Microsoft Word) and that of the current document file.

Undo Reverses a previous editing or typing step. You can usually undo several word processing steps in reverse order.

Wizard Asks a series of questions about a document format and uses your answers to build a document for you to use.

word processing Using a computer to write, edit, format, store, and print documents.

word wrap A word processing feature that determines where line breaks need to fall and automatically begins a new line where necessary. You should press (ENTER) only to start a new paragraph.

WordArt A miniprogram built into Word that allows you to create typographical special effects. To create a WordArt object, choose Object from the Insert menu and then select Microsoft WordArt.

WYSIWYG An acronym for "what you see is what you get," which refers to the fact that the Word screen shows the document formatted as it will be printed.

Index